CONTENTS

EVEN THO' YO' HEART BE BREAKIN', LAUGH CLOWN, LAUGH

Dean Haspiel is a mass of contradictions. Moreover, he is easy to misjudge. See, when Dean walks into a room, be it crowded or near empty, he fills it up with his abundant...personality (the room can't be totally empty because he needs an audience, although even there I can't be certain--Dean might be compulsive enough to try to entertain the curtains). He's loud, brash, and unapologetically clownish. And that's where the first part of the split comes in. He laments being that clown, the jovial Pagliacci who laughs on the outside while crying on the inside. He'll say, "I'm *tired* of being the *buffoon*. Let some-one *else* do the work for a change. *I* want to be entertained." But then he continues his act.

As stated, he's often underestimated. Because Haspiel favors the bowlegged swagger of a gangsta-stylee, ebonically loquacious, Caucasian **Redd Foxx** (the bowlegged part due to an ancient, alcohol-induced injury), some folks make the mistake of thinking he's less intelligent than he actually is--*much* less intelligent. Unlike most white folks Dean uses words like *dope*, *def*, *diss*, *hype*, *whack*, *fresh*, *chillin'*, *ill*, ad nauseam, in daily conver-sation, and without irony. I'll repeat that for the punters in the cheap seats: *without irony.* Dean is no Jerome-come-lately, suburban mall-rat, "wigger." He likes **Wu Tang Clan** because he thinks they're good. He was listening to all that shit, back in the day (know'm say'n', kid?)--back when most of the current crop of tyro rap artistes were just a glint in their now (probably) absent father's eyes.

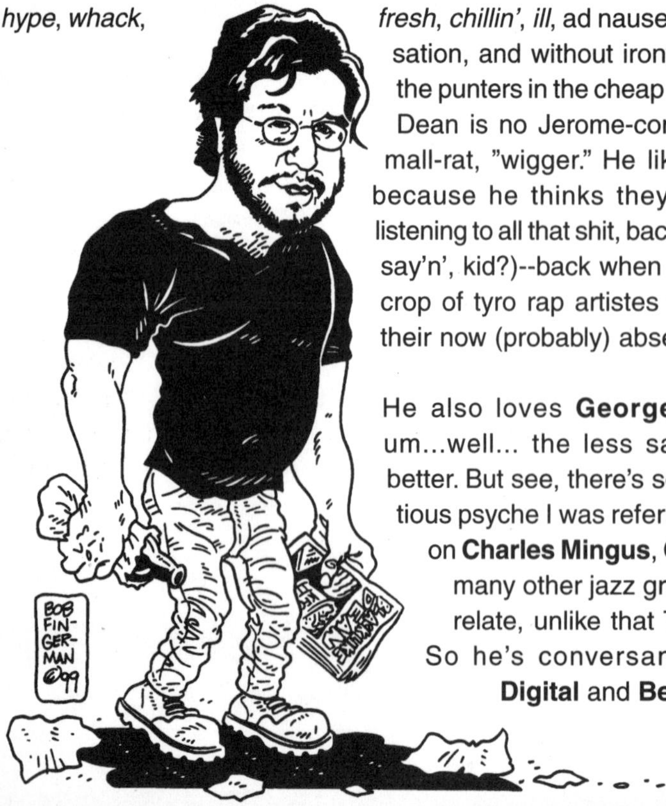
BOB FIN-GER-MAN ©99

He also loves **George Michael**, and I, um...well... the less said about that the better. But see, there's some of that conten-tious psyche I was referring to. He also digs on **Charles Mingus**, **Charlie Parker**, and many other jazz greats (to which I *can* relate, unlike that Tangy Clan of Wu). So he's conversant in both **Bobby Digital** and **Ben Webster**.

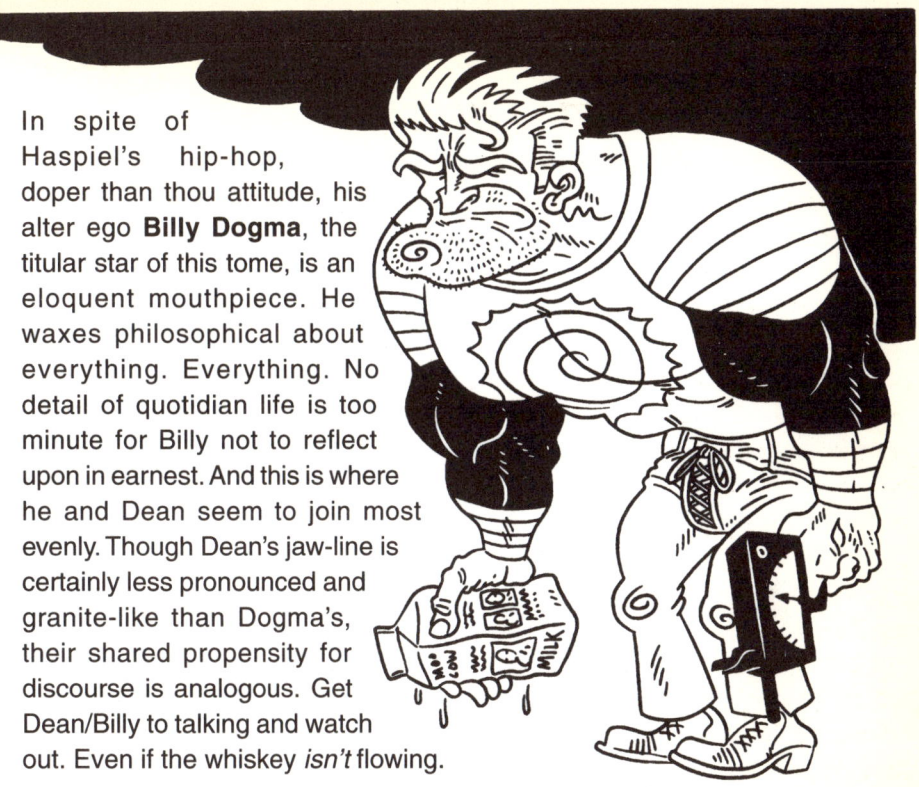

In spite of Haspiel's hip-hop, doper than thou attitude, his alter ego **Billy Dogma**, the titular star of this tome, is an eloquent mouthpiece. He waxes philosophical about everything. Everything. No detail of quotidian life is too minute for Billy not to reflect upon in earnest. And this is where he and Dean seem to join most evenly. Though Dean's jaw-line is certainly less pronounced and granite-like than Dogma's, their shared propensity for discourse is analogous. Get Dean/Billy to talking and watch out. Even if the whiskey *isn't* flowing.

They also share a masochistic streak of romanticism. It's not for nothing that Billy's tag line is, "the last romantic antihero." Both foster great reverence for that sticky commodity called love. One of Dean's quotes has been, "It's all about hugs." Sure he says it with a wink, but he means it, too, which imbues it with more than just cheap laugh value. Dean is more Hallmark card than rap sheet, dig? Dean is a "very special episode," with a booming soundtrack.

And so, without any further meandering prose, allow me to congratulate you on taking the bold step to purchase this volume. I wish you great pleasure in reading it. Though the characters and situations in this book are oft times surreal, the strong themes of love, longing and loyalty will anchor you in a reality that really isn't all that different from your own. Especially if you live in New York.

Enjoy.

Bob Fingerman
New York City
March 1, 1999

This experience is dedicated to Linda Perkins, the original Jane Legit.

Thanks to: Josh Neufeld, **Jessica Abel**,

Chris Staros, **Brett Warnock**, Peter Tunnell,

Nick Bertozzi, Pete Sickman-Garner,

Chris Oarr, Greg Bennett, **The Haspiel Family**,

Heidi Grygiel, **Inverna Lockpez**, James Sturm,

Don Haring, Jason Palmer Little,

Lisa Lippman, Robert Lippman,

Heidi MacDonald, Seth Dinnerman,

Christian Urich, Lorie Reilly, **Bob Fingerman**,

Amanda Williams, **John Battistini**, Tim Hall,

Vanessa Weiman, Howard Chaykin,

Walter Simonson, Matt Madden, **Steve**

Weissman, and Comix@.

Daydream Lullabies: A Billy Dogma Experience, May 1999. Published by Top Shelf Productions, Brett Warnock and Chris Staros. PO Box 1282, Marietta GA, 30061-1282. Unless specified otherwise, all stories and art © 1999 by Dean Haspiel. All other stuff © 1999 by Top Shelf Productions, Inc. Top Shelf Productions and the Top Shelf logo are TM and © 1999 Top Shelf Productions, Inc. *Courtney Clare* © 1999 Jessica Abel. *Lovely Prudence*, *Thesaurus Black*, and *Corset Face* © 1999 Peter Tunnell. *Viva Muerte* © 1999 Nick Bertozzi. *Hey, Mister* © 1999 Pete Sickman-Garner. No part of this book may be reproduced without permission, except for purposes of review. Get hip, look at the web page **www.topshelfcomix.com**. Write for a free catalog. Thanks to Grey Matter Design for everything under the sun. Cover and endpapers designed by Brad Engle/ Highball Design. (Brad, you kick ass!) Printed in Canada by the fine folks at Quebecor.

Haspiel, Dean
Daydream Lullabies / Dean Haspiel
1st Top Shelf Productions ed.
ISBN 1-891830-07-4
1. Humor   2. Cartoons

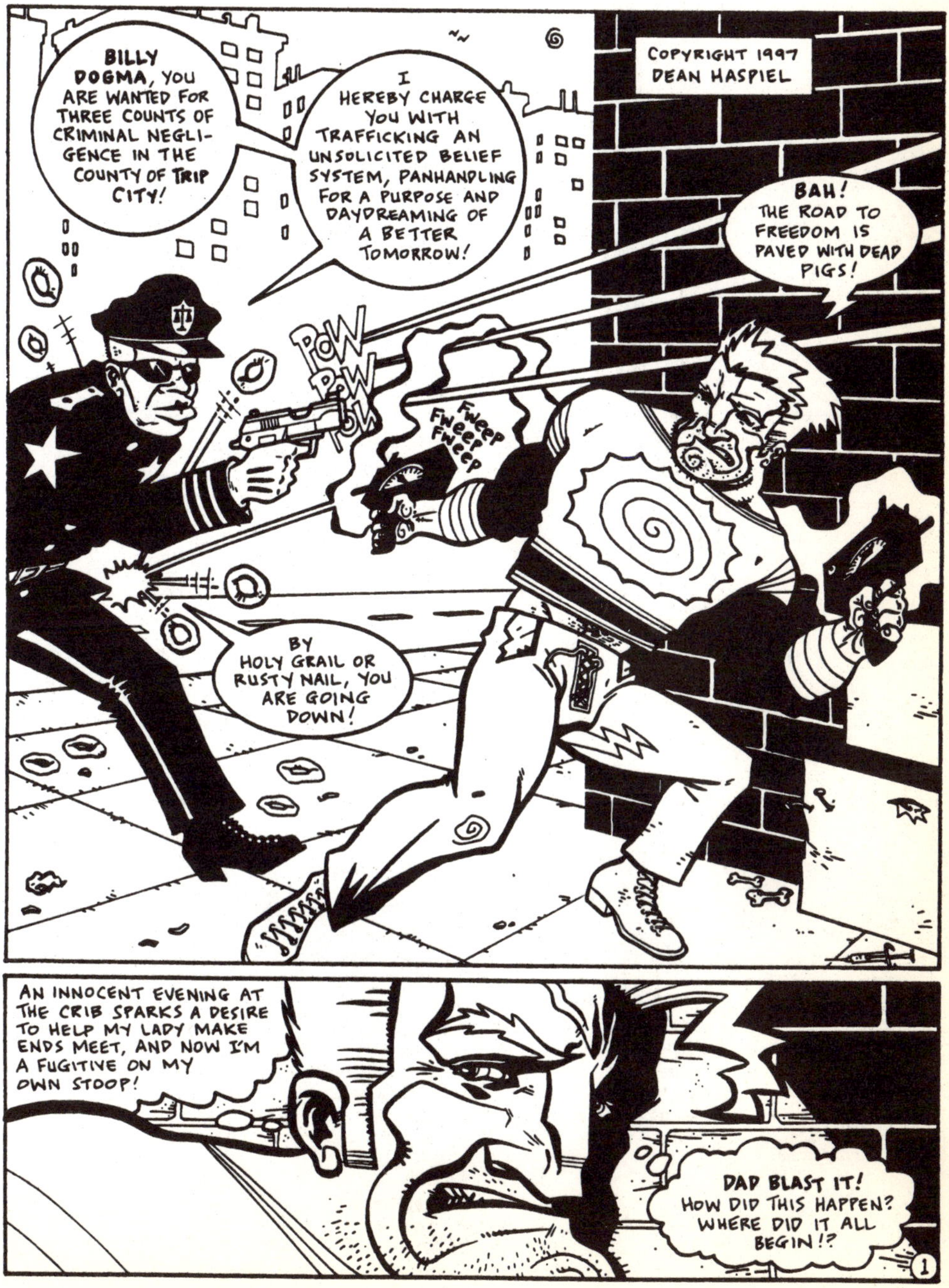
BILLY DOGMA, YOU ARE WANTED FOR THREE COUNTS OF CRIMINAL NEGLI-GENCE IN THE COUNTY OF TRIP CITY!
I HEREBY CHARGE YOU WITH TRAFFICKING AN UNSOLICITED BELIEF SYSTEM, PANHANDLING FOR A PURPOSE AND DAYDREAMING OF A BETTER TOMORROW!
COPYRIGHT 1997 DEAN HASPIEL
BAH! THE ROAD TO FREEDOM IS PAVED WITH DEAD PIGS!
POW POW POW
FWEEP FWEEP FWEEP
BY HOLY GRAIL OR RUSTY NAIL, YOU ARE GOING DOWN!
AN INNOCENT EVENING AT THE CRIB SPARKS A DESIRE TO HELP MY LADY MAKE ENDS MEET, AND NOW I'M A FUGITIVE ON MY OWN STOOP!
DAD BLAST IT! HOW DID THIS HAPPEN? WHERE DID IT ALL BEGIN!?
1

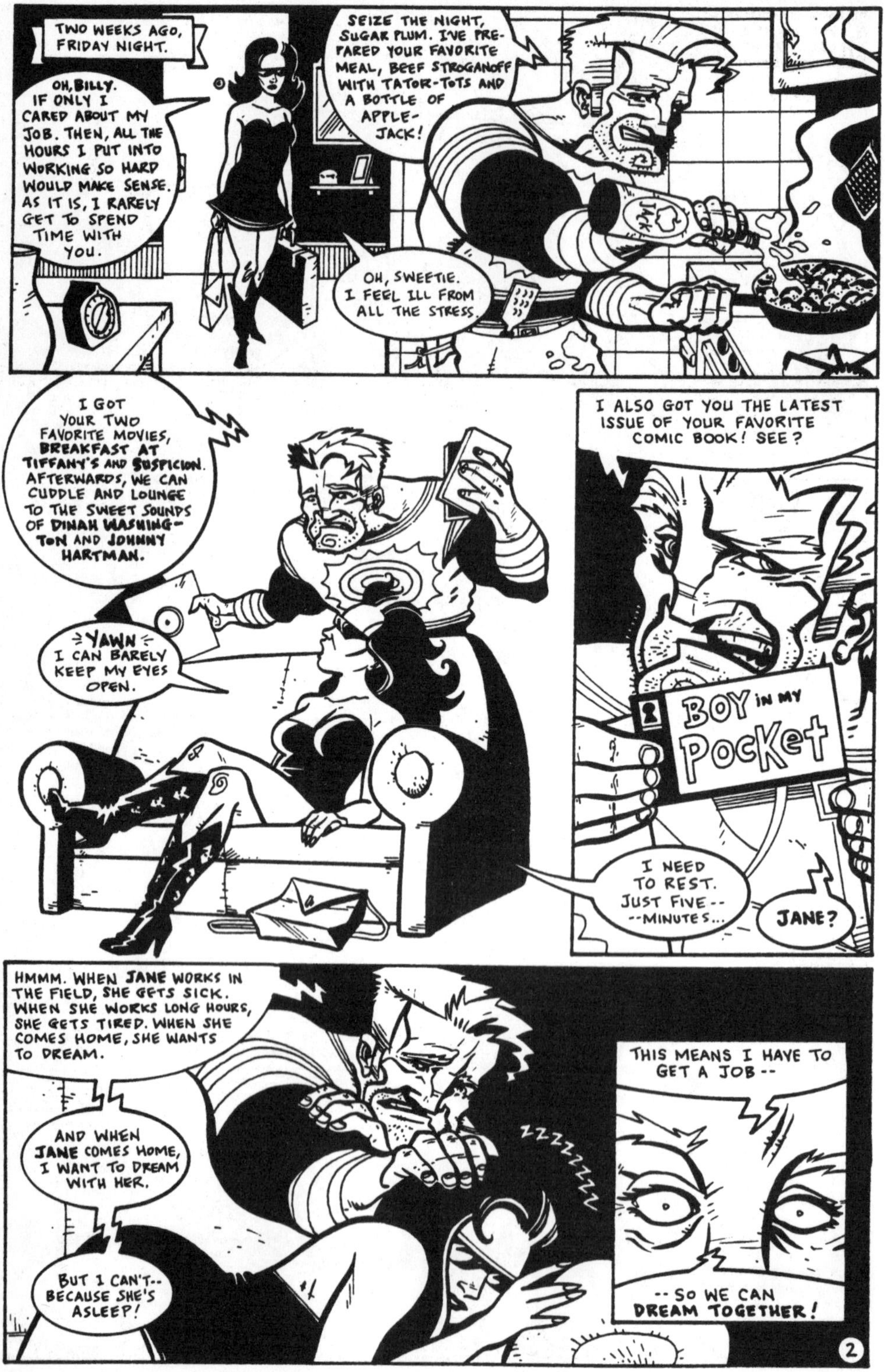
TWO WEEKS AGO, FRIDAY NIGHT.
OH, BILLY. IF ONLY I CARED ABOUT MY JOB. THEN, ALL THE HOURS I PUT INTO WORKING SO HARD WOULD MAKE SENSE. AS IT IS, I RARELY GET TO SPEND TIME WITH YOU.
SEIZE THE NIGHT, SUGAR PLUM. I'VE PREPARED YOUR FAVORITE MEAL, BEEF STROGANOFF WITH TATOR-TOTS AND A BOTTLE OF APPLE-JACK!
OH, SWEETIE. I FEEL ILL FROM ALL THE STRESS.
JACK
I GOT YOUR TWO FAVORITE MOVIES, BREAKFAST AT TIFFANY'S AND SUSPICION. AFTERWARDS, WE CAN CUDDLE AND LOUNGE TO THE SWEET SOUNDS OF DINAH WASHINGTON AND JOHNNY HARTMAN.
YAWN I CAN BARELY KEEP MY EYES OPEN.
I ALSO GOT YOU THE LATEST ISSUE OF YOUR FAVORITE COMIC BOOK! SEE?
BOY IN MY POCKET
I NEED TO REST. JUST FIVE-- --MINUTES...
JANE?
HMMM. WHEN JANE WORKS IN THE FIELD, SHE GETS SICK. WHEN SHE WORKS LONG HOURS, SHE GETS TIRED. WHEN SHE COMES HOME, SHE WANTS TO DREAM.
AND WHEN JANE COMES HOME, I WANT TO DREAM WITH HER.
BUT I CAN'T-- BECAUSE SHE'S ASLEEP!
ZZZZZZZZ
THIS MEANS I HAVE TO GET A JOB --
-- SO WE CAN DREAM TOGETHER!
2

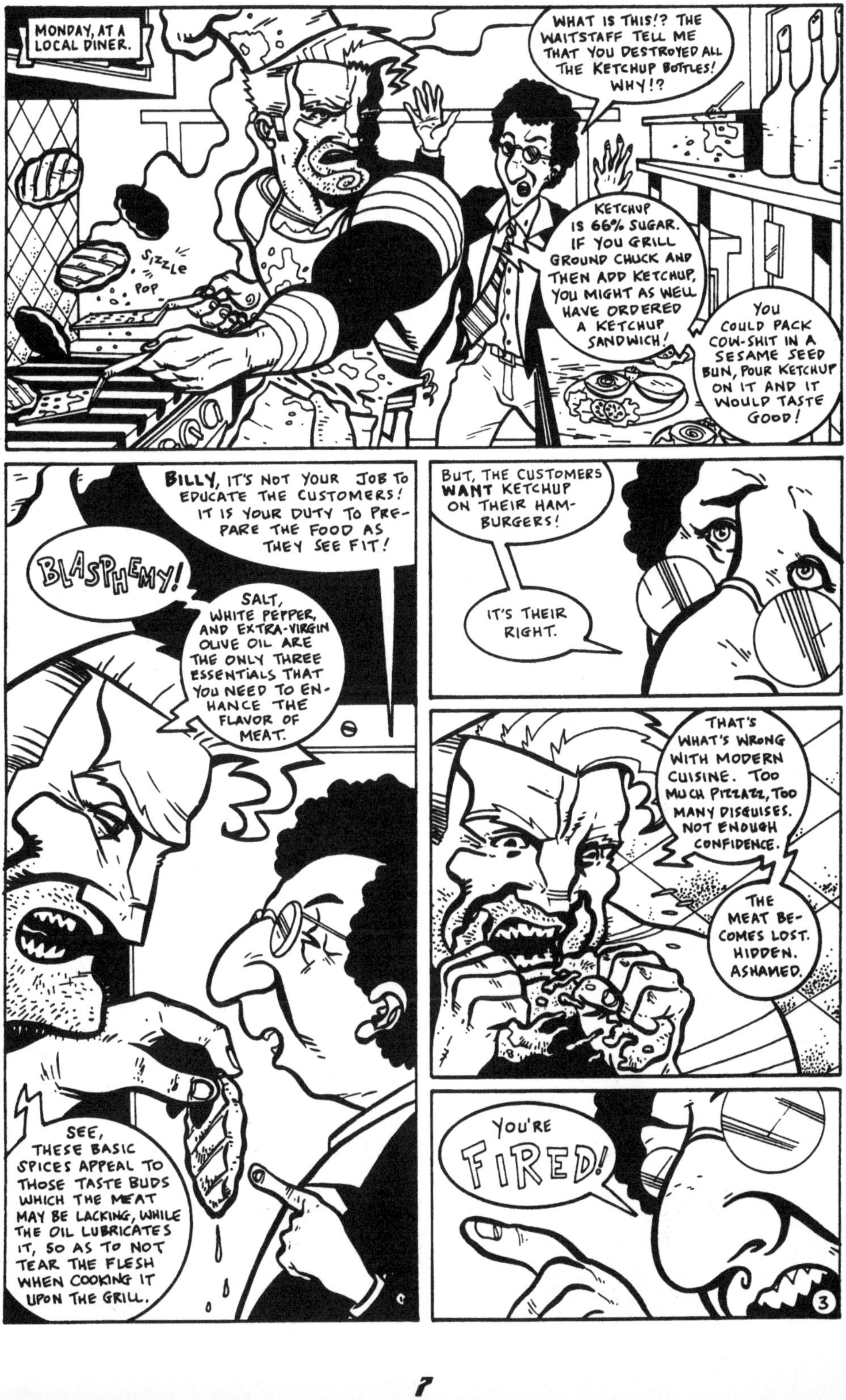
MONDAY, AT A LOCAL DINER.
WHAT IS THIS!? THE WAITSTAFF TELL ME THAT YOU DESTROYED ALL THE KETCHUP BOTTLES! WHY!?
SIZZLE
POP
KETCHUP IS 66% SUGAR. IF YOU GRILL GROUND CHUCK AND THEN ADD KETCHUP, YOU MIGHT AS WELL HAVE ORDERED A KETCHUP SANDWICH!
YOU COULD PACK COW-SHIT IN A SESAME SEED BUN, POUR KETCHUP ON IT AND IT WOULD TASTE GOOD!
BILLY, IT'S NOT YOUR JOB TO EDUCATE THE CUSTOMERS! IT IS YOUR DUTY TO PREPARE THE FOOD AS THEY SEE FIT!
BLASPHEMY!
SALT, WHITE PEPPER, AND EXTRA-VIRGIN OLIVE OIL ARE THE ONLY THREE ESSENTIALS THAT YOU NEED TO ENHANCE THE FLAVOR OF MEAT.
SEE, THESE BASIC SPICES APPEAL TO THOSE TASTE BUDS WHICH THE MEAT MAY BE LACKING, WHILE THE OIL LUBRICATES IT, SO AS TO NOT TEAR THE FLESH WHEN COOKING IT UPON THE GRILL.
BUT, THE CUSTOMERS WANT KETCHUP ON THEIR HAMBURGERS!
IT'S THEIR RIGHT.
THAT'S WHAT'S WRONG WITH MODERN CUISINE. TOO MUCH PIZZAZZ, TOO MANY DISGUISES. NOT ENOUGH CONFIDENCE.
THE MEAT BECOMES LOST. HIDDEN. ASHAMED.
YOU'RE FIRED!
3

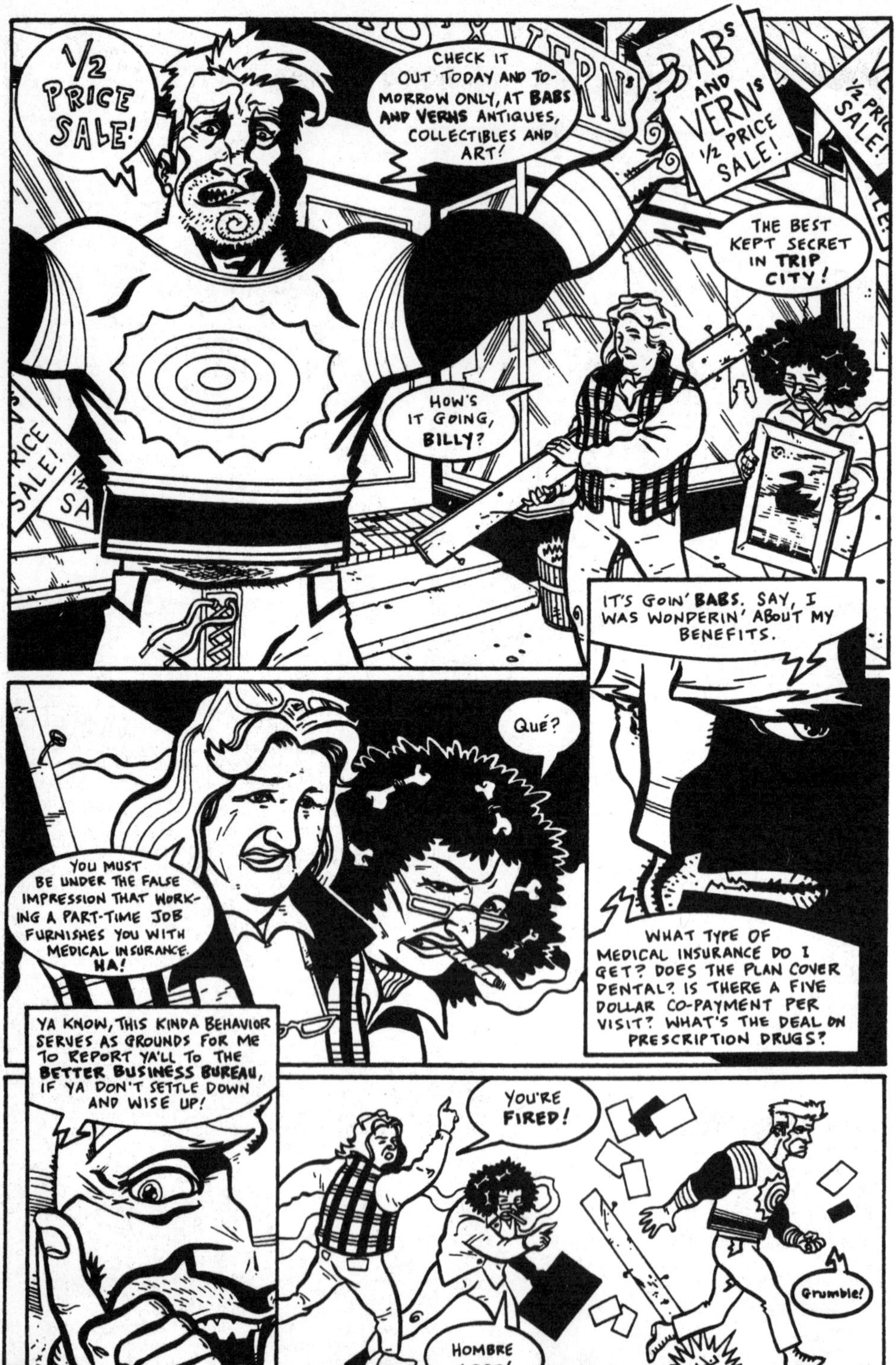
1/2 PRICE SALE!
CHECK IT OUT TODAY AND TOMORROW ONLY, AT BABS AND VERNS ANTIQUES, COLLECTIBLES AND ART!
BABS AND VERNS 1/2 PRICE SALE!
1/2 PRICE SALE!
THE BEST KEPT SECRET IN TRIP CITY!
HOW'S IT GOING, BILLY?
PRICE SALE!
IT'S GOIN' BABS. SAY, I WAS WONDERIN' ABOUT MY BENEFITS.
QUÉ?
WHAT TYPE OF MEDICAL INSURANCE DO I GET? DOES THE PLAN COVER DENTAL? IS THERE A FIVE DOLLAR CO-PAYMENT PER VISIT? WHAT'S THE DEAL ON PRESCRIPTION DRUGS?
YOU MUST BE UNDER THE FALSE IMPRESSION THAT WORKING A PART-TIME JOB FURNISHES YOU WITH MEDICAL INSURANCE. HA!
YA KNOW, THIS KINDA BEHAVIOR SERVES AS GROUNDS FOR ME TO REPORT YA'LL TO THE BETTER BUSINESS BUREAU, IF YA DON'T SETTLE DOWN AND WISE UP!
YOU'RE FIRED!
HOMBRE LOCO!
Grumble!
4

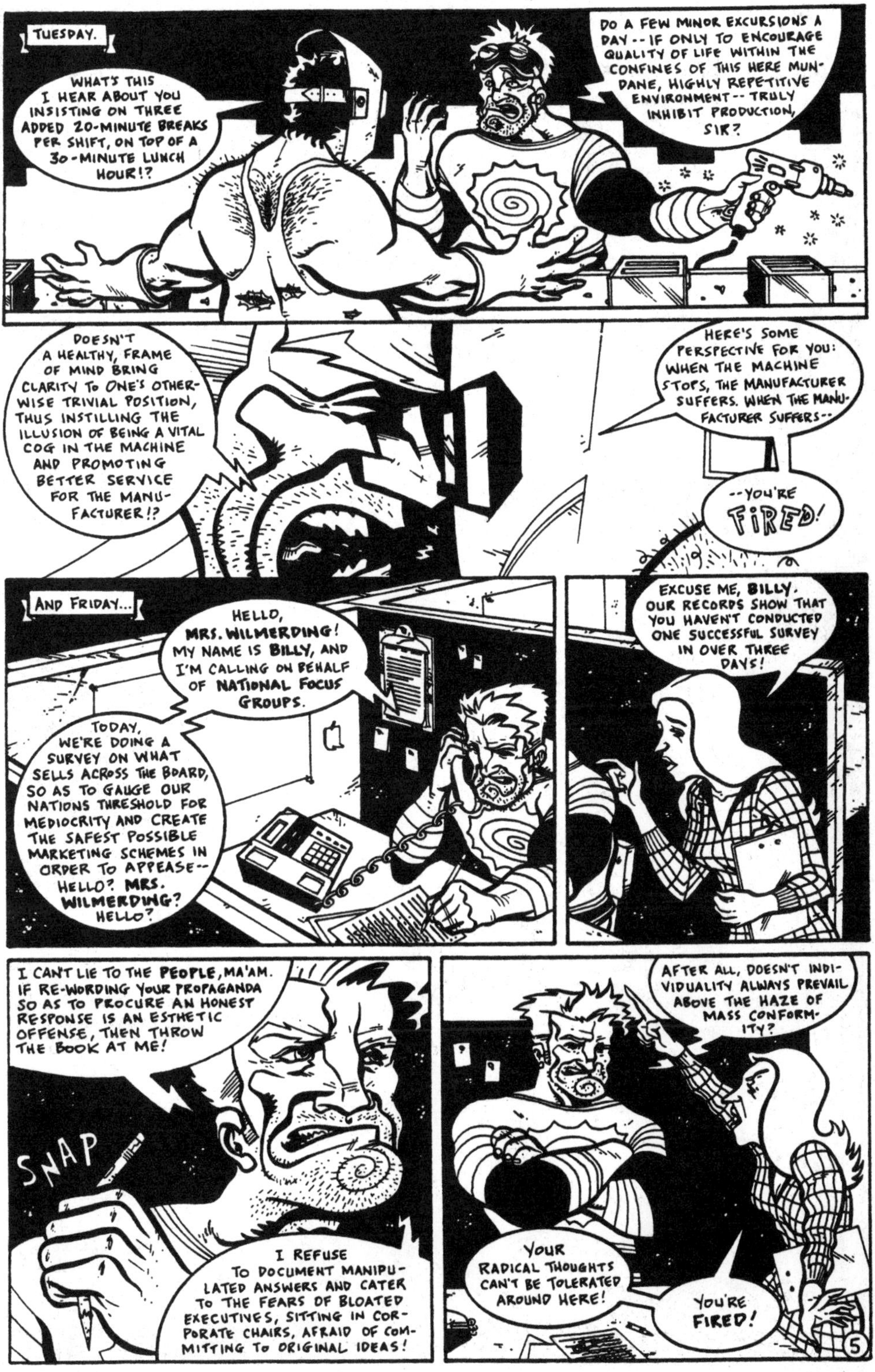
TUESDAY.
WHAT'S THIS I HEAR ABOUT YOU INSISTING ON THREE ADDED 20-MINUTE BREAKS PER SHIFT, ON TOP OF A 30-MINUTE LUNCH HOUR!?
DO A FEW MINOR EXCURSIONS A DAY -- IF ONLY TO ENCOURAGE QUALITY OF LIFE WITHIN THE CONFINES OF THIS HERE MUNDANE, HIGHLY REPETITIVE ENVIRONMENT -- TRULY INHIBIT PRODUCTION, SIR?
DOESN'T A HEALTHY, FRAME OF MIND BRING CLARITY TO ONE'S OTHERWISE TRIVIAL POSITION, THUS INSTILLING THE ILLUSION OF BEING A VITAL COG IN THE MACHINE AND PROMOTING BETTER SERVICE FOR THE MANUFACTURER!?
HERE'S SOME PERSPECTIVE FOR YOU: WHEN THE MACHINE STOPS, THE MANUFACTURER SUFFERS. WHEN THE MANUFACTURER SUFFERS--
--YOU'RE FIRED!
AND FRIDAY...
HELLO, MRS. WILMERDING! MY NAME IS BILLY, AND I'M CALLING ON BEHALF OF NATIONAL FOCUS GROUPS.
TODAY, WE'RE DOING A SURVEY ON WHAT SELLS ACROSS THE BOARD, SO AS TO GAUGE OUR NATIONS THRESHOLD FOR MEDIOCRITY AND CREATE THE SAFEST POSSIBLE MARKETING SCHEMES IN ORDER TO APPEASE-- HELLO? MRS. WILMERDING? HELLO?
EXCUSE ME, BILLY. OUR RECORDS SHOW THAT YOU HAVEN'T CONDUCTED ONE SUCCESSFUL SURVEY IN OVER THREE DAYS!
I CAN'T LIE TO THE PEOPLE, MA'AM. IF RE-WORDING YOUR PROPAGANDA SO AS TO PROCURE AN HONEST RESPONSE IS AN ESTHETIC OFFENSE, THEN THROW THE BOOK AT ME!
SNAP
I REFUSE TO DOCUMENT MANIPULATED ANSWERS AND CATER TO THE FEARS OF BLOATED EXECUTIVES, SITTING IN CORPORATE CHAIRS, AFRAID OF COMMITTING TO ORIGINAL IDEAS!
AFTER ALL, DOESN'T INDIVIDUALITY ALWAYS PREVAIL ABOVE THE HAZE OF MASS CONFORMITY?
YOUR RADICAL THOUGHTS CAN'T BE TOLERATED AROUND HERE!
YOU'RE FIRED!
5

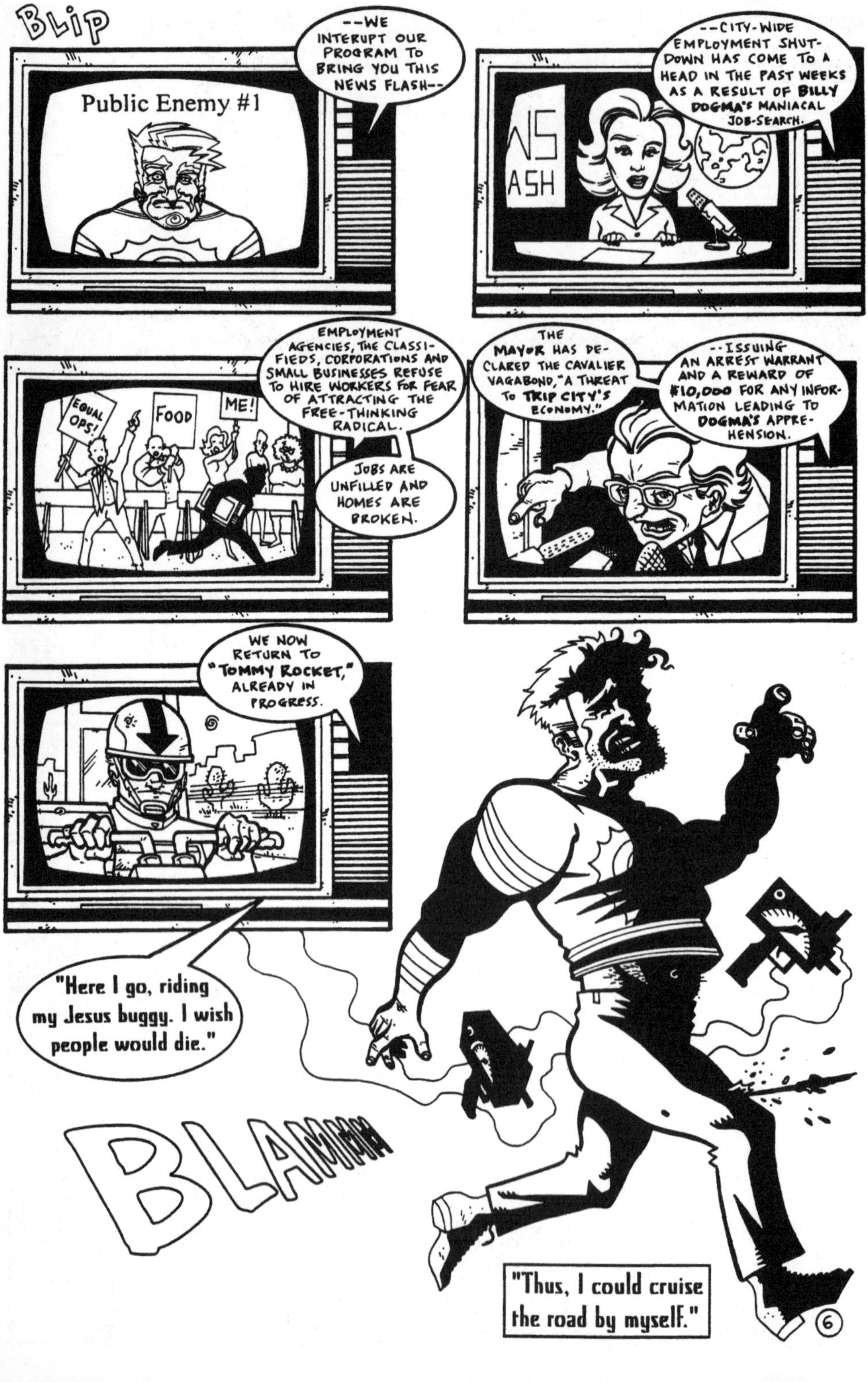
Blip
Public Enemy #1
--We interupt our program to bring you this news flash--
--City-wide employment shut-down has come to a head in the past weeks as a result of Billy Dogma's maniacal job-search.
Employment agencies, the classifieds, corporations and small businesses refuse to hire workers for fear of attracting the free-thinking radical.
Equal ops!
Food
Me!
Jobs are unfilled and homes are broken.
The Mayor has declared the cavalier vagabond, "a threat to Trip City's economy."
--Issuing an arrest warrant and a reward of $10,000 for any information leading to Dogma's apprehension.
We now return to "Tommy Rocket," already in progress.
"Here I go, riding my Jesus buggy. I wish people would die."
BLAMMM
"Thus, I could cruise the road by myself."
6

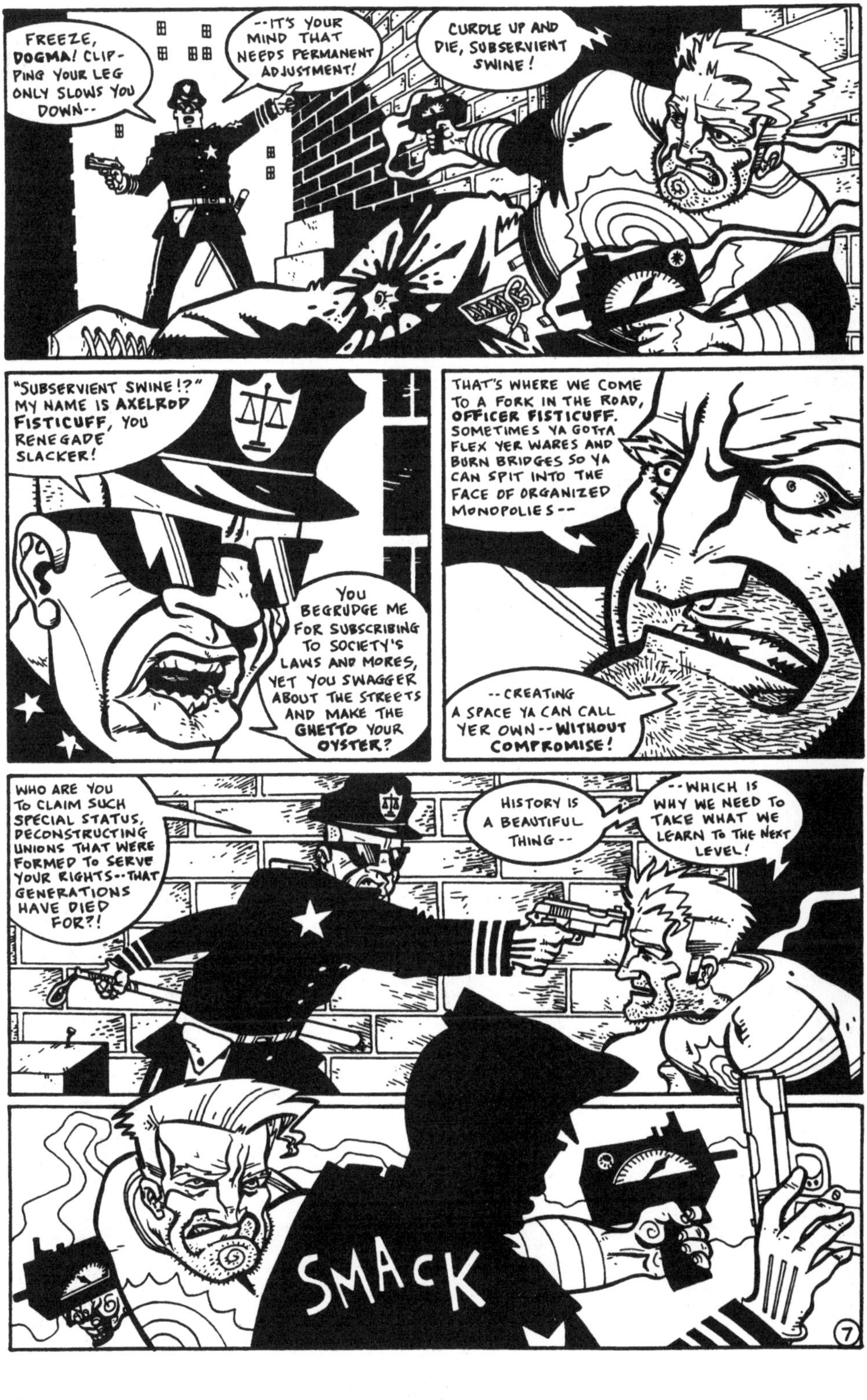
FREEZE, DOGMA! CLIPPING YOUR LEG ONLY SLOWS YOU DOWN--
--IT'S YOUR MIND THAT NEEDS PERMANENT ADJUSTMENT!
CURDLE UP AND DIE, SUBSERVIENT SWINE!
"SUBSERVIENT SWINE!?" MY NAME IS AXELROD FISTICUFF, YOU RENEGADE SLACKER!
YOU BEGRUDGE ME FOR SUBSCRIBING TO SOCIETY'S LAWS AND MORES, YET YOU SWAGGER ABOUT THE STREETS AND MAKE THE GHETTO YOUR OYSTER?
THAT'S WHERE WE COME TO A FORK IN THE ROAD, OFFICER FISTICUFF. SOMETIMES YA GOTTA FLEX YER WARES AND BURN BRIDGES SO YA CAN SPIT INTO THE FACE OF ORGANIZED MONOPOLIES--
--CREATING A SPACE YA CAN CALL YER OWN--WITHOUT COMPROMISE!
WHO ARE YOU TO CLAIM SUCH SPECIAL STATUS, DECONSTRUCTING UNIONS THAT WERE FORMED TO SERVE YOUR RIGHTS--THAT GENERATIONS HAVE DIED FOR?!
HISTORY IS A BEAUTIFUL THING--
--WHICH IS WHY WE NEED TO TAKE WHAT WE LEARN TO THE NEXT LEVEL!
SMACK
7

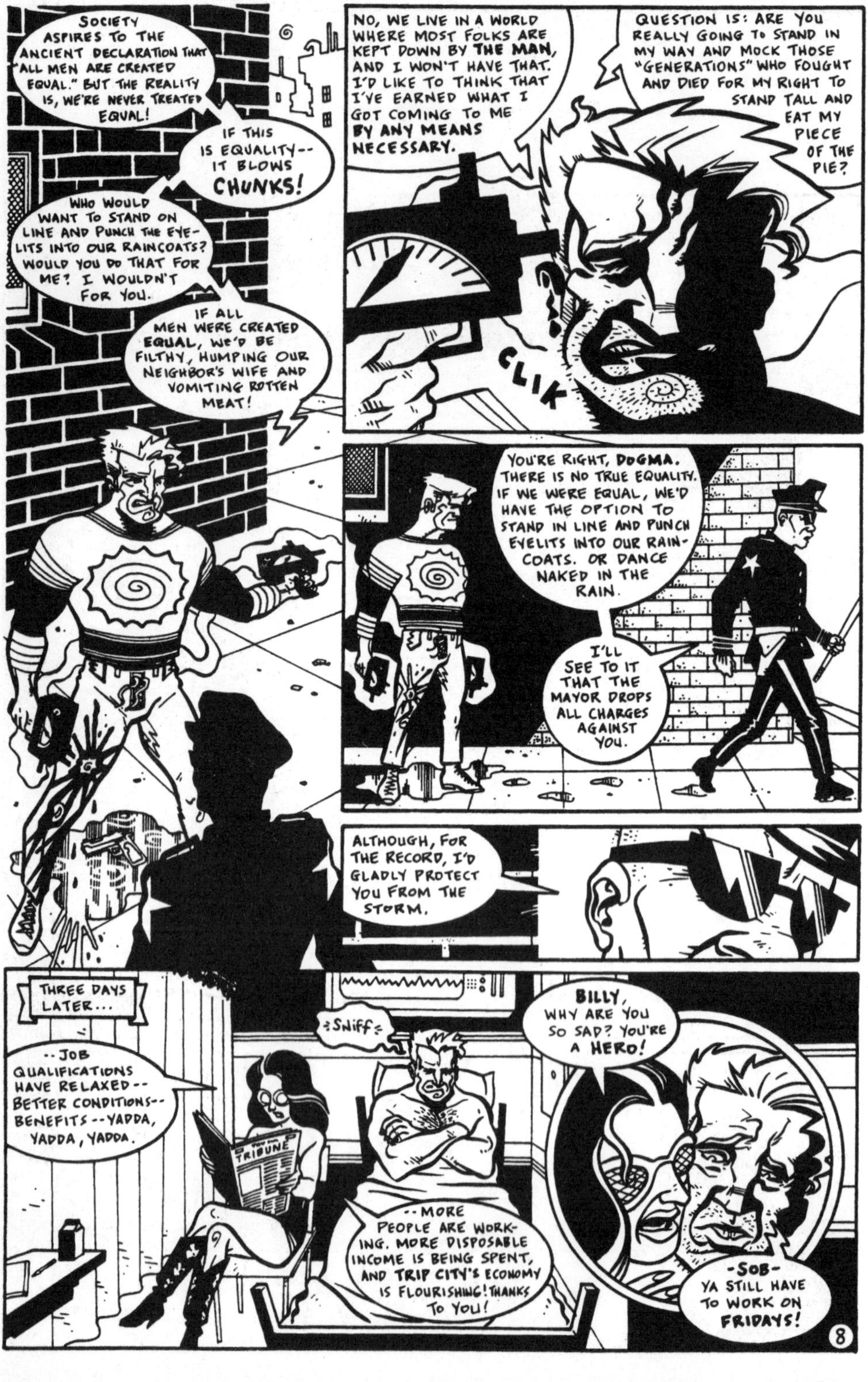
SOCIETY ASPIRES TO THE ANCIENT DECLARATION THAT "ALL MEN ARE CREATED EQUAL." BUT THE REALITY IS, WE'RE NEVER TREATED EQUAL!
IF THIS IS EQUALITY-- IT BLOWS CHUNKS!
WHO WOULD WANT TO STAND ON LINE AND PUNCH THE EYE-LITS INTO OUR RAINCOATS? WOULD YOU DO THAT FOR ME? I WOULDN'T FOR YOU.
IF ALL MEN WERE CREATED EQUAL, WE'D BE FILTHY, HUMPING OUR NEIGHBOR'S WIFE AND VOMITING ROTTEN MEAT!
NO, WE LIVE IN A WORLD WHERE MOST FOLKS ARE KEPT DOWN BY THE MAN, AND I WON'T HAVE THAT. I'D LIKE TO THINK THAT I'VE EARNED WHAT I GOT COMING TO ME BY ANY MEANS NECESSARY.
QUESTION IS: ARE YOU REALLY GOING TO STAND IN MY WAY AND MOCK THOSE "GENERATIONS" WHO FOUGHT AND DIED FOR MY RIGHT TO STAND TALL AND EAT MY PIECE OF THE PIE?
CLIK
YOU'RE RIGHT, DOGMA. THERE IS NO TRUE EQUALITY. IF WE WERE EQUAL, WE'D HAVE THE OPTION TO STAND IN LINE AND PUNCH EYELITS INTO OUR RAIN-COATS. OR DANCE NAKED IN THE RAIN.
I'LL SEE TO IT THAT THE MAYOR DROPS ALL CHARGES AGAINST YOU.
ALTHOUGH, FOR THE RECORD, I'D GLADLY PROTECT YOU FROM THE STORM.
THREE DAYS LATER...
--JOB QUALIFICATIONS HAVE RELAXED-- BETTER CONDITIONS-- BENEFITS --YADDA, YADDA, YADDA.
SNIFF
TRIBUNE
BILLY, WHY ARE YOU SO SAD? YOU'RE A HERO!
--MORE PEOPLE ARE WORK-ING. MORE DISPOSABLE INCOME IS BEING SPENT, AND TRIP CITY'S ECONOMY IS FLOURISHING! THANKS TO YOU!
-SOB-
YA STILL HAVE TO WORK ON FRIDAYS!
8

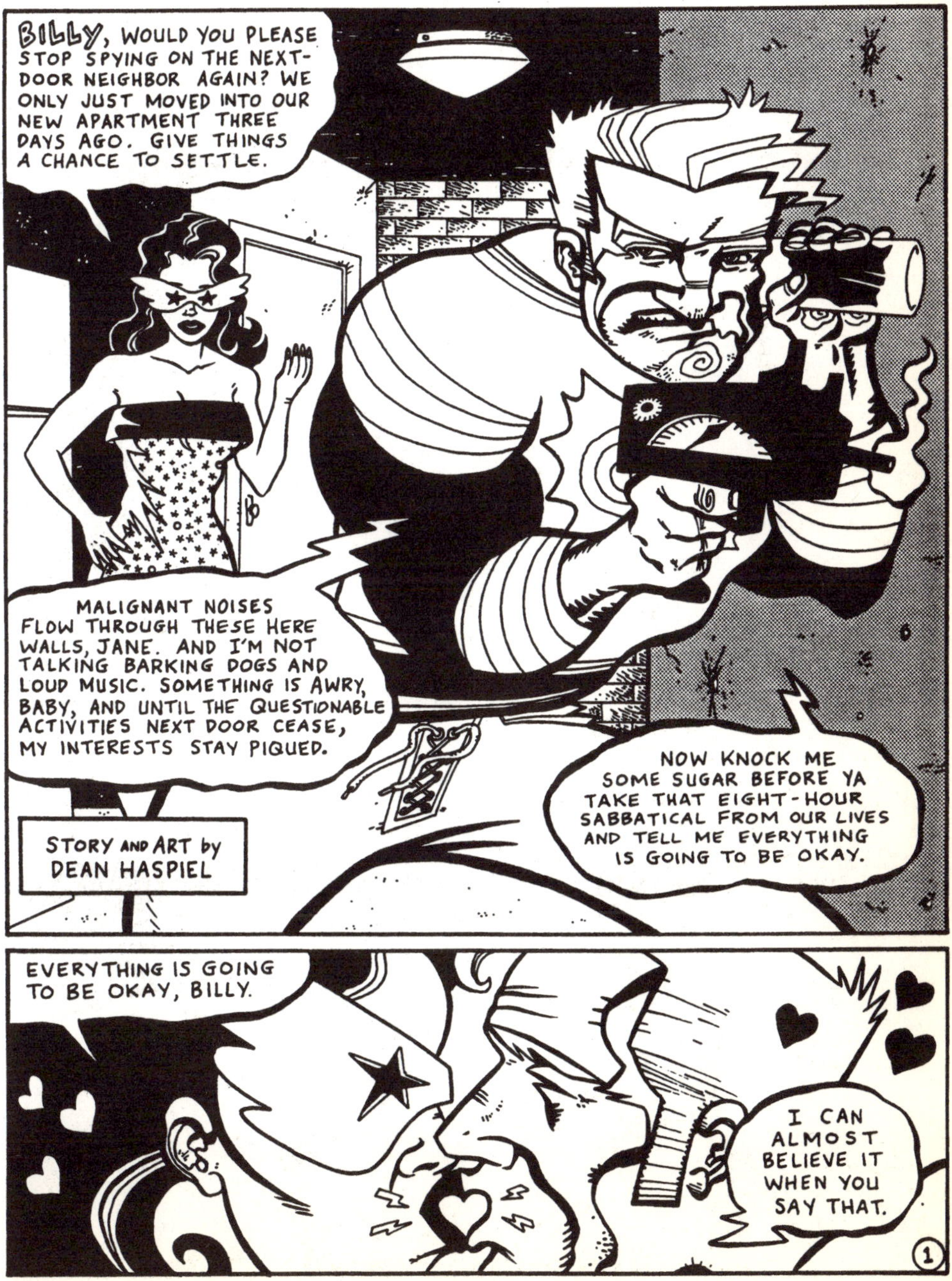
BILLY, WOULD YOU PLEASE STOP SPYING ON THE NEXT-DOOR NEIGHBOR AGAIN? WE ONLY JUST MOVED INTO OUR NEW APARTMENT THREE DAYS AGO. GIVE THINGS A CHANCE TO SETTLE.
MALIGNANT NOISES FLOW THROUGH THESE HERE WALLS, JANE. AND I'M NOT TALKING BARKING DOGS AND LOUD MUSIC. SOMETHING IS AWRY, BABY, AND UNTIL THE QUESTIONABLE ACTIVITIES NEXT DOOR CEASE, MY INTERESTS STAY PIQUED.
NOW KNOCK ME SOME SUGAR BEFORE YA TAKE THAT EIGHT-HOUR SABBATICAL FROM OUR LIVES AND TELL ME EVERYTHING IS GOING TO BE OKAY.
STORY AND ART by DEAN HASPIEL
EVERYTHING IS GOING TO BE OKAY, BILLY.
I CAN ALMOST BELIEVE IT WHEN YOU SAY THAT.
1

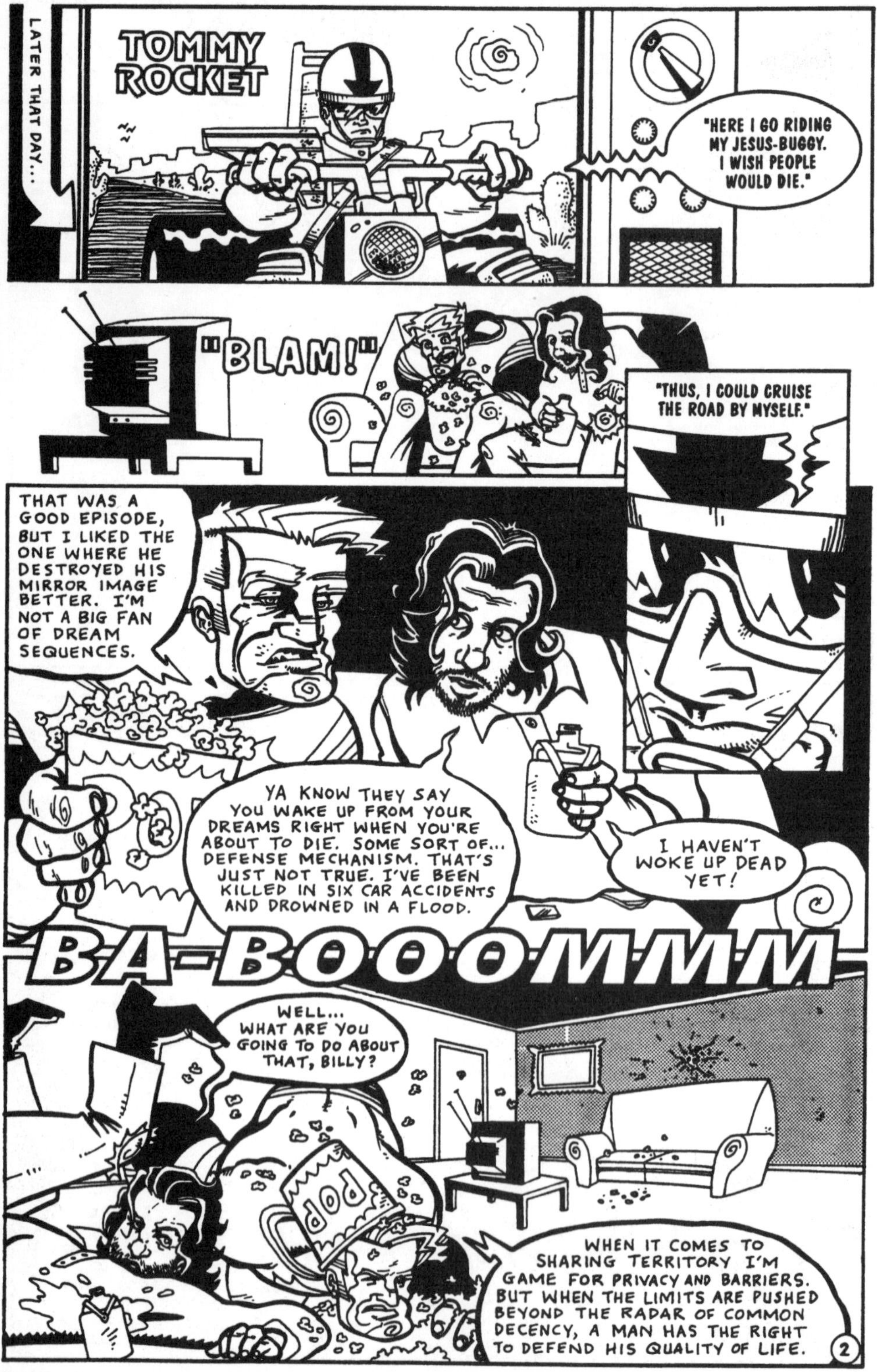
LATER THAT DAY...
TOMMY ROCKET
"HERE I GO RIDING MY JESUS-BUGGY. I WISH PEOPLE WOULD DIE."
"BLAM!"
"THUS, I COULD CRUISE THE ROAD BY MYSELF."
THAT WAS A GOOD EPISODE, BUT I LIKED THE ONE WHERE HE DESTROYED HIS MIRROR IMAGE BETTER. I'M NOT A BIG FAN OF DREAM SEQUENCES.
YA KNOW THEY SAY YOU WAKE UP FROM YOUR DREAMS RIGHT WHEN YOU'RE ABOUT TO DIE. SOME SORT OF... DEFENSE MECHANISM. THAT'S JUST NOT TRUE. I'VE BEEN KILLED IN SIX CAR ACCIDENTS AND DROWNED IN A FLOOD.
I HAVEN'T WOKE UP DEAD YET!
BA-BOOOMMM
WELL... WHAT ARE YOU GOING TO DO ABOUT THAT, BILLY?
POP
WHEN IT COMES TO SHARING TERRITORY I'M GAME FOR PRIVACY AND BARRIERS. BUT WHEN THE LIMITS ARE PUSHED BEYOND THE RADAR OF COMMON DECENCY, A MAN HAS THE RIGHT TO DEFEND HIS QUALITY OF LIFE.
2

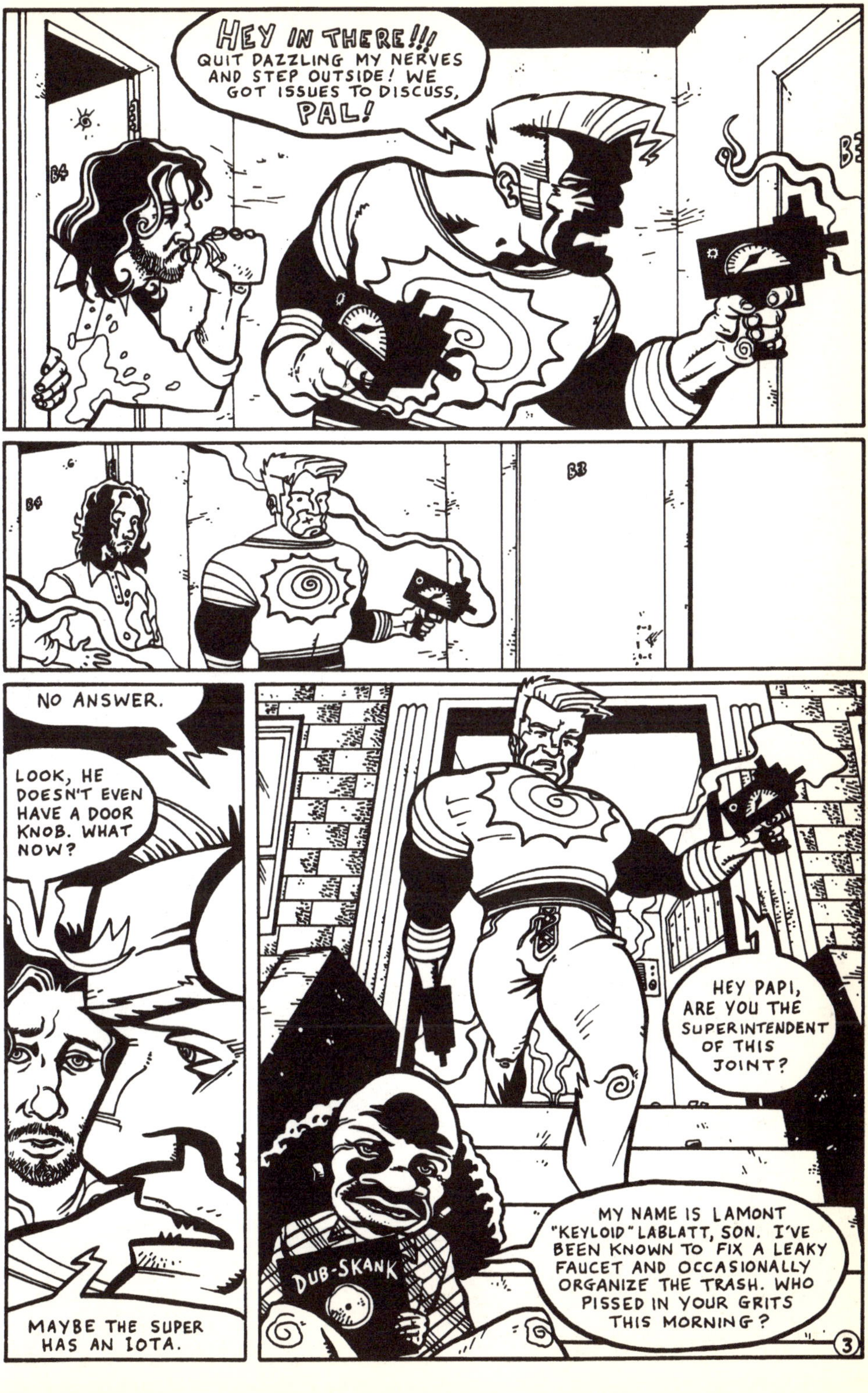
HEY IN THERE!!! QUIT DAZZLING MY NERVES AND STEP OUTSIDE! WE GOT ISSUES TO DISCUSS, PAL!
B4
B3
B3
B4
NO ANSWER.
LOOK, HE DOESN'T EVEN HAVE A DOOR KNOB. WHAT NOW?
MAYBE THE SUPER HAS AN IOTA.
HEY PAPI, ARE YOU THE SUPERINTENDENT OF THIS JOINT?
MY NAME IS LAMONT "KEYLOID" LABLATT, SON. I'VE BEEN KNOWN TO FIX A LEAKY FAUCET AND OCCASIONALLY ORGANIZE THE TRASH. WHO PISSED IN YOUR GRITS THIS MORNING?
DUB-SKANK
3

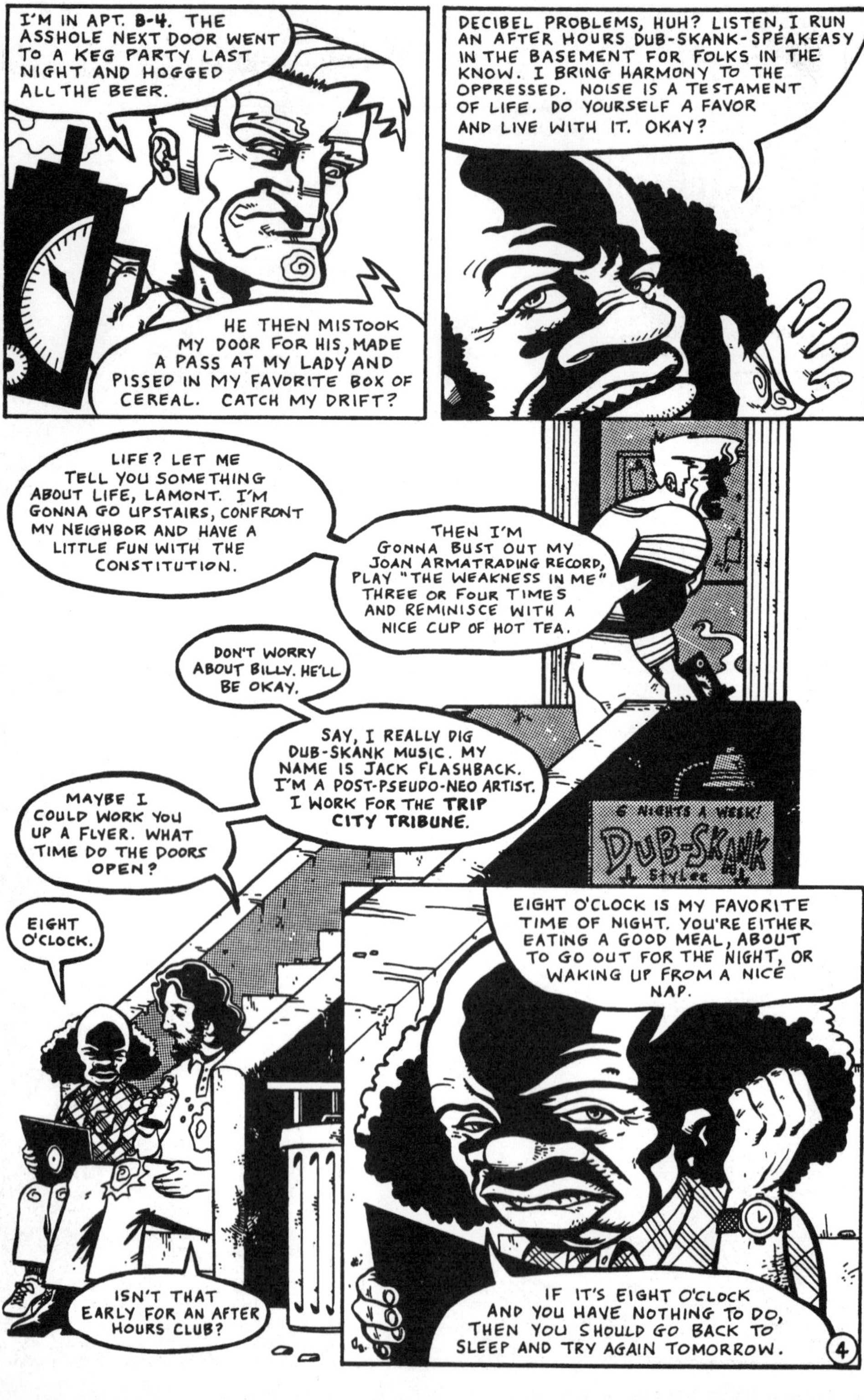
I'M IN APT. B-4. THE ASSHOLE NEXT DOOR WENT TO A KEG PARTY LAST NIGHT AND HOGGED ALL THE BEER.
HE THEN MISTOOK MY DOOR FOR HIS, MADE A PASS AT MY LADY AND PISSED IN MY FAVORITE BOX OF CEREAL. CATCH MY DRIFT?
DECIBEL PROBLEMS, HUH? LISTEN, I RUN AN AFTER HOURS DUB-SKANK-SPEAKEASY IN THE BASEMENT FOR FOLKS IN THE KNOW. I BRING HARMONY TO THE OPPRESSED. NOISE IS A TESTAMENT OF LIFE. DO YOURSELF A FAVOR AND LIVE WITH IT. OKAY?
LIFE? LET ME TELL YOU SOMETHING ABOUT LIFE, LAMONT. I'M GONNA GO UPSTAIRS, CONFRONT MY NEIGHBOR AND HAVE A LITTLE FUN WITH THE CONSTITUTION.
THEN I'M GONNA BUST OUT MY JOAN ARMATRADING RECORD, PLAY "THE WEAKNESS IN ME" THREE OR FOUR TIMES AND REMINISCE WITH A NICE CUP OF HOT TEA.
DON'T WORRY ABOUT BILLY. HE'LL BE OKAY.
SAY, I REALLY DIG DUB-SKANK MUSIC. MY NAME IS JACK FLASHBACK. I'M A POST-PSEUDO-NEO ARTIST. I WORK FOR THE TRIP CITY TRIBUNE.
MAYBE I COULD WORK YOU UP A FLYER. WHAT TIME DO THE DOORS OPEN?
6 NIGHTS A WEEK!
DUB-SKANK
STYLEE
EIGHT O'CLOCK.
ISN'T THAT EARLY FOR AN AFTER HOURS CLUB?
EIGHT O'CLOCK IS MY FAVORITE TIME OF NIGHT. YOU'RE EITHER EATING A GOOD MEAL, ABOUT TO GO OUT FOR THE NIGHT, OR WAKING UP FROM A NICE NAP.
IF IT'S EIGHT O'CLOCK AND YOU HAVE NOTHING TO DO, THEN YOU SHOULD GO BACK TO SLEEP AND TRY AGAIN TOMORROW.
4

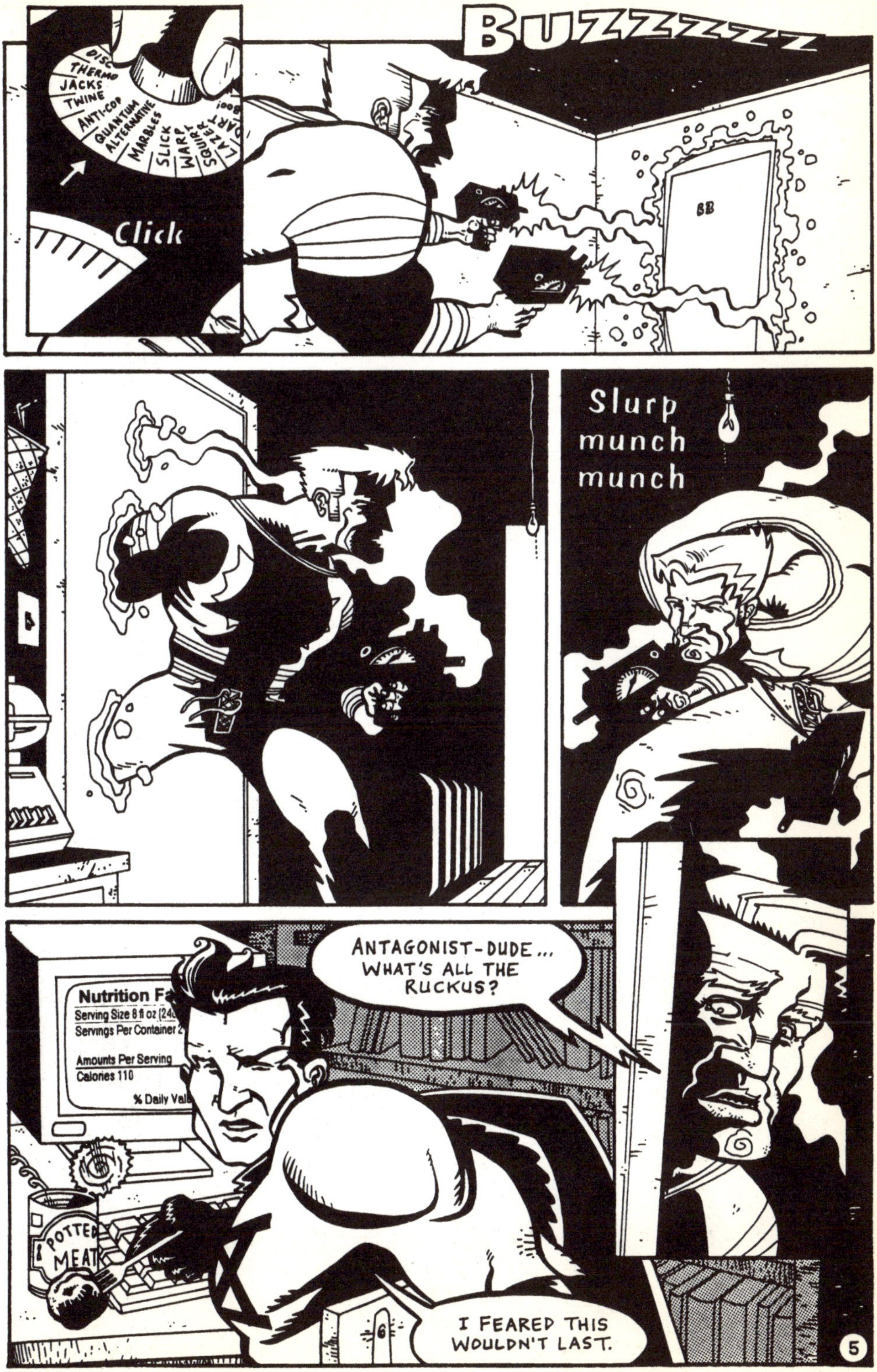
DISC
THERMO
JACKS
TWINE
ANTI-COP
QUANTUM
ALTERNATIVE
MARBLES
SLICK
WARP
SQUIRT
SQUEEZE
LAZER
DART
BOOT
Click
BUZZZZZZZ
BB
Slurp
munch
munch
ANTAGONIST-DUDE...
WHAT'S ALL THE
RUCKUS?
I FEARED THIS
WOULDN'T LAST.
Nutrition Fa
Serving Size 8 fl oz (24
Servings Per Container 2
Amounts Per Serving
Calories 110
% Daily Valu
POTTED
MEAT
5

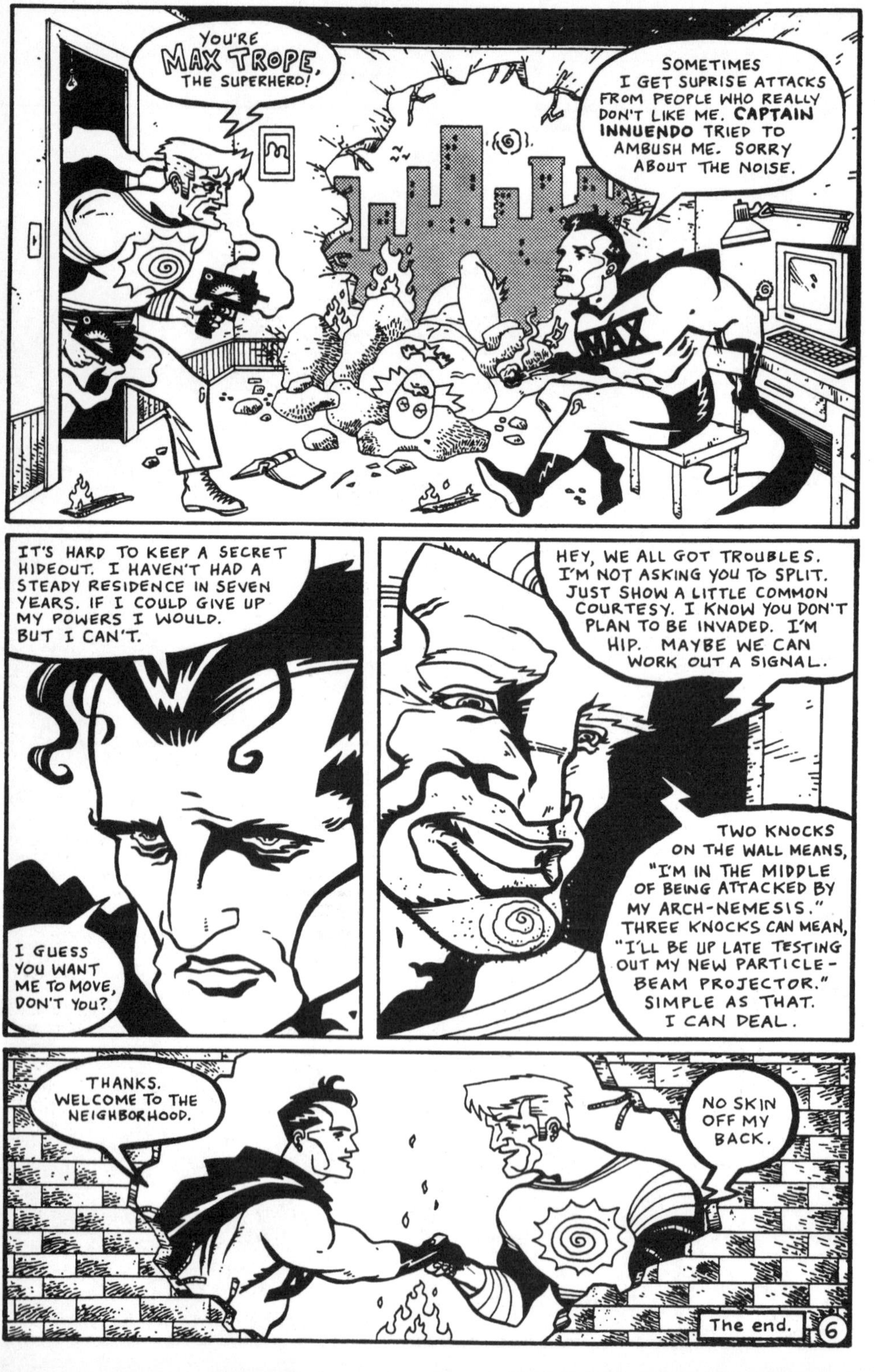

YOU'RE MAX TROPE, THE SUPERHERO!
SOMETIMES I GET SUPRISE ATTACKS FROM PEOPLE WHO REALLY DON'T LIKE ME. CAPTAIN INNUENDO TRIED TO AMBUSH ME. SORRY ABOUT THE NOISE.
MAX
IT'S HARD TO KEEP A SECRET HIDEOUT. I HAVEN'T HAD A STEADY RESIDENCE IN SEVEN YEARS. IF I COULD GIVE UP MY POWERS I WOULD. BUT I CAN'T.
I GUESS YOU WANT ME TO MOVE, DON'T YOU?
HEY, WE ALL GOT TROUBLES. I'M NOT ASKING YOU TO SPLIT. JUST SHOW A LITTLE COMMON COURTESY. I KNOW YOU DON'T PLAN TO BE INVADED. I'M HIP. MAYBE WE CAN WORK OUT A SIGNAL.
TWO KNOCKS ON THE WALL MEANS, "I'M IN THE MIDDLE OF BEING ATTACKED BY MY ARCH-NEMESIS." THREE KNOCKS CAN MEAN, "I'LL BE UP LATE TESTING OUT MY NEW PARTICLE-BEAM PROJECTOR." SIMPLE AS THAT. I CAN DEAL.
THANKS. WELCOME TO THE NEIGHBORHOOD.
NO SKIN OFF MY BACK.
The end.
6

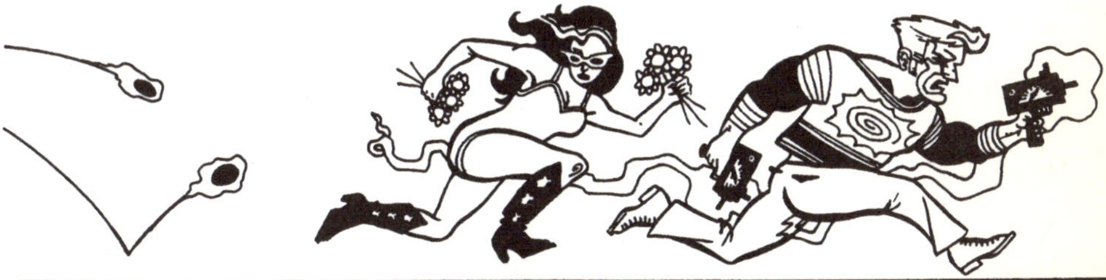

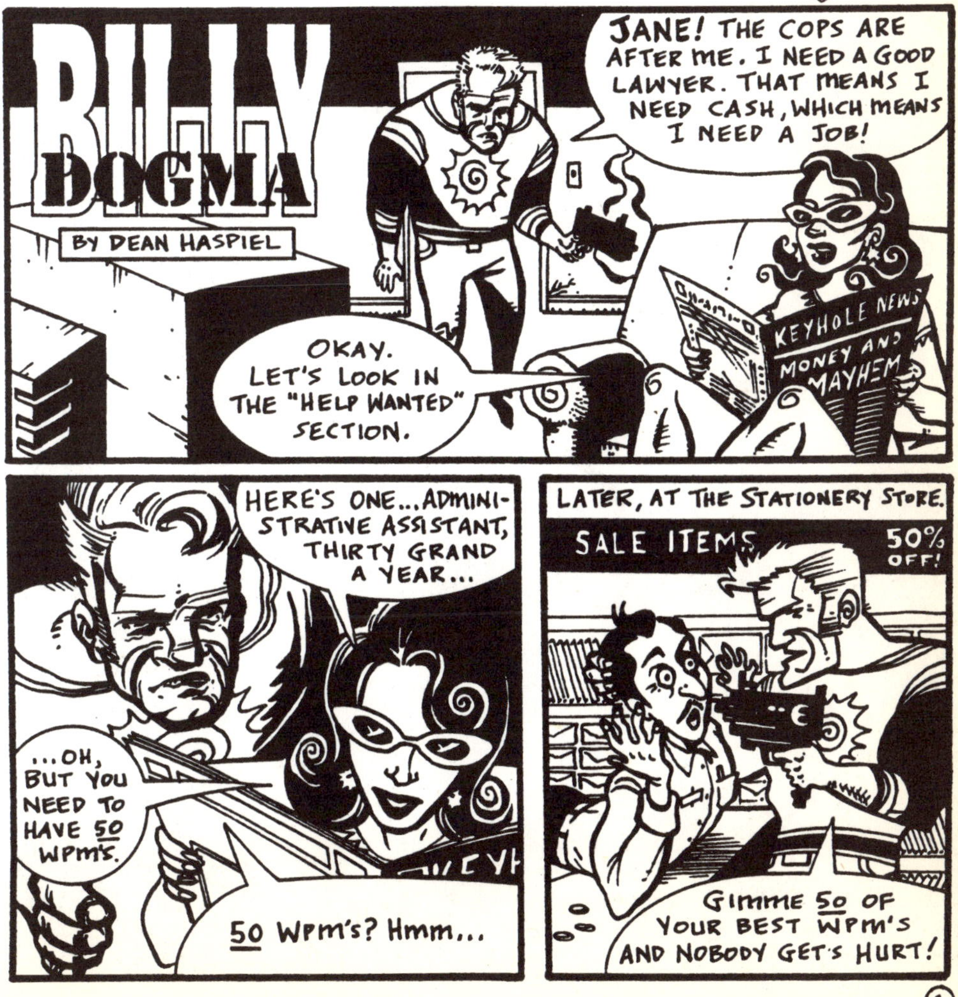
BILLY DOGMA
BY DEAN HASPIEL
JANE! THE COPS ARE AFTER ME. I NEED A GOOD LAWYER. THAT MEANS I NEED CASH, WHICH MEANS I NEED A JOB!
KEYHOLE NEWS
MONEY AND MAYHEM
OKAY. LET'S LOOK IN THE "HELP WANTED" SECTION.
HERE'S ONE...ADMINISTRATIVE ASSISTANT, THIRTY GRAND A YEAR...
...OH, BUT YOU NEED TO HAVE 50 WPM'S.
50 WPM'S? HMM...
LATER, AT THE STATIONERY STORE.
SALE ITEMS
50% OFF!
GIMME 50 OF YOUR BEST WPM'S AND NOBODY GET'S HURT!
1

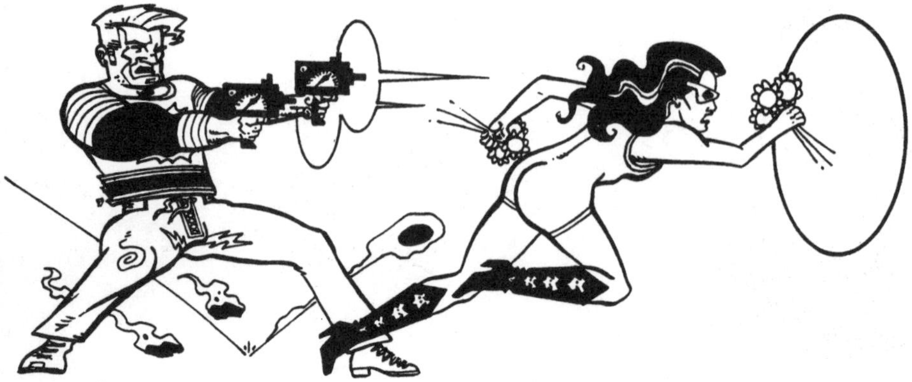

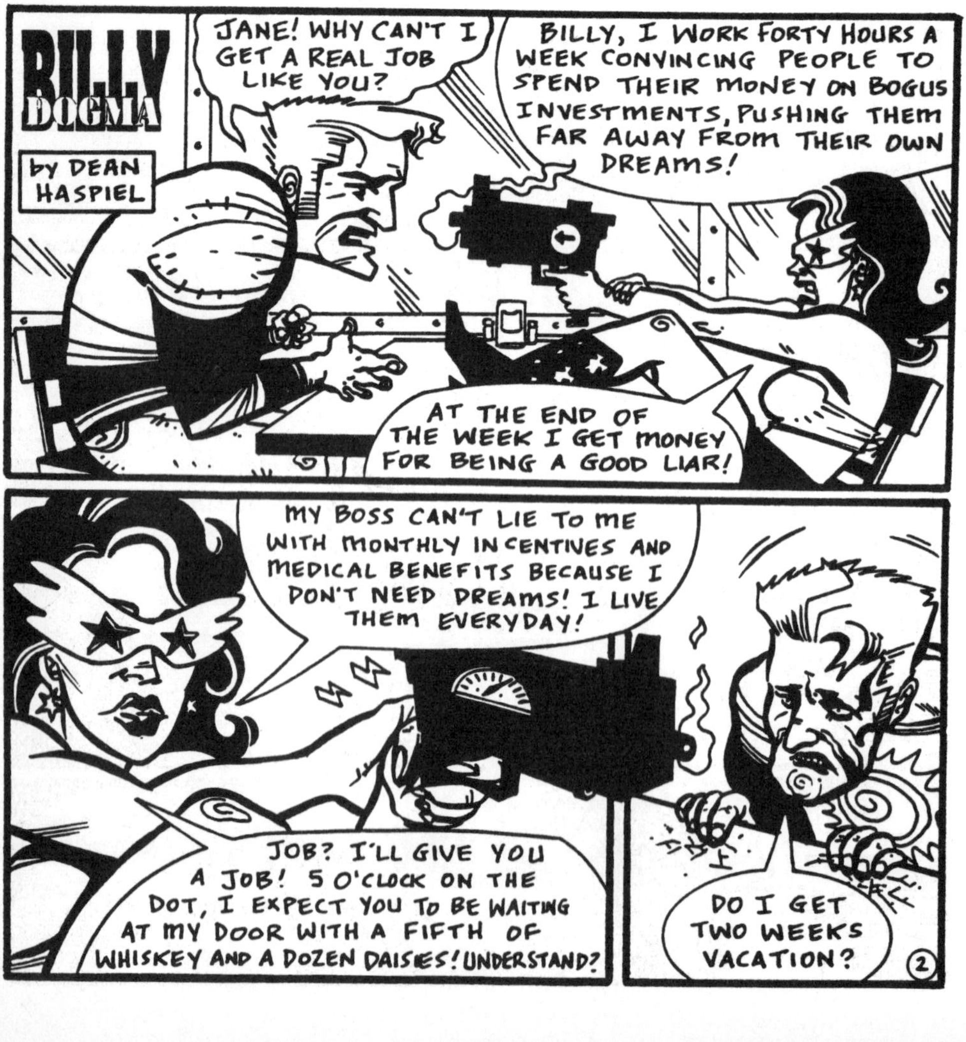
BILLY DOGMA
by DEAN HASPIEL
JANE! WHY CAN'T I GET A REAL JOB LIKE YOU?
BILLY, I WORK FORTY HOURS A WEEK CONVINCING PEOPLE TO SPEND THEIR MONEY ON BOGUS INVESTMENTS, PUSHING THEM FAR AWAY FROM THEIR OWN DREAMS!
AT THE END OF THE WEEK I GET MONEY FOR BEING A GOOD LIAR!
MY BOSS CAN'T LIE TO ME WITH MONTHLY INCENTIVES AND MEDICAL BENEFITS BECAUSE I DON'T NEED DREAMS! I LIVE THEM EVERYDAY!
JOB? I'LL GIVE YOU A JOB! 5 O'CLOCK ON THE DOT, I EXPECT YOU TO BE WAITING AT MY DOOR WITH A FIFTH OF WHISKEY AND A DOZEN DAISIES! UNDERSTAND?
DO I GET TWO WEEKS VACATION?
2

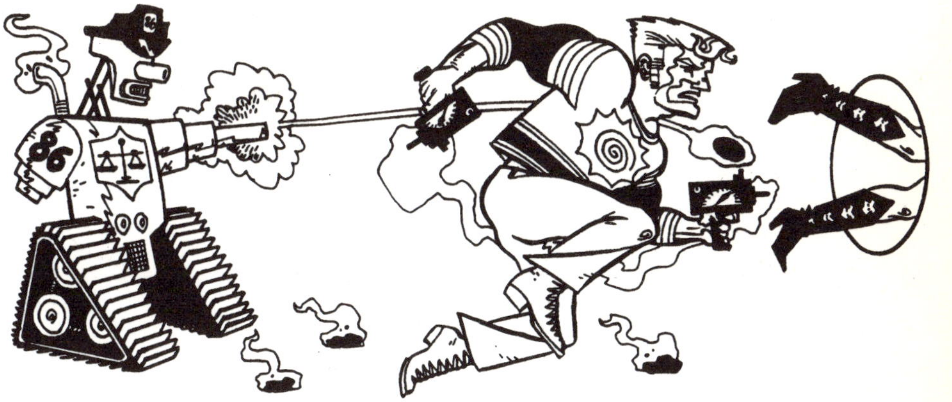

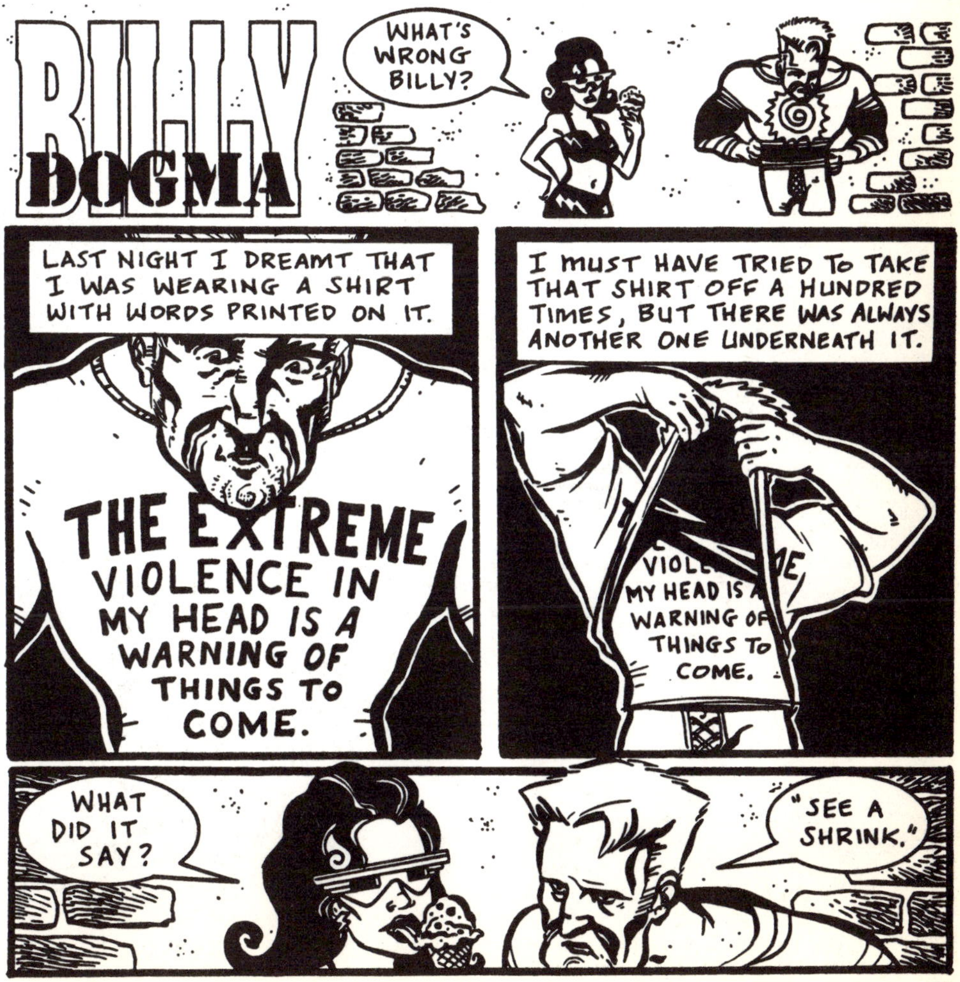

BILLY
DOGMA
WHAT'S WRONG BILLY?
LAST NIGHT I DREAMT THAT I WAS WEARING A SHIRT WITH WORDS PRINTED ON IT.
THE EXTREME VIOLENCE IN MY HEAD IS A WARNING OF THINGS TO COME.
I MUST HAVE TRIED TO TAKE THAT SHIRT OFF A HUNDRED TIMES, BUT THERE WAS ALWAYS ANOTHER ONE UNDERNEATH IT.
MY HEAD IS A WARNING OF THINGS TO COME.
WHAT DID IT SAY?
"SEE A SHRINK."

3

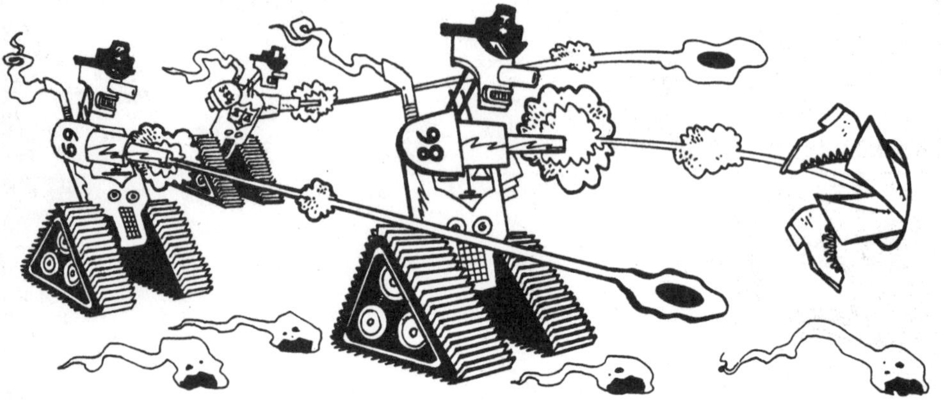
69
86

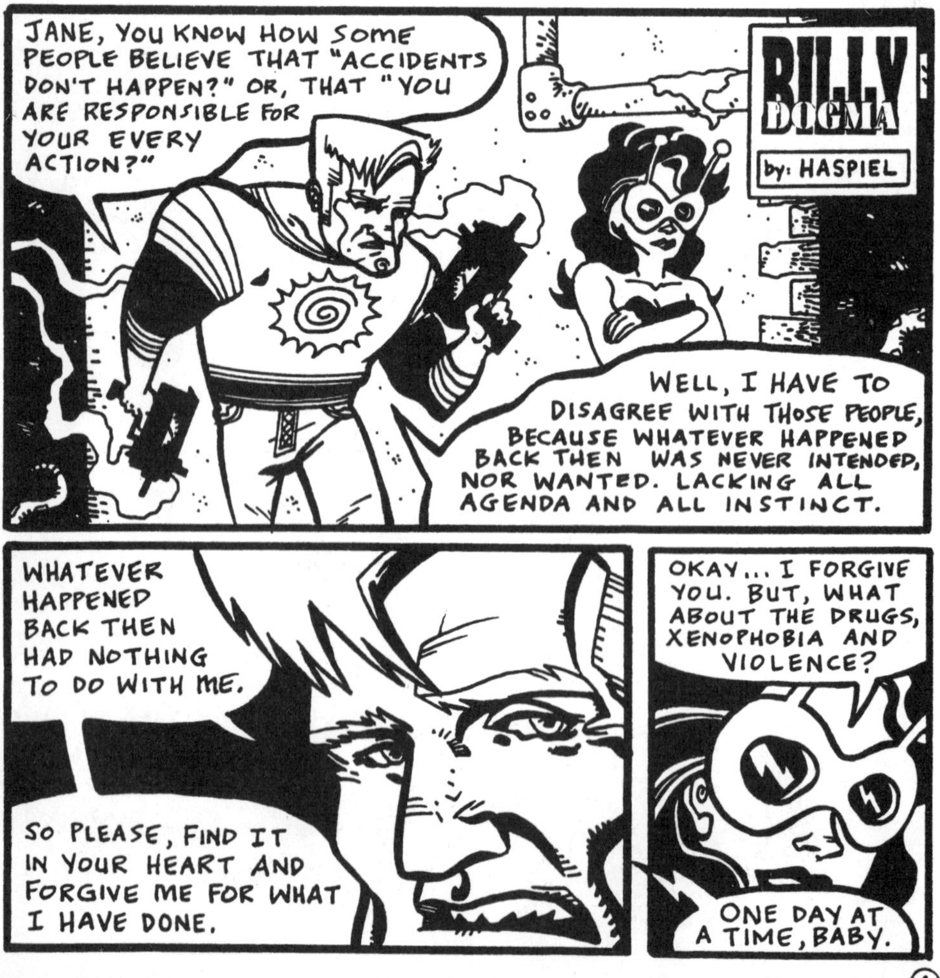
BILLY DOGMA
by: HASPIEL
JANE, YOU KNOW HOW SOME PEOPLE BELIEVE THAT "ACCIDENTS DON'T HAPPEN?" OR, THAT "YOU ARE RESPONSIBLE FOR YOUR EVERY ACTION?"
WELL, I HAVE TO DISAGREE WITH THOSE PEOPLE, BECAUSE WHATEVER HAPPENED BACK THEN WAS NEVER INTENDED, NOR WANTED. LACKING ALL AGENDA AND ALL INSTINCT.
WHATEVER HAPPENED BACK THEN HAD NOTHING TO DO WITH ME.
SO PLEASE, FIND IT IN YOUR HEART AND FORGIVE ME FOR WHAT I HAVE DONE.
OKAY... I FORGIVE YOU. BUT, WHAT ABOUT THE DRUGS, XENOPHOBIA AND VIOLENCE?
ONE DAY AT A TIME, BABY.

4

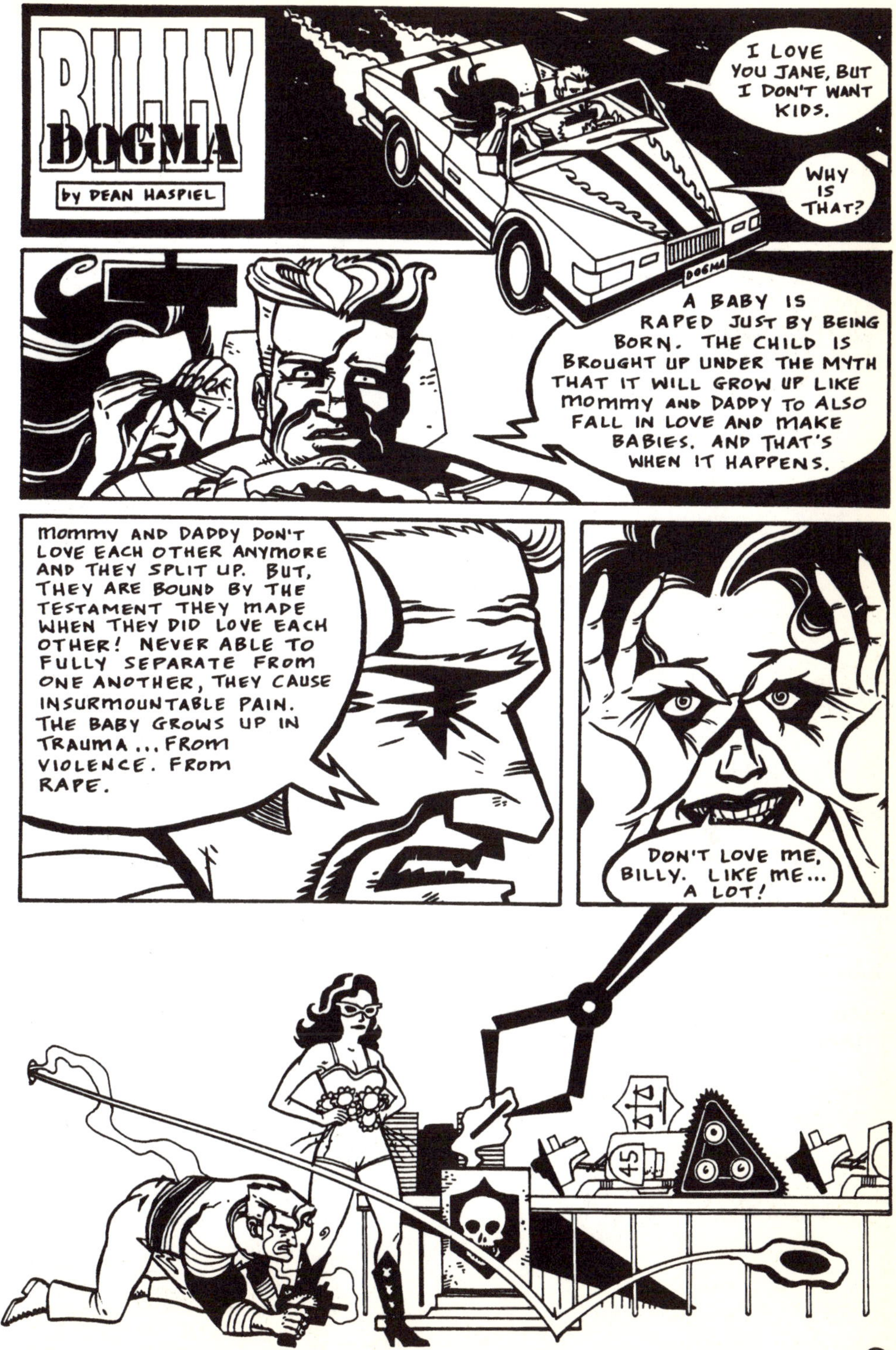
BILLY DOGMA
by DEAN HASPIEL
I LOVE YOU JANE, BUT I DON'T WANT KIDS.
WHY IS THAT?
DOGMA
A BABY IS RAPED JUST BY BEING BORN. THE CHILD IS BROUGHT UP UNDER THE MYTH THAT IT WILL GROW UP LIKE MOMMY AND DADDY TO ALSO FALL IN LOVE AND MAKE BABIES. AND THAT'S WHEN IT HAPPENS.
MOMMY AND DADDY DON'T LOVE EACH OTHER ANYMORE AND THEY SPLIT UP. BUT, THEY ARE BOUND BY THE TESTAMENT THEY MADE WHEN THEY DID LOVE EACH OTHER! NEVER ABLE TO FULLY SEPARATE FROM ONE ANOTHER, THEY CAUSE INSURMOUNTABLE PAIN. THE BABY GROWS UP IN TRAUMA... FROM VIOLENCE. FROM RAPE.
DON'T LOVE ME, BILLY. LIKE ME... A LOT!
45
5

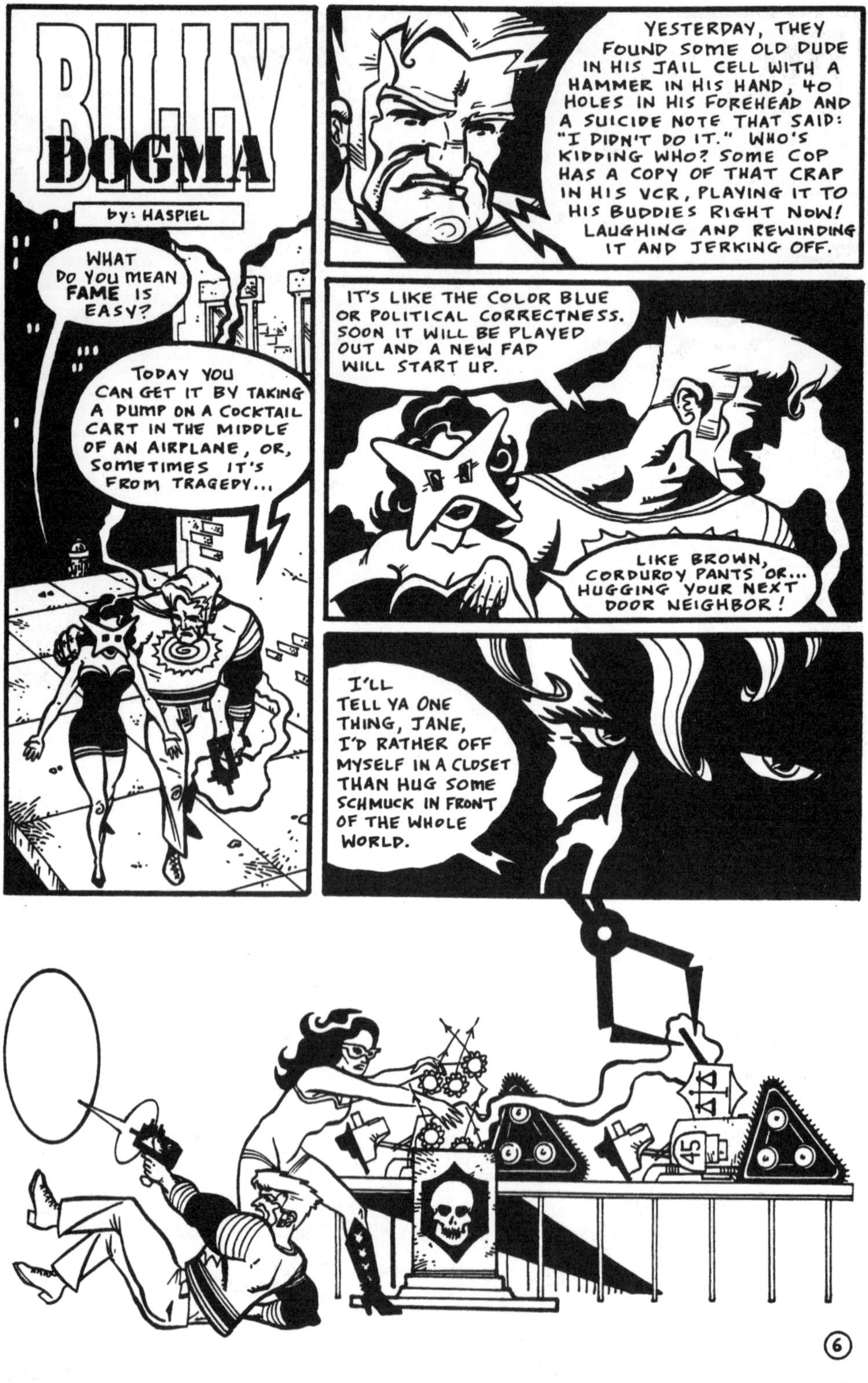
BILLY DOGMA
by: HASPIEL
WHAT DO YOU MEAN FAME IS EASY?
TODAY YOU CAN GET IT BY TAKING A DUMP ON A COCKTAIL CART IN THE MIDDLE OF AN AIRPLANE, OR, SOMETIMES IT'S FROM TRAGEDY...
YESTERDAY, THEY FOUND SOME OLD DUDE IN HIS JAIL CELL WITH A HAMMER IN HIS HAND, 40 HOLES IN HIS FOREHEAD AND A SUICIDE NOTE THAT SAID: "I DIDN'T DO IT." WHO'S KIDDING WHO? SOME COP HAS A COPY OF THAT CRAP IN HIS VCR, PLAYING IT TO HIS BUDDIES RIGHT NOW! LAUGHING AND REWINDING IT AND JERKING OFF.
IT'S LIKE THE COLOR BLUE OR POLITICAL CORRECTNESS. SOON IT WILL BE PLAYED OUT AND A NEW FAD WILL START UP.
LIKE BROWN, CORDUROY PANTS OR... HUGGING YOUR NEXT DOOR NEIGHBOR!
I'LL TELL YA ONE THING, JANE, I'D RATHER OFF MYSELF IN A CLOSET THAN HUG SOME SCHMUCK IN FRONT OF THE WHOLE WORLD.
45
6

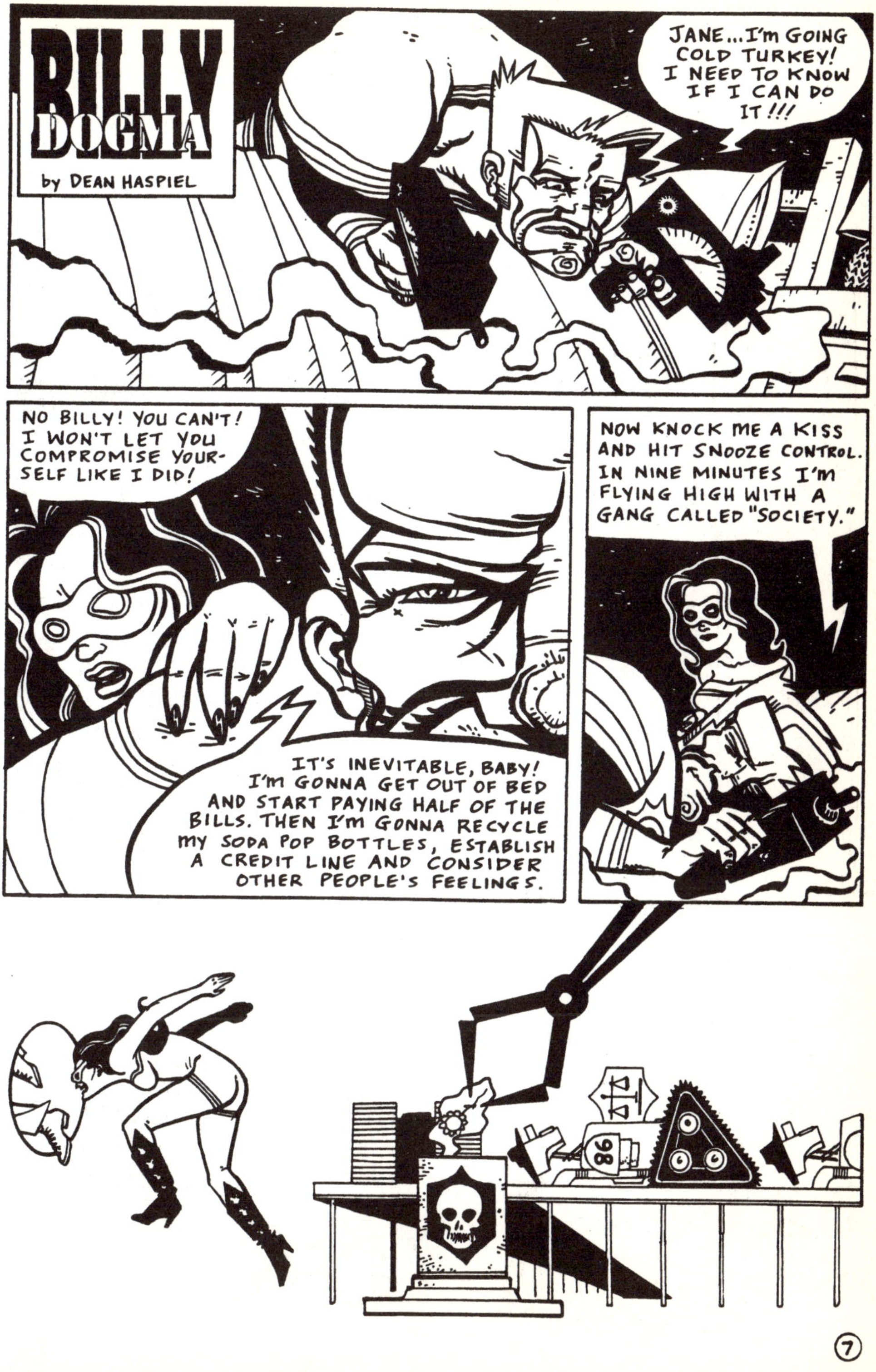
BILLY DOGMA
by DEAN HASPIEL
JANE... I'M GOING COLD TURKEY! I NEED TO KNOW IF I CAN DO IT!!!
NO BILLY! YOU CAN'T! I WON'T LET YOU COMPROMISE YOURSELF LIKE I DID!
IT'S INEVITABLE, BABY! I'M GONNA GET OUT OF BED AND START PAYING HALF OF THE BILLS. THEN I'M GONNA RECYCLE MY SODA POP BOTTLES, ESTABLISH A CREDIT LINE AND CONSIDER OTHER PEOPLE'S FEELINGS.
NOW KNOCK ME A KISS AND HIT SNOOZE CONTROL. IN NINE MINUTES I'M FLYING HIGH WITH A GANG CALLED "SOCIETY."
98
7

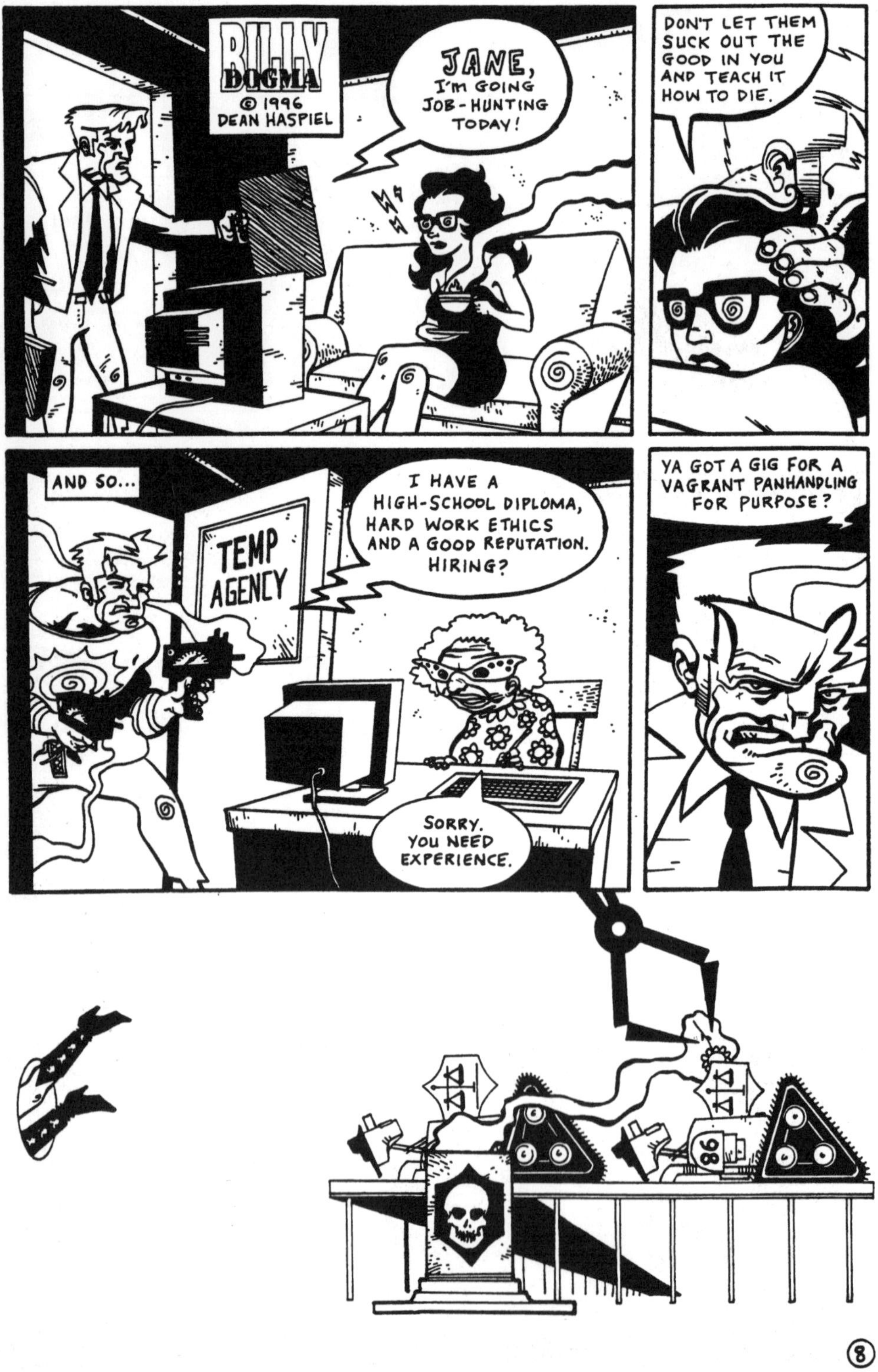
BILLY DOGMA
© 1996 DEAN HASPIEL
JANE, I'M GOING JOB-HUNTING TODAY!
DON'T LET THEM SUCK OUT THE GOOD IN YOU AND TEACH IT HOW TO DIE.
AND SO...
TEMP AGENCY
I HAVE A HIGH-SCHOOL DIPLOMA, HARD WORK ETHICS AND A GOOD REPUTATION. HIRING?
SORRY. YOU NEED EXPERIENCE.
YA GOT A GIG FOR A VAGRANT PANHANDLING FOR PURPOSE?
86
8

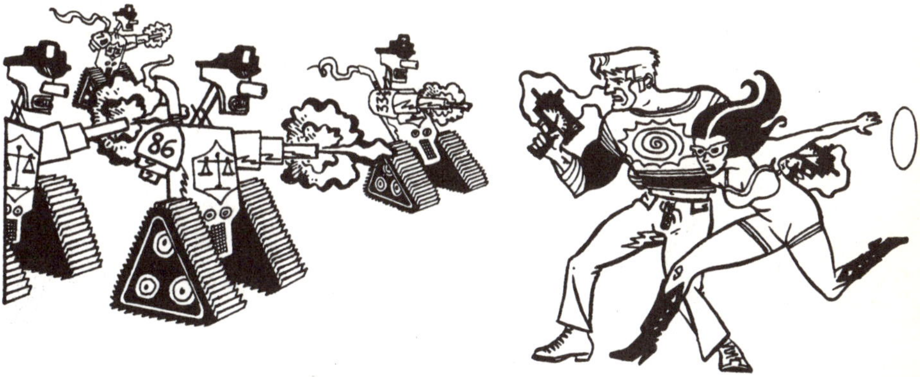

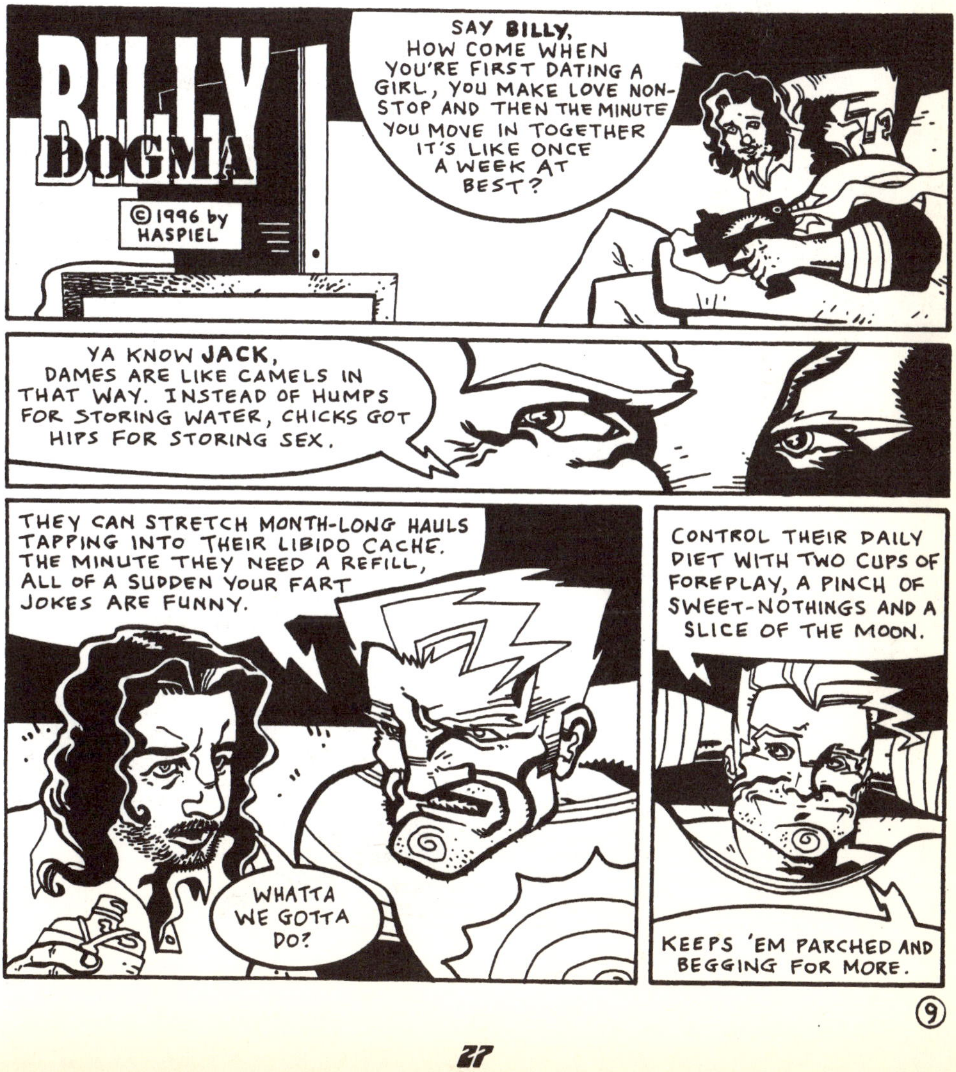

BILLY DOGMA
©1996 by HASPIEL
SAY BILLY, HOW COME WHEN YOU'RE FIRST DATING A GIRL, YOU MAKE LOVE NON-STOP AND THEN THE MINUTE YOU MOVE IN TOGETHER IT'S LIKE ONCE A WEEK AT BEST?
YA KNOW JACK, DAMES ARE LIKE CAMELS IN THAT WAY. INSTEAD OF HUMPS FOR STORING WATER, CHICKS GOT HIPS FOR STORING SEX.
THEY CAN STRETCH MONTH-LONG HAULS TAPPING INTO THEIR LIBIDO CACHE. THE MINUTE THEY NEED A REFILL, ALL OF A SUDDEN YOUR FART JOKES ARE FUNNY.
WHATTA WE GOTTA DO?
CONTROL THEIR DAILY DIET WITH TWO CUPS OF FOREPLAY, A PINCH OF SWEET-NOTHINGS AND A SLICE OF THE MOON.
KEEPS 'EM PARCHED AND BEGGING FOR MORE.
9

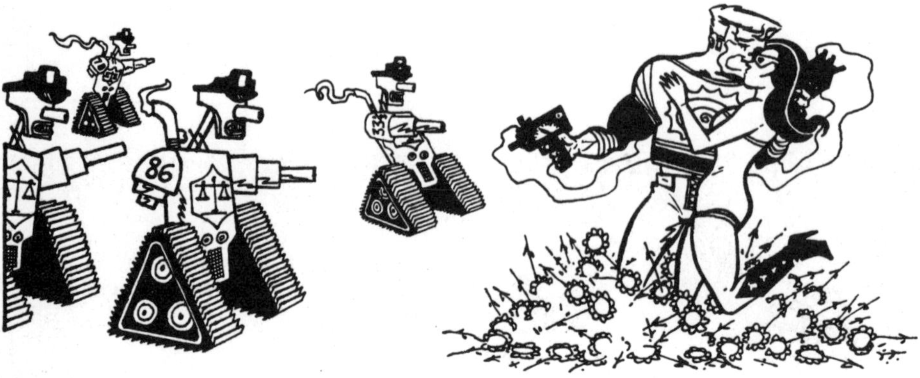

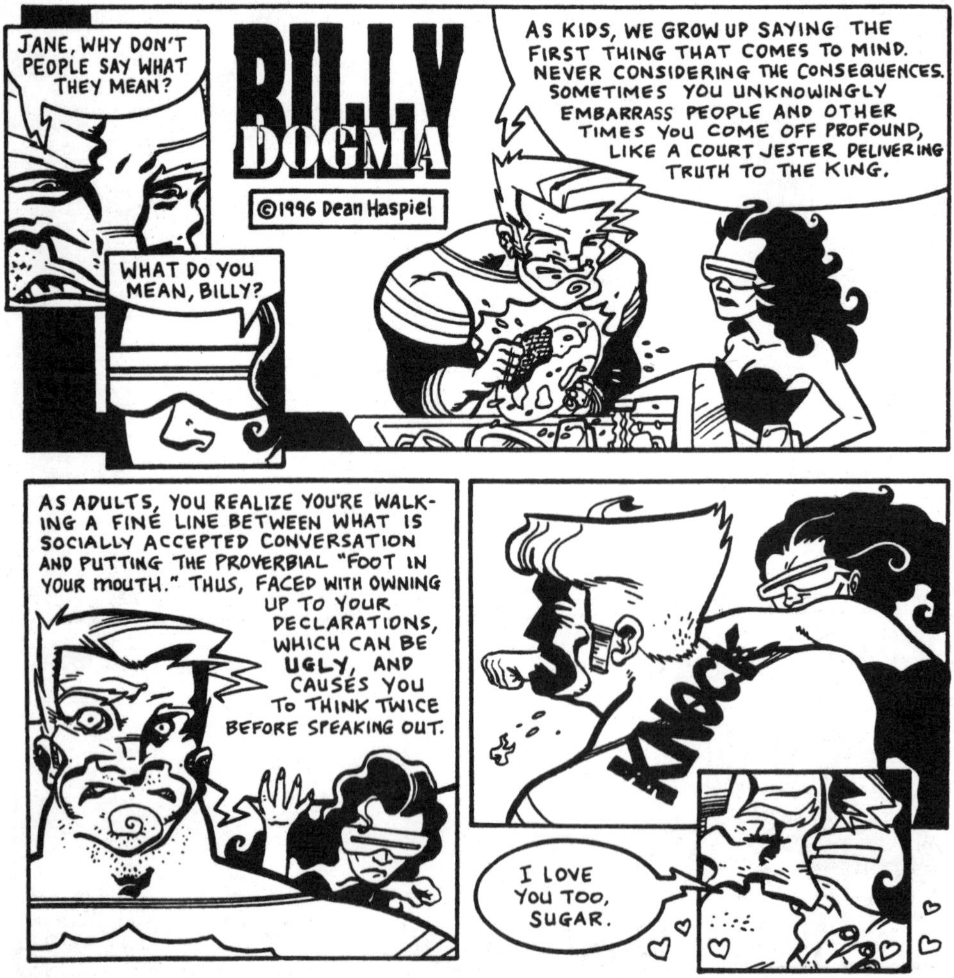

BILLY DOGMA
©1996 Dean Haspiel
JANE, WHY DON'T PEOPLE SAY WHAT THEY MEAN?
WHAT DO YOU MEAN, BILLY?
AS KIDS, WE GROW UP SAYING THE FIRST THING THAT COMES TO MIND. NEVER CONSIDERING THE CONSEQUENCES. SOMETIMES YOU UNKNOWINGLY EMBARRASS PEOPLE AND OTHER TIMES YOU COME OFF PROFOUND, LIKE A COURT JESTER DELIVERING TRUTH TO THE KING.
AS ADULTS, YOU REALIZE YOU'RE WALKING A FINE LINE BETWEEN WHAT IS SOCIALLY ACCEPTED CONVERSATION AND PUTTING THE PROVERBIAL "FOOT IN YOUR MOUTH." THUS, FACED WITH OWNING UP TO YOUR DECLARATIONS, WHICH CAN BE UGLY, AND CAUSES YOU TO THINK TWICE BEFORE SPEAKING OUT.
KNOCK
I LOVE YOU TOO, SUGAR.
10

billy dogma and his better half are snapshot poets in ***PHOTOBOOTH FOLLIES***

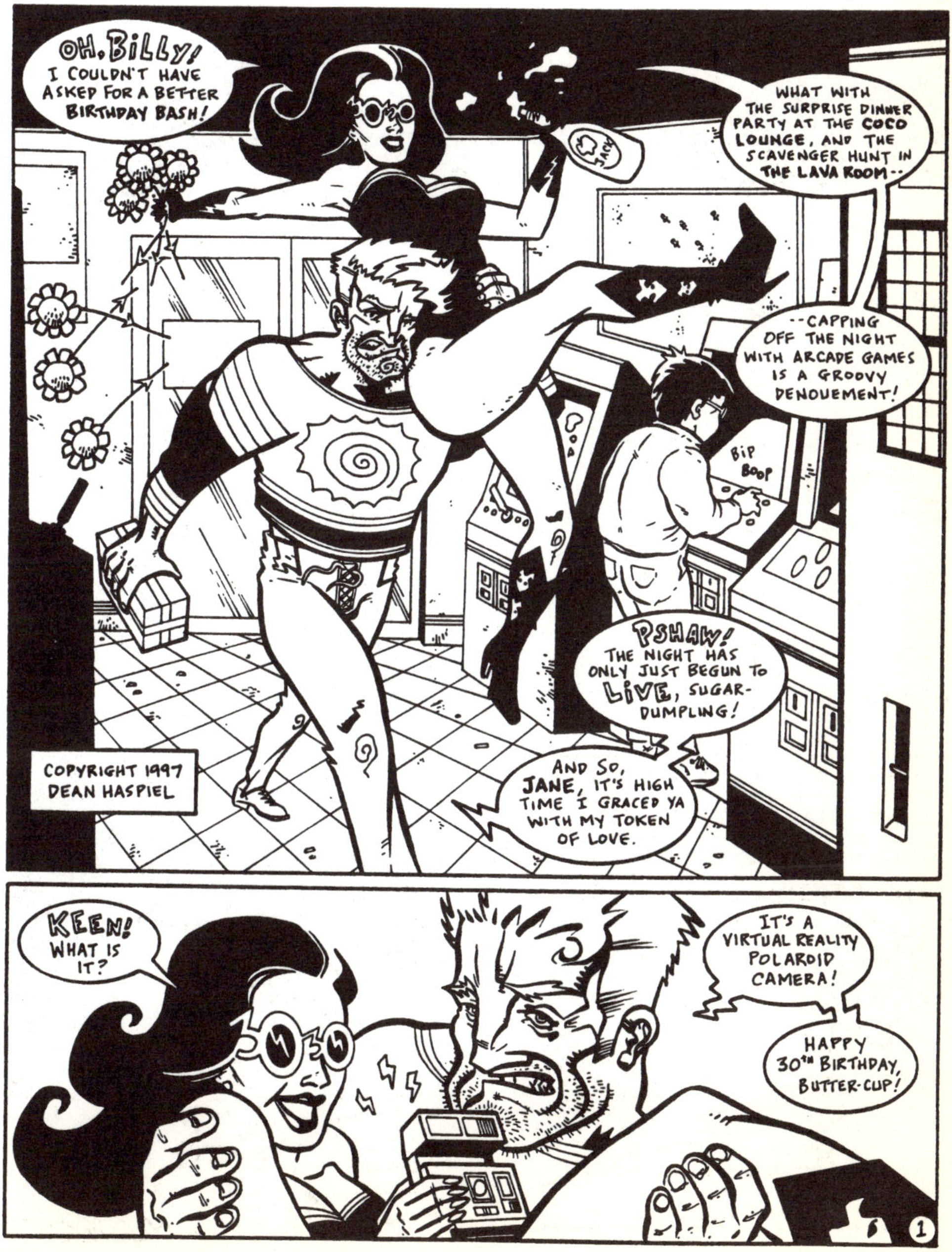
OH, BILLY! I COULDN'T HAVE ASKED FOR A BETTER BIRTHDAY BASH!
WHAT WITH THE SURPRISE DINNER PARTY AT THE COCO LOUNGE, AND THE SCAVENGER HUNT IN THE LAVA ROOM--
--CAPPING OFF THE NIGHT WITH ARCADE GAMES IS A GROOVY DENOUEMENT!
BIP BOOP
PSHAW! THE NIGHT HAS ONLY JUST BEGUN TO LIVE, SUGAR-DUMPLING!
AND SO, JANE, IT'S HIGH TIME I GRACED YA WITH MY TOKEN OF LOVE.
COPYRIGHT 1997 DEAN HASPIEL
KEEN! WHAT IS IT?
IT'S A VIRTUAL REALITY POLAROID CAMERA!
HAPPY 30th BIRTHDAY, BUTTER-CUP!
1

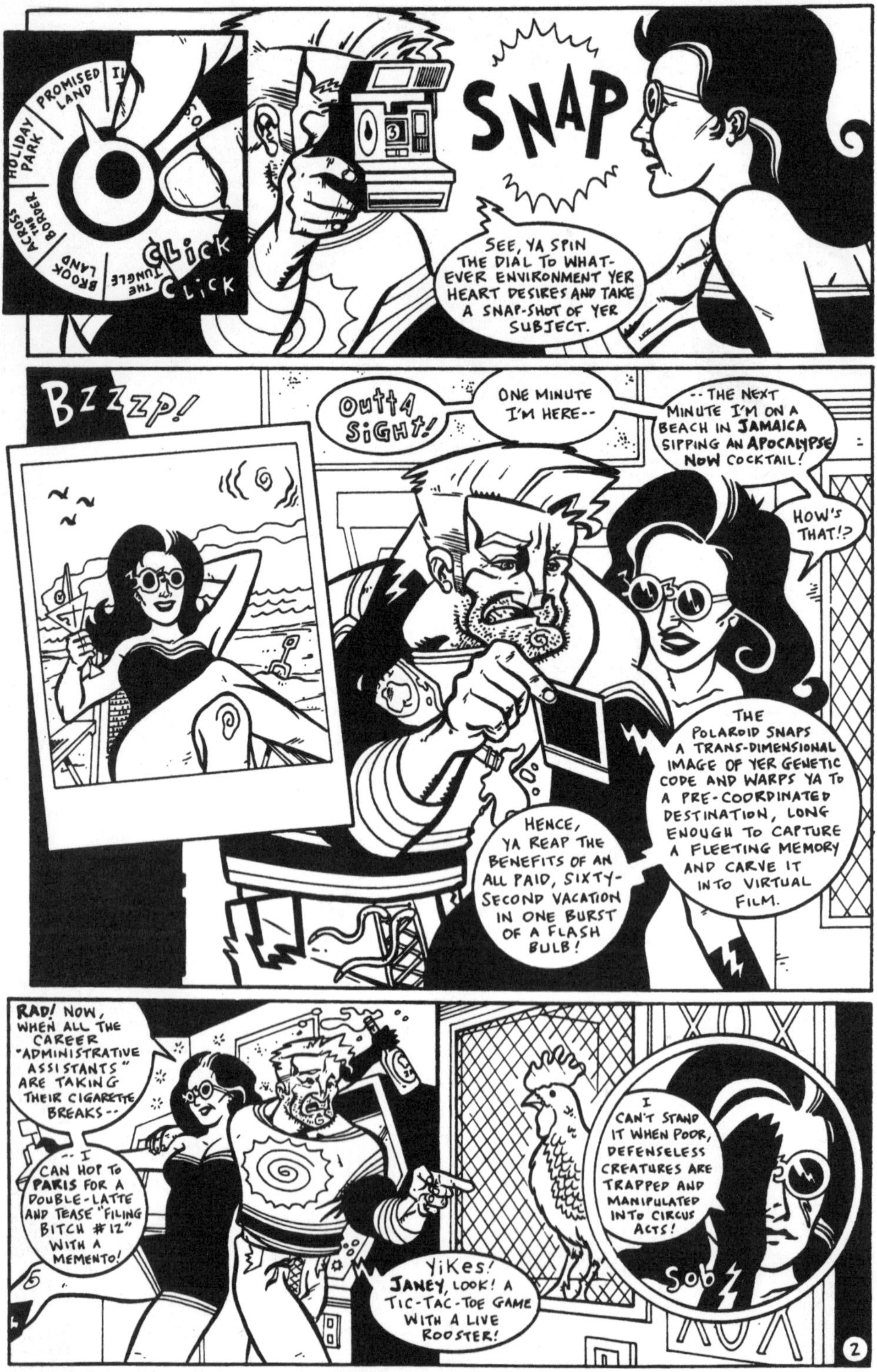
PROMISED LAND
HOLIDAY PARK
ACROSS THE BORDER
BROOK LAND
THE JUNGLE
CLICK CLICK
SNAP
SEE, YA SPIN THE DIAL TO WHAT-EVER ENVIRONMENT YER HEART DESIRES AND TAKE A SNAP-SHOT OF YER SUBJECT.
BZZZP!
OUTTA SIGHT!
ONE MINUTE I'M HERE--
--THE NEXT MINUTE I'M ON A BEACH IN JAMAICA SIPPING AN APOCALYPSE NOW COCKTAIL!
HOW'S THAT!?
THE POLAROID SNAPS A TRANS-DIMENSIONAL IMAGE OF YER GENETIC CODE AND WARPS YA TO A PRE-COORDINATED DESTINATION, LONG ENOUGH TO CAPTURE A FLEETING MEMORY AND CARVE IT INTO VIRTUAL FILM.
HENCE, YA REAP THE BENEFITS OF AN ALL PAID, SIXTY-SECOND VACATION IN ONE BURST OF A FLASH BULB!
RAD! NOW, WHEN ALL THE CAREER "ADMINISTRATIVE ASSISTANTS" ARE TAKING THEIR CIGARETTE BREAKS--
--I CAN HOP TO PARIS FOR A DOUBLE-LATTE AND TEASE "FILING BITCH #12" WITH A MEMENTO!
YIKES! JANEY, LOOK! A TIC-TAC-TOE GAME WITH A LIVE ROOSTER!
I CAN'T STAND IT WHEN POOR, DEFENSELESS CREATURES ARE TRAPPED AND MANIPULATED INTO CIRCUS ACTS!
SOB
2

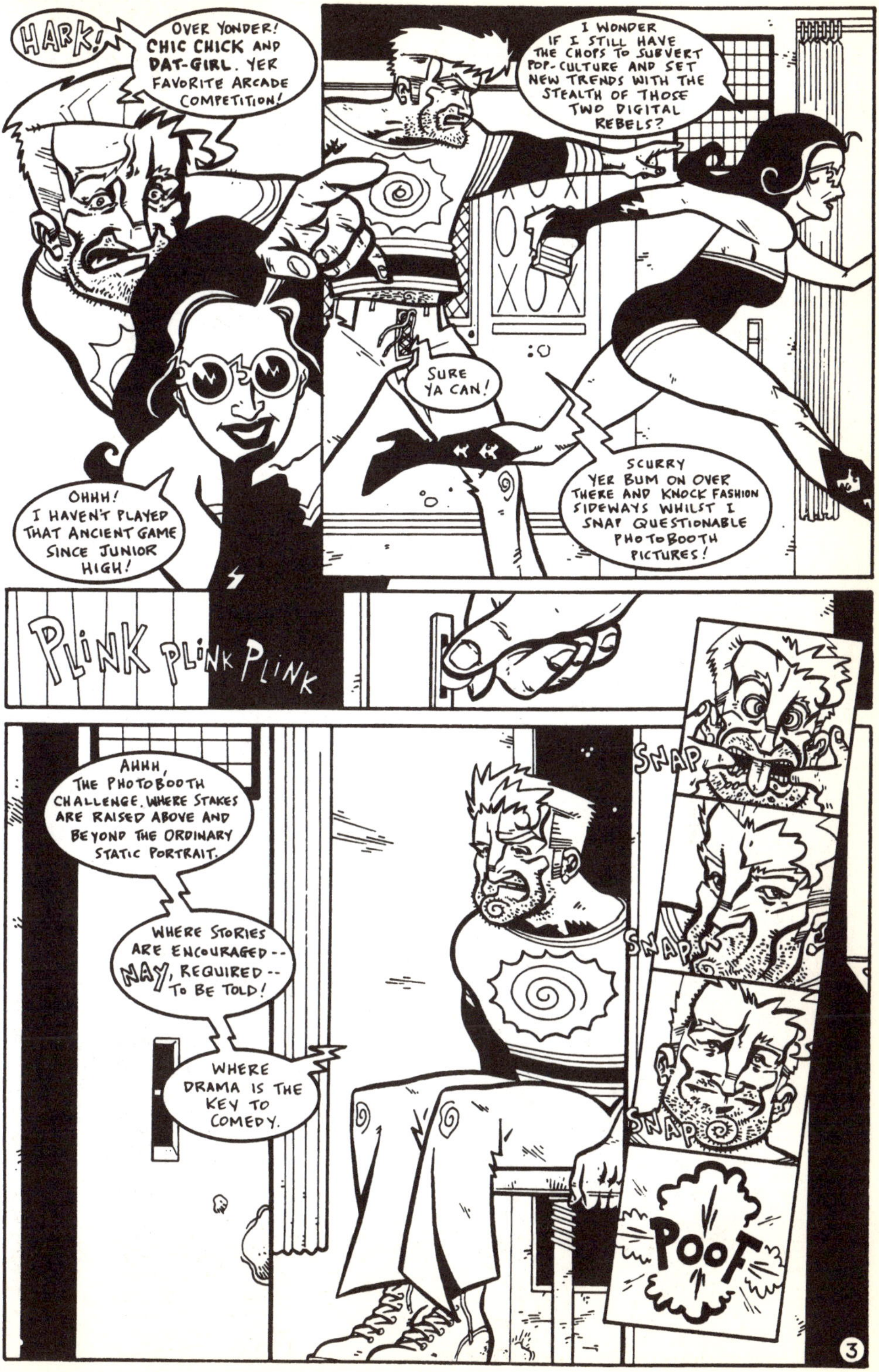
HARK!
OVER YONDER! CHIC CHICK AND DAT-GIRL. YER FAVORITE ARCADE COMPETITION!
I WONDER IF I STILL HAVE THE CHOPS TO SUBVERT POP-CULTURE AND SET NEW TRENDS WITH THE STEALTH OF THOSE TWO DIGITAL REBELS?
SURE YA CAN!
SCURRY YER BUM ON OVER THERE AND KNOCK FASHION SIDEWAYS WHILST I SNAP QUESTIONABLE PHOTOBOOTH PICTURES!
OHHH! I HAVEN'T PLAYED THAT ANCIENT GAME SINCE JUNIOR HIGH!
PLINK PLINK PLINK
AHHH, THE PHOTOBOOTH CHALLENGE. WHERE STAKES ARE RAISED ABOVE AND BEYOND THE ORDINARY STATIC PORTRAIT.
WHERE STORIES ARE ENCOURAGED -- NAY, REQUIRED -- TO BE TOLD!
WHERE DRAMA IS THE KEY TO COMEDY.
SNAP
SNAP
SNAP
POOF
3

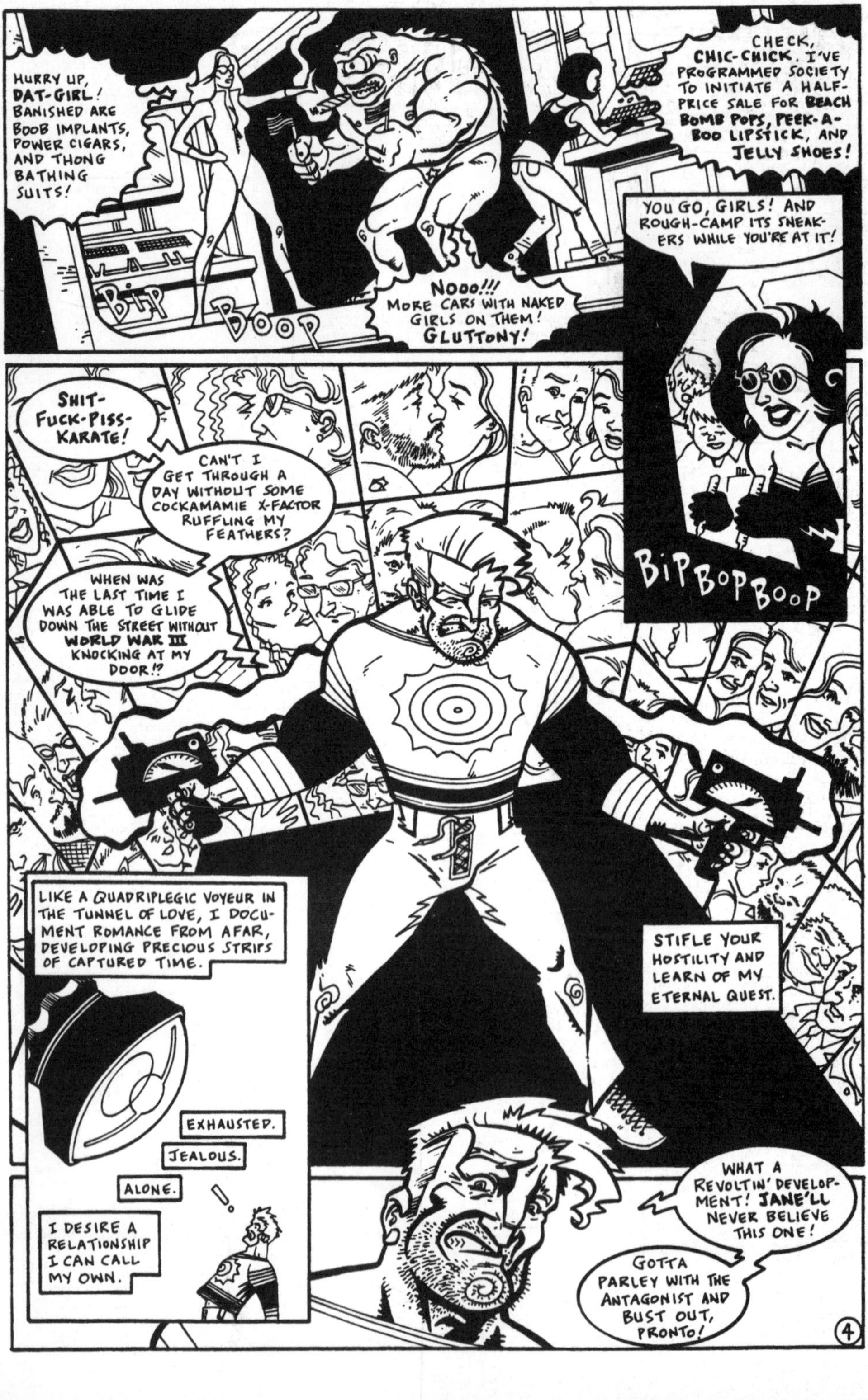

HURRY UP, DAT-GIRL! BANISHED ARE BOOB IMPLANTS, POWER CIGARS, AND THONG BATHING SUITS!
CHECK, CHIC-CHICK. I'VE PROGRAMMED SOCIETY TO INITIATE A HALF-PRICE SALE FOR BEACH BOMB POPS, PEEK-A-BOO LIPSTICK, AND JELLY SHOES!
BIP
BOOP
NOOO!!! MORE CARS WITH NAKED GIRLS ON THEM! GLUTTONY!
YOU GO, GIRLS! AND ROUGH-CAMP ITS SNEAKERS WHILE YOU'RE AT IT!
BIP BOP BOOP
SHIT-FUCK-PISS-KARATE!
CAN'T I GET THROUGH A DAY WITHOUT SOME COCKAMAMIE X-FACTOR RUFFLING MY FEATHERS?
WHEN WAS THE LAST TIME I WAS ABLE TO GLIDE DOWN THE STREET WITHOUT WORLD WAR III KNOCKING AT MY DOOR!?
LIKE A QUADRIPLEGIC VOYEUR IN THE TUNNEL OF LOVE, I DOCUMENT ROMANCE FROM AFAR, DEVELOPING PRECIOUS STRIPS OF CAPTURED TIME.
STIFLE YOUR HOSTILITY AND LEARN OF MY ETERNAL QUEST.
EXHAUSTED.
JEALOUS.
ALONE.
I DESIRE A RELATIONSHIP I CAN CALL MY OWN.
!
WHAT A REVOLTIN' DEVELOPMENT! JANE'LL NEVER BELIEVE THIS ONE!
GOTTA PARLEY WITH THE ANTAGONIST AND BUST OUT, PRONTO!
4

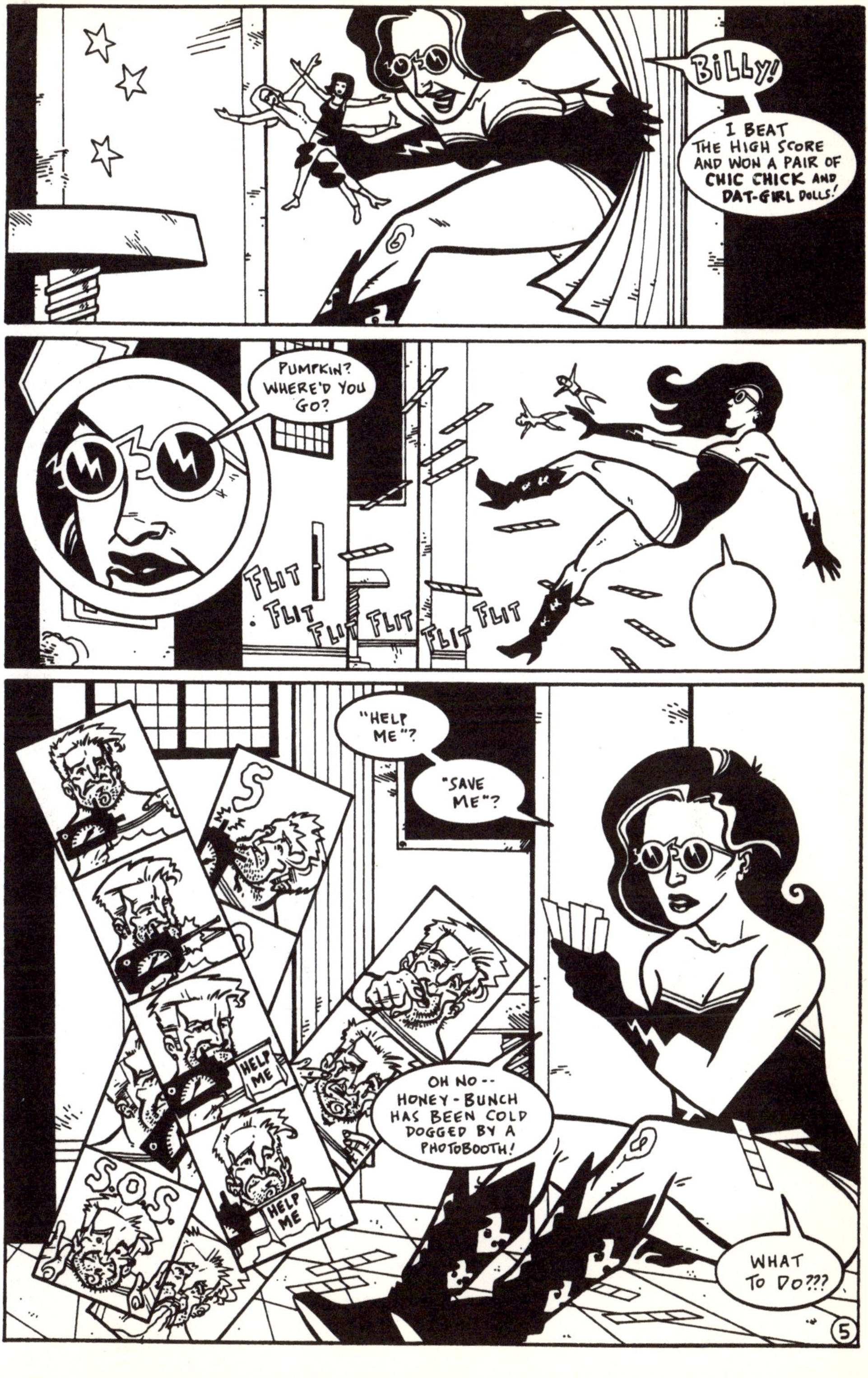
BILLY!
I BEAT THE HIGH SCORE AND WON A PAIR OF CHIC CHICK AND DAT-GIRL DOLLS!
PUMPKIN? WHERE'D YOU GO?
FLIT FLIT FLIT FLIT FLIT FLIT
"HELP ME"?
"SAVE ME"?
S
HELP ME
S.O.S.
HELP ME
OH NO -- HONEY-BUNCH HAS BEEN COLD DOGGED BY A PHOTOBOOTH!
WHAT TO DO???
5

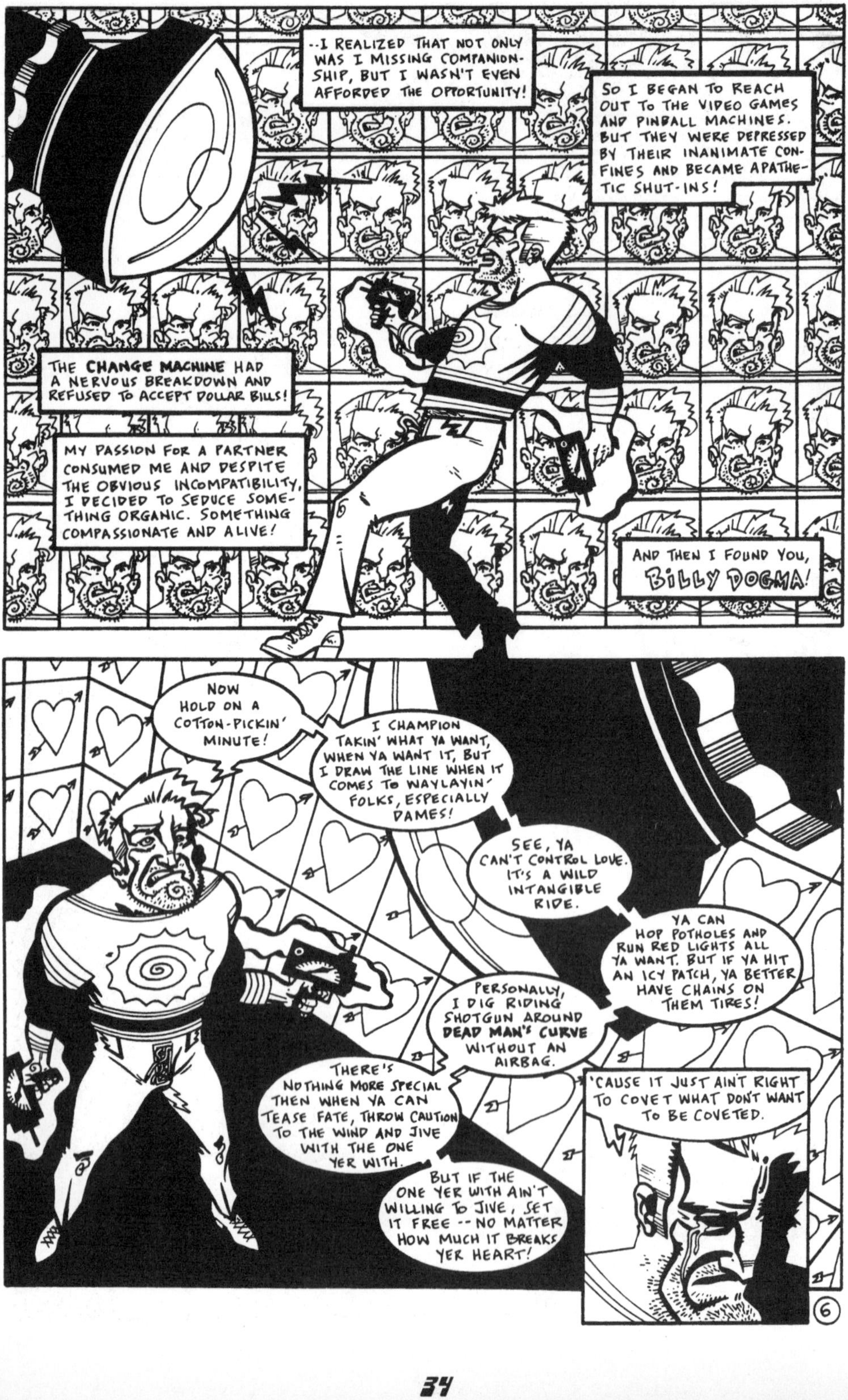

--I REALIZED THAT NOT ONLY WAS I MISSING COMPANIONSHIP, BUT I WASN'T EVEN AFFORDED THE OPPORTUNITY!
SO I BEGAN TO REACH OUT TO THE VIDEO GAMES AND PINBALL MACHINES. BUT THEY WERE DEPRESSED BY THEIR INANIMATE CONFINES AND BECAME APATHETIC SHUT-INS!
THE CHANGE MACHINE HAD A NERVOUS BREAKDOWN AND REFUSED TO ACCEPT DOLLAR BILLS!
MY PASSION FOR A PARTNER CONSUMED ME AND DESPITE THE OBVIOUS INCOMPATIBILITY, I DECIDED TO SEDUCE SOMETHING ORGANIC. SOMETHING COMPASSIONATE AND ALIVE!
AND THEN I FOUND YOU, BILLY DOGMA!
NOW HOLD ON A COTTON-PICKIN' MINUTE!
I CHAMPION TAKIN' WHAT YA WANT, WHEN YA WANT IT, BUT I DRAW THE LINE WHEN IT COMES TO WAYLAYIN' FOLKS, ESPECIALLY DAMES!
SEE, YA CAN'T CONTROL LOVE. IT'S A WILD INTANGIBLE RIDE.
YA CAN HOP POTHOLES AND RUN RED LIGHTS ALL YA WANT. BUT IF YA HIT AN ICY PATCH, YA BETTER HAVE CHAINS ON THEM TIRES!
PERSONALLY, I DIG RIDING SHOTGUN AROUND DEAD MAN'S CURVE WITHOUT AN AIRBAG.
THERE'S NOTHING MORE SPECIAL THEN WHEN YA CAN TEASE FATE, THROW CAUTION TO THE WIND AND JIVE WITH THE ONE YER WITH.
BUT IF THE ONE YER WITH AIN'T WILLING TO JIVE, SET IT FREE -- NO MATTER HOW MUCH IT BREAKS YER HEART!
'CAUSE IT JUST AIN'T RIGHT TO COVET WHAT DON'T WANT TO BE COVETED.
6

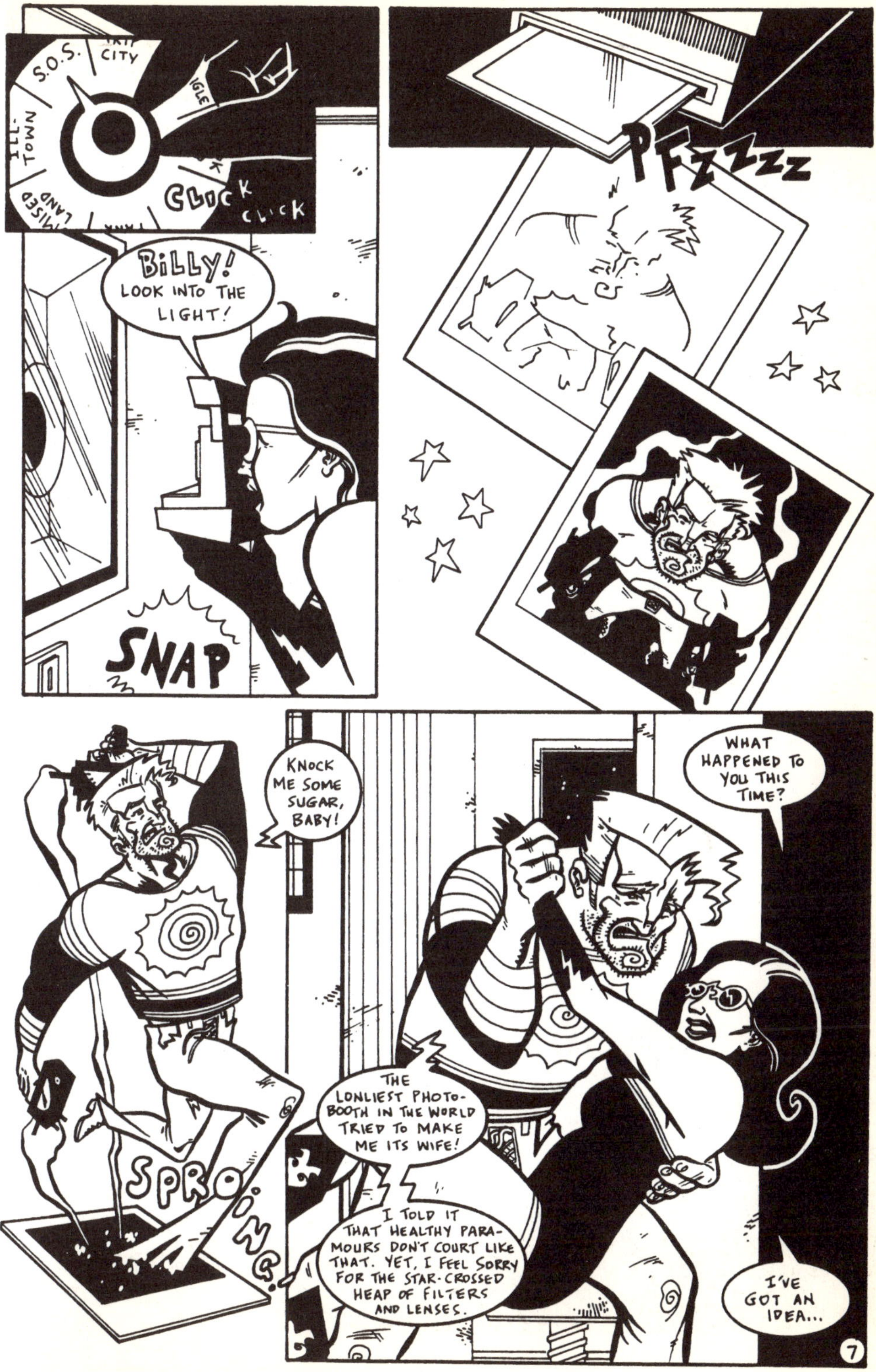
S.O.S.
CITY
IGLE
ILL-TOWN
LAND
CLICK
CLICK
BILLY! LOOK INTO THE LIGHT!
SNAP
PFZZZZ
KNOCK ME SOME SUGAR, BABY!
SPROING!
WHAT HAPPENED TO YOU THIS TIME?
THE LONLIEST PHOTO-BOOTH IN THE WORLD TRIED TO MAKE ME ITS WIFE!
I TOLD IT THAT HEALTHY PARA-MOURS DON'T COURT LIKE THAT. YET, I FEEL SORRY FOR THE STAR-CROSSED HEAP OF FILTERS AND LENSES.
I'VE GOT AN IDEA...
7

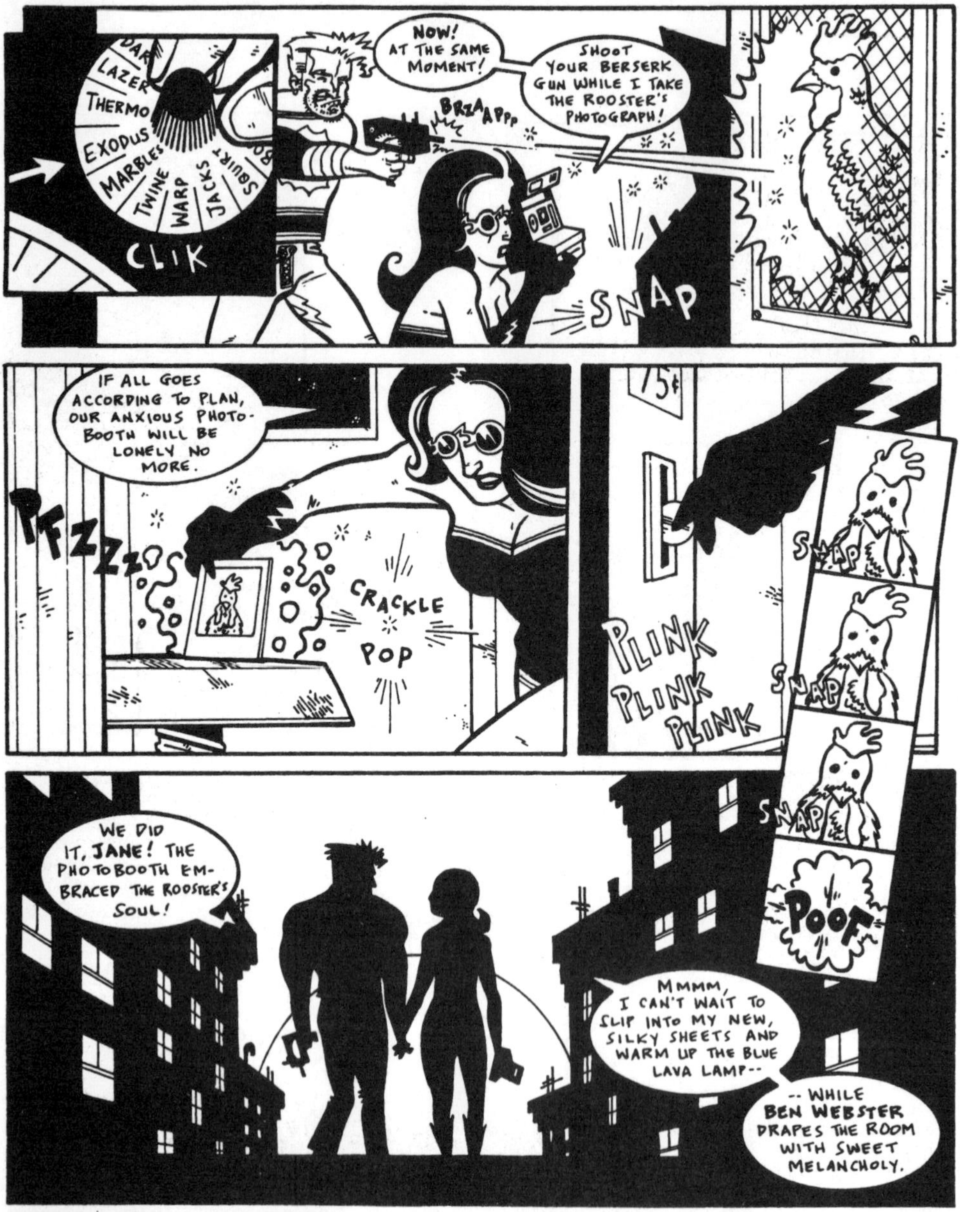
DART
LAZER
THERMO
EXODUS
MARBLES
TWINE
WARP
JACKS
SQUIRT
BOO
CLIK
NOW! AT THE SAME MOMENT!
SHOOT YOUR BERSERK GUN WHILE I TAKE THE ROOSTER'S PHOTOGRAPH!
BRZAAPPP
SNAP
IF ALL GOES ACCORDING TO PLAN, OUR ANXIOUS PHOTO-BOOTH WILL BE LONELY NO MORE.
PFZZZZ
CRACKLE
POP
75¢
PLINK
PLINK
PLINK
SNAP
SNAP
SNAP
POOF
WE DID IT, JANE! THE PHOTOBOOTH EM-BRACED THE ROOSTER'S SOUL!
MMMM, I CAN'T WAIT TO SLIP INTO MY NEW, SILKY SHEETS AND WARM UP THE BLUE LAVA LAMP--
-- WHILE BEN WEBSTER DRAPES THE ROOM WITH SWEET MELANCHOLY.
THREE MONTHS LATER...
NOT ONLY IS IT ANNOYING, BUT YOU COULD SET A CLOCK TO IT!!! IT'S THE SAME THING EVERY MORNING "COCK-A-DOODLE-DOO!"
COO?
8

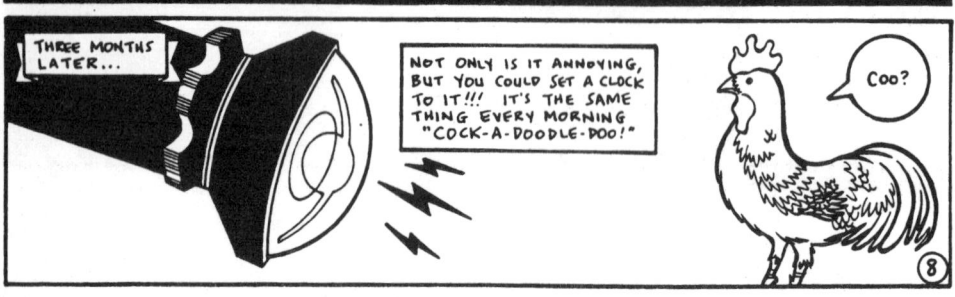

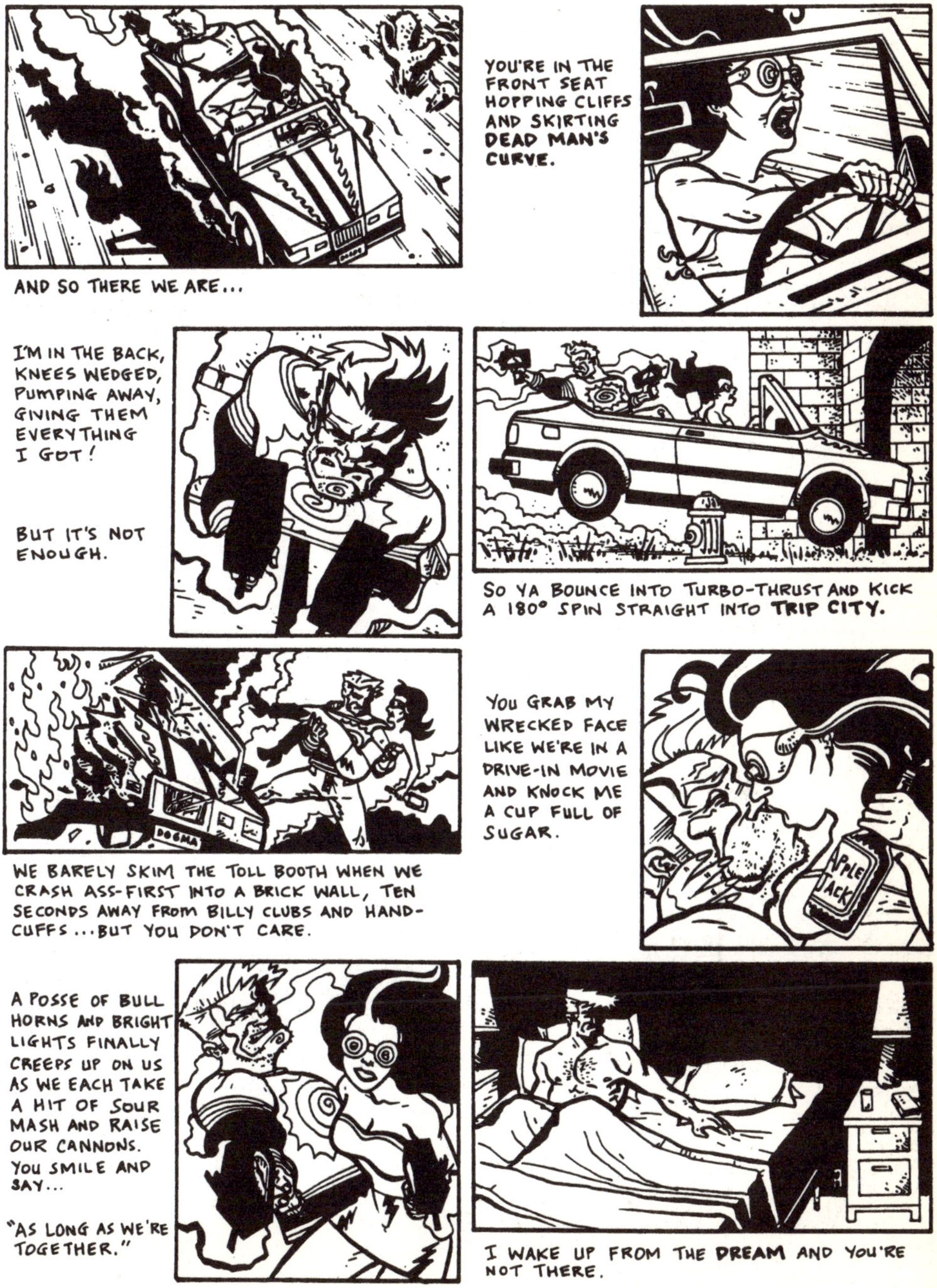
AND SO THERE WE ARE...
YOU'RE IN THE FRONT SEAT HOPPING CLIFFS AND SKIRTING DEAD MAN'S CURVE.
I'M IN THE BACK, KNEES WEDGED, PUMPING AWAY, GIVING THEM EVERYTHING I GOT!
BUT IT'S NOT ENOUGH.
SO YA BOUNCE INTO TURBO-THRUST AND KICK A 180° SPIN STRAIGHT INTO TRIP CITY.
DOGMA
WE BARELY SKIM THE TOLL BOOTH WHEN WE CRASH ASS-FIRST INTO A BRICK WALL, TEN SECONDS AWAY FROM BILLY CLUBS AND HAND-CUFFS ...BUT YOU DON'T CARE.
YOU GRAB MY WRECKED FACE LIKE WE'RE IN A DRIVE-IN MOVIE AND KNOCK ME A CUP FULL OF SUGAR.
APPLE JACK
A POSSE OF BULL HORNS AND BRIGHT LIGHTS FINALLY CREEPS UP ON US AS WE EACH TAKE A HIT OF SOUR MASH AND RAISE OUR CANNONS. YOU SMILE AND SAY...
"AS LONG AS WE'RE TOGETHER."
I WAKE UP FROM THE DREAM AND YOU'RE NOT THERE.

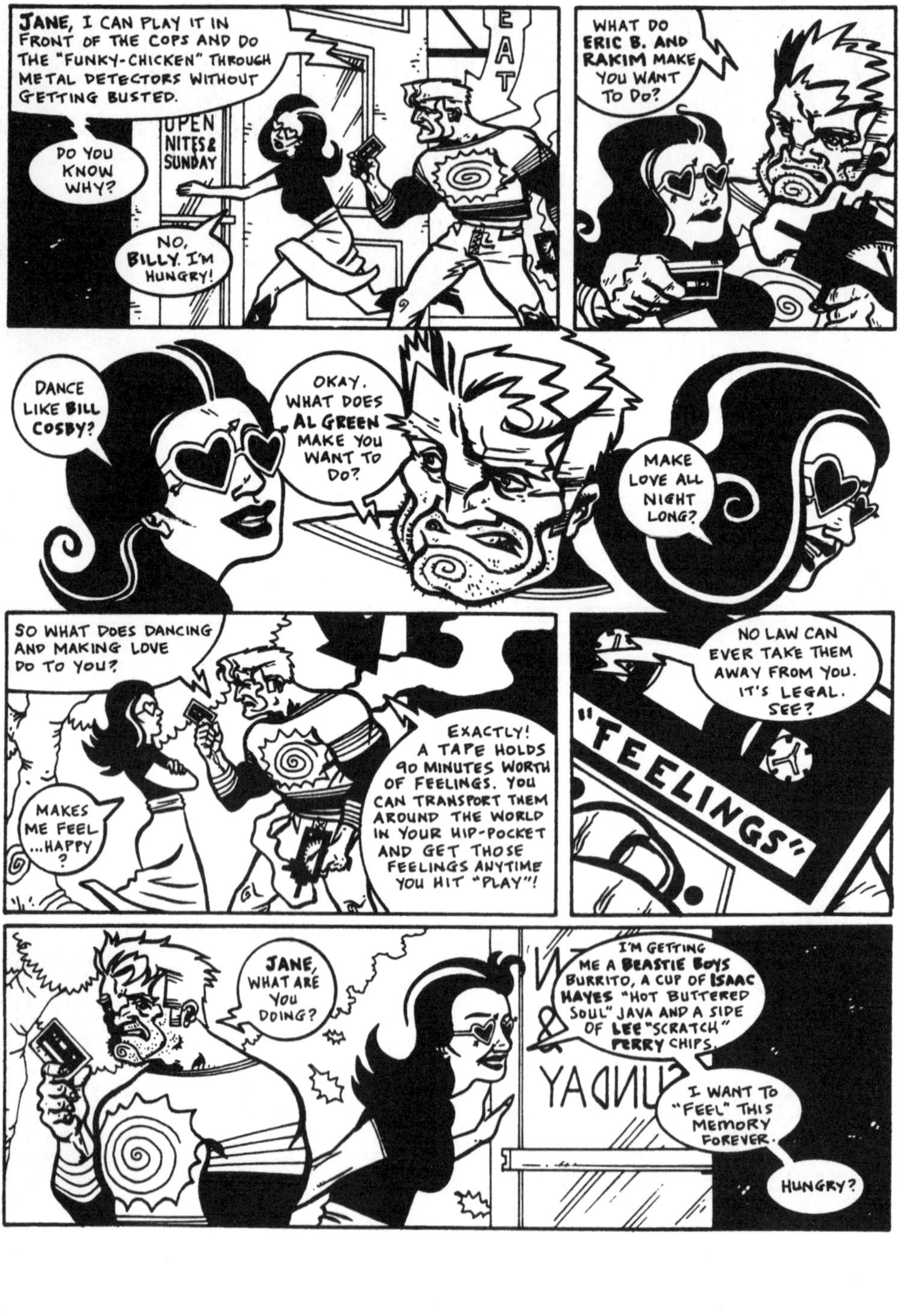
JANE, I CAN PLAY IT IN FRONT OF THE COPS AND DO THE "FUNKY-CHICKEN" THROUGH METAL DETECTORS WITHOUT GETTING BUSTED.
DO YOU KNOW WHY?
NO, BILLY. I'M HUNGRY!
EAT
OPEN NITES & SUNDAY
WHAT DO ERIC B. AND RAKIM MAKE YOU WANT TO DO?
DANCE LIKE BILL COSBY?
OKAY. WHAT DOES AL GREEN MAKE YOU WANT TO DO?
MAKE LOVE ALL NIGHT LONG?
SO WHAT DOES DANCING AND MAKING LOVE DO TO YOU?
MAKES ME FEEL ...HAPPY?
EXACTLY! A TAPE HOLDS 90 MINUTES WORTH OF FEELINGS. YOU CAN TRANSPORT THEM AROUND THE WORLD IN YOUR HIP-POCKET AND GET THOSE FEELINGS ANYTIME YOU HIT "PLAY"!
NO LAW CAN EVER TAKE THEM AWAY FROM YOU. IT'S LEGAL. SEE?
"FEELINGS"
JANE, WHAT ARE YOU DOING?
I'M GETTING ME A BEASTIE BOYS BURRITO, A CUP OF ISAAC HAYES "HOT BUTTERED SOUL" JAVA AND A SIDE OF LEE "SCRATCH" PERRY CHIPS.
I WANT TO "FEEL" THIS MEMORY FOREVER.
HUNGRY?

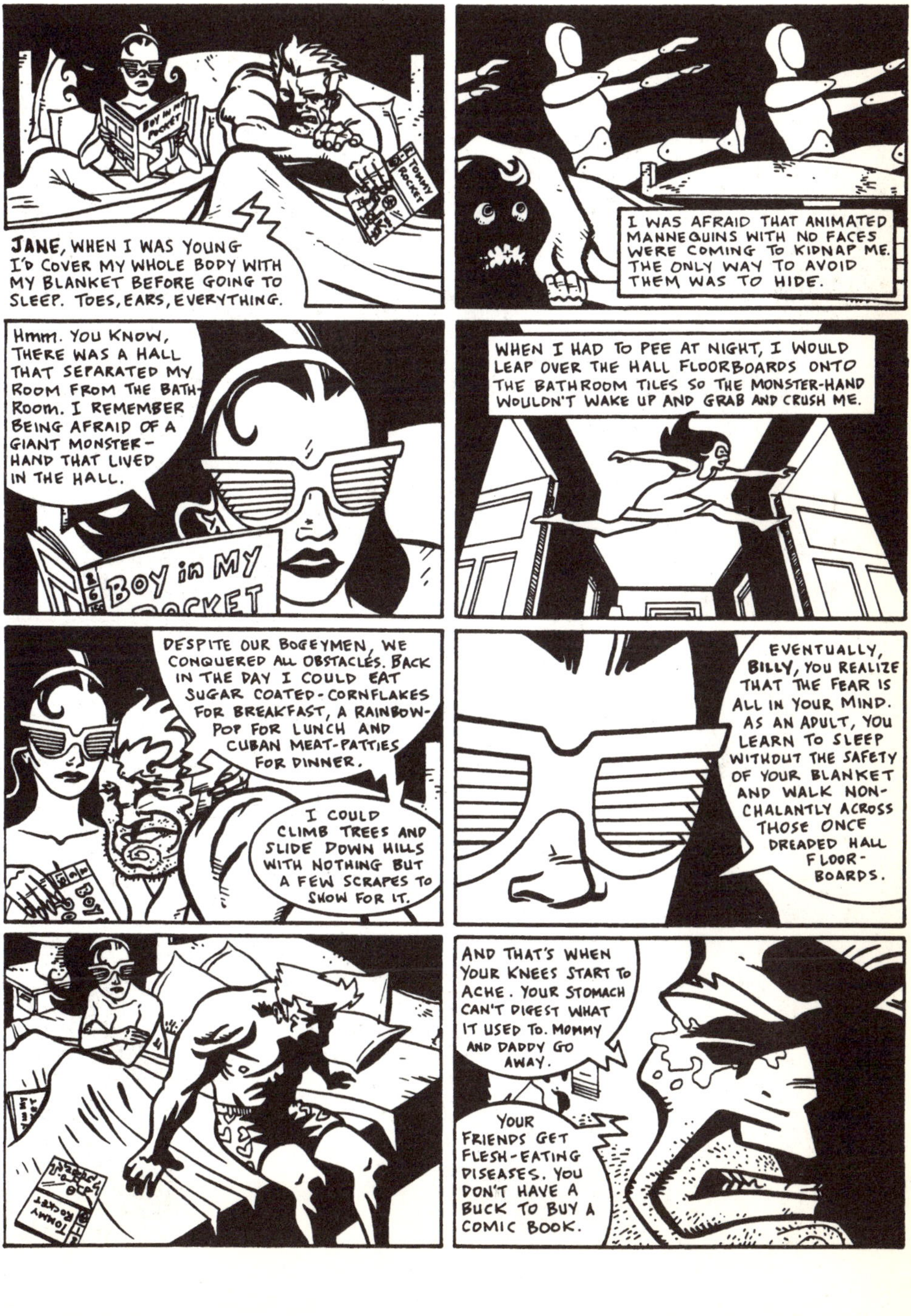
BOY IN MY POCKET
TOMMY ROCKET
JANE, WHEN I WAS YOUNG I'D COVER MY WHOLE BODY WITH MY BLANKET BEFORE GOING TO SLEEP. TOES, EARS, EVERYTHING.
I WAS AFRAID THAT ANIMATED MANNEQUINS WITH NO FACES WERE COMING TO KIDNAP ME. THE ONLY WAY TO AVOID THEM WAS TO HIDE.
Hmm. YOU KNOW, THERE WAS A HALL THAT SEPARATED MY ROOM FROM THE BATH-ROOM. I REMEMBER BEING AFRAID OF A GIANT MONSTER-HAND THAT LIVED IN THE HALL.
Boy in My
WHEN I HAD TO PEE AT NIGHT, I WOULD LEAP OVER THE HALL FLOORBOARDS ONTO THE BATHROOM TILES SO THE MONSTER-HAND WOULDN'T WAKE UP AND GRAB AND CRUSH ME.
DESPITE OUR BOGEYMEN, WE CONQUERED ALL OBSTACLES. BACK IN THE DAY I COULD EAT SUGAR COATED-CORNFLAKES FOR BREAKFAST, A RAINBOW-POP FOR LUNCH AND CUBAN MEAT-PATTIES FOR DINNER.
I COULD CLIMB TREES AND SLIDE DOWN HILLS WITH NOTHING BUT A FEW SCRAPES TO SHOW FOR IT.
EVENTUALLY, BILLY, YOU REALIZE THAT THE FEAR IS ALL IN YOUR MIND. AS AN ADULT, YOU LEARN TO SLEEP WITHOUT THE SAFETY OF YOUR BLANKET AND WALK NON-CHALANTLY ACROSS THOSE ONCE DREADED HALL FLOOR-BOARDS.
AND THAT'S WHEN YOUR KNEES START TO ACHE. YOUR STOMACH CAN'T DIGEST WHAT IT USED TO. MOMMY AND DADDY GO AWAY.
YOUR FRIENDS GET FLESH-EATING DISEASES. YOU DON'T HAVE A BUCK TO BUY A COMIC BOOK.

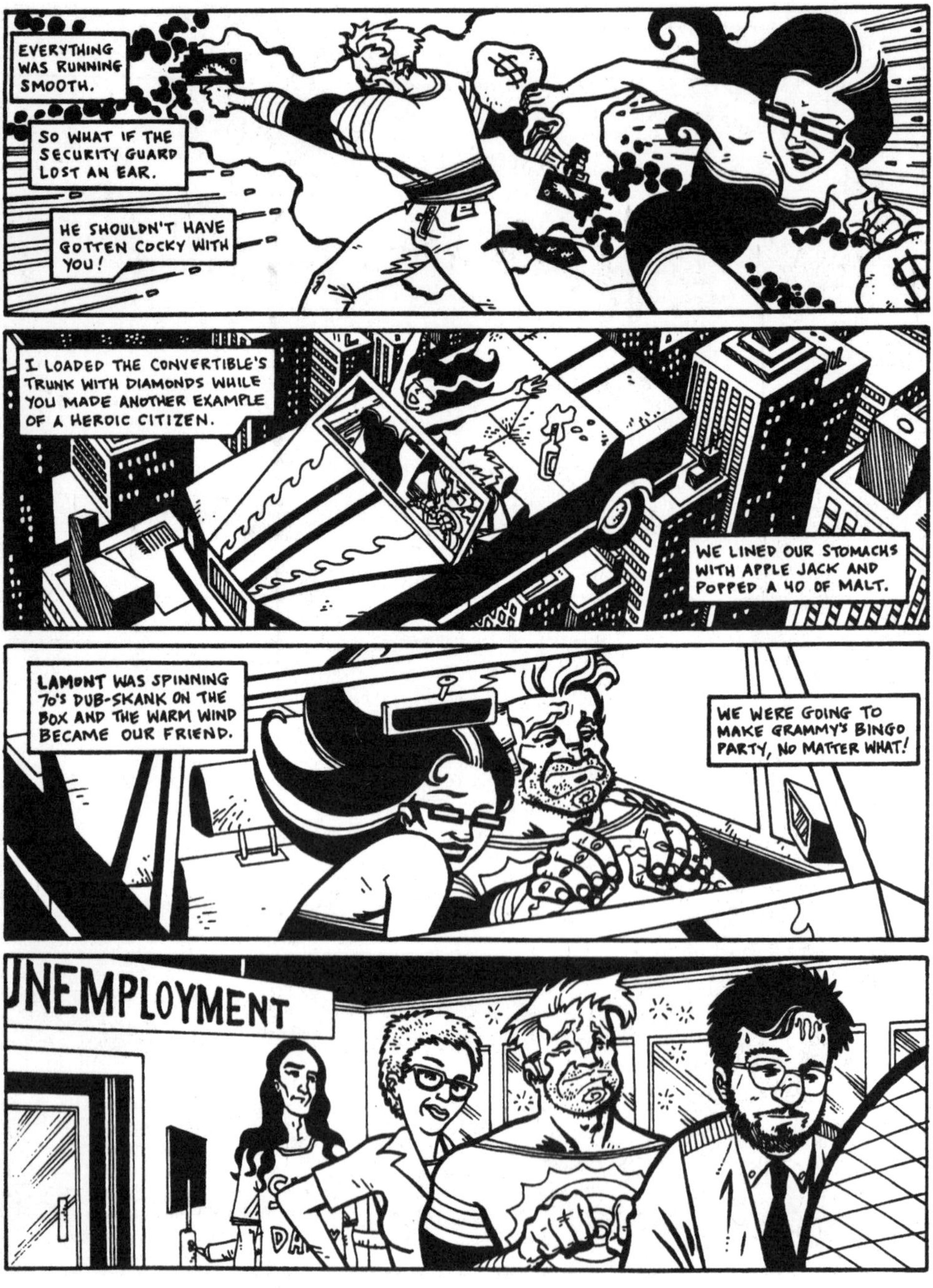
EVERYTHING WAS RUNNING SMOOTH.
SO WHAT IF THE SECURITY GUARD LOST AN EAR.
HE SHOULDN'T HAVE GOTTEN COCKY WITH YOU!
I LOADED THE CONVERTIBLE'S TRUNK WITH DIAMONDS WHILE YOU MADE ANOTHER EXAMPLE OF A HEROIC CITIZEN.
WE LINED OUR STOMACHS WITH APPLE JACK AND POPPED A 40 OF MALT.
LAMONT WAS SPINNING 70'S DUB-SKANK ON THE BOX AND THE WARM WIND BECAME OUR FRIEND.
WE WERE GOING TO MAKE GRAMMY'S BINGO PARTY, NO MATTER WHAT!
UNEMPLOYMENT

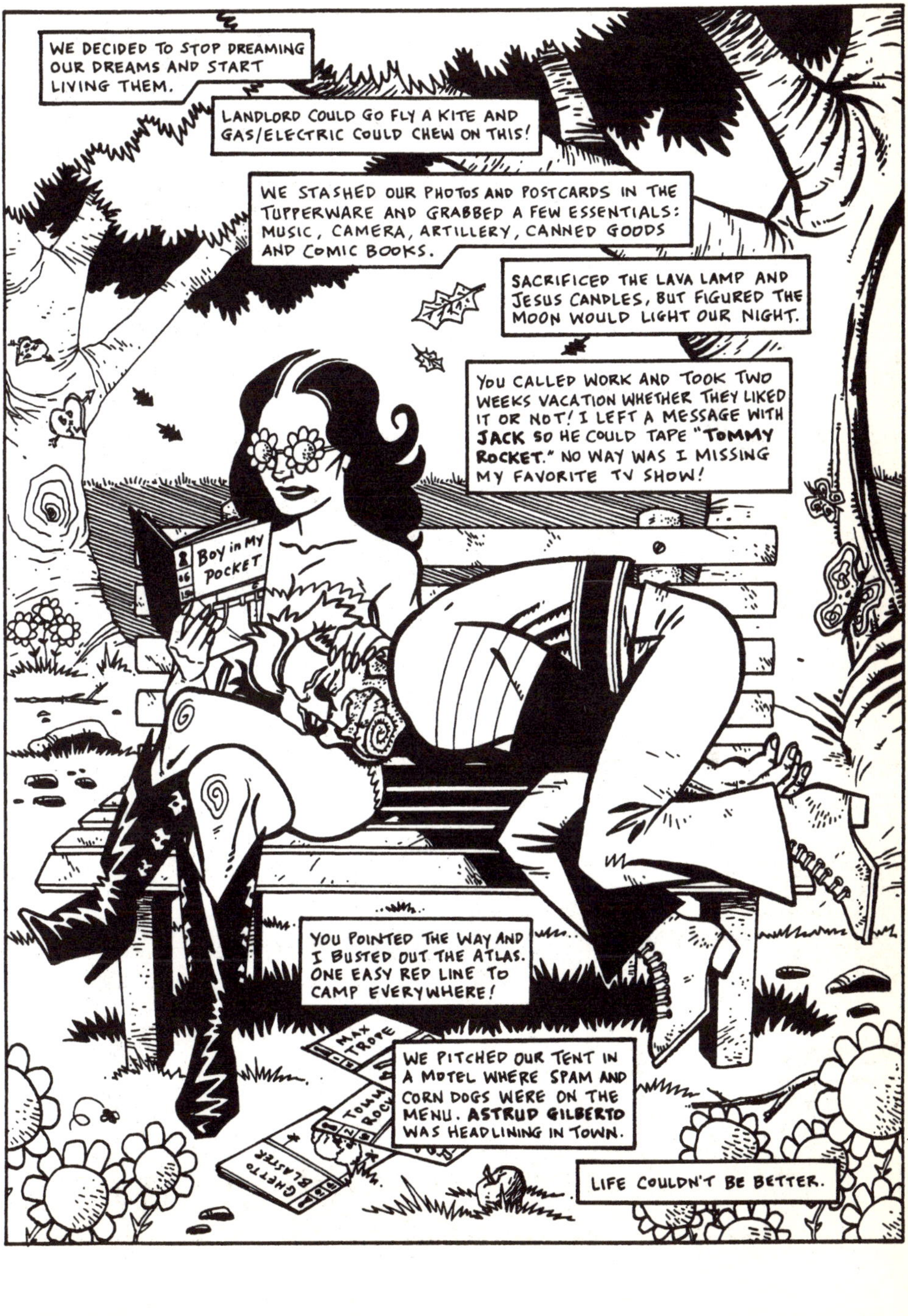
WE DECIDED TO STOP DREAMING OUR DREAMS AND START LIVING THEM.
LANDLORD COULD GO FLY A KITE AND GAS/ELECTRIC COULD CHEW ON THIS!
WE STASHED OUR PHOTOS AND POSTCARDS IN THE TUPPERWARE AND GRABBED A FEW ESSENTIALS: MUSIC, CAMERA, ARTILLERY, CANNED GOODS AND COMIC BOOKS.
SACRIFICED THE LAVA LAMP AND JESUS CANDLES, BUT FIGURED THE MOON WOULD LIGHT OUR NIGHT.
YOU CALLED WORK AND TOOK TWO WEEKS VACATION WHETHER THEY LIKED IT OR NOT! I LEFT A MESSAGE WITH JACK SO HE COULD TAPE "TOMMY ROCKET." NO WAY WAS I MISSING MY FAVORITE TV SHOW!
Boy in My POCKET
YOU POINTED THE WAY AND I BUSTED OUT THE ATLAS. ONE EASY RED LINE TO CAMP EVERYWHERE!
MAX TROPE
WE PITCHED OUR TENT IN A MOTEL WHERE SPAM AND CORN DOGS WERE ON THE MENU. ASTRUD GILBERTO WAS HEADLINING IN TOWN.
GHETTO BLASTER
LIFE COULDN'T BE BETTER.

BILLY DOGMA in The DOUBLE DARE TANGO
C.1997 DEAN HASPIEL
YA KNOW JANE, LIFE IS A LOT LIKE BOWLING.
MOST TIMES YOU HURL THE BALL, YA CAN CLOCK 6 OR 7 PINS...
...LEAVING A FEW OBSTACLES LEFT TO CONSIDER.
BUT, IF YA CONCENTRATE REAL HARD AND DON'T LET THE DOGS OF CHAOS CORRUPT YER COMMIT-MENT TO FOLLOW THRU--
--THEN YA CAN SWAY THE CONTEST IN YER FAVOR WITH A SURE GLANCE AND A STEADY PAW.

CLUNKITY
CLUNK
CLUNK
THEN THERE ARE THOSE TIMES WHEN YA STUMBLE, CRAWLING AIMLESSLY IN THE GUTTER, WONDERING WHETHER KNOCKING DOWN ALL TEN PINS IS THE POINT OF IT ALL ...
AND THAT'S WHEN YOU WATCH WITH BATED BREATH AS YOU PLAY MUMBLETY-PEG WITH A RUSTY SWITCHBLADE--
TAP TAP TAP
--WHILE THE MAN OF YOUR DREAMS CONTEMPLATES THE PROS AND CONS OF WAKING UP IN THE MORNING.

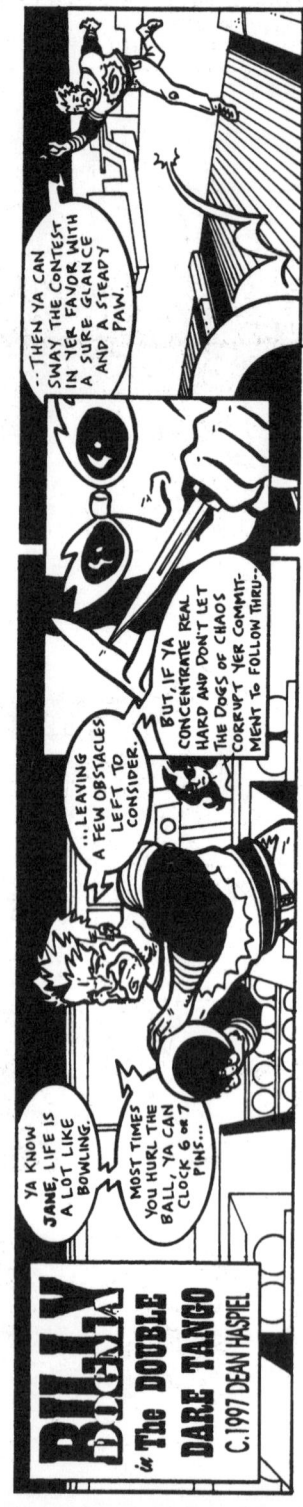

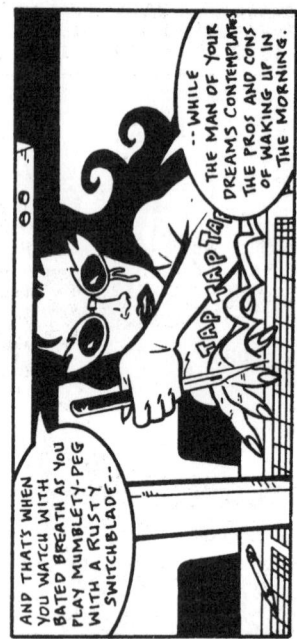

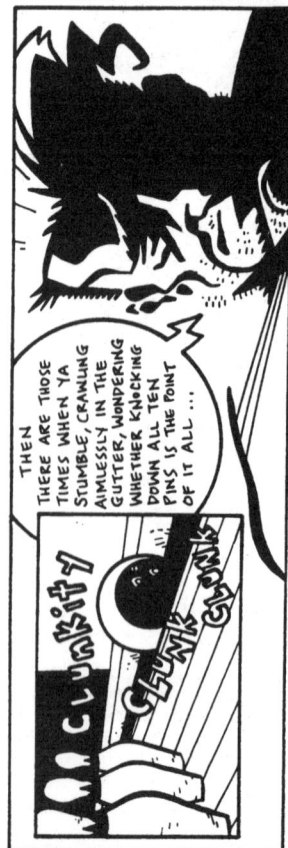

BILLY DOGMA IS A CAVALIER VAGABOND, SO CONFUSED THAT HIS BERSERK GUNS SHOOT EVERYTHING BUT BULLETS. HIS CAREER-DRIVEN GIRLFRIEND JANE LEGIT ENCOURAGES BILLY TO MANIFEST THEIR INNERMOST DESIRES IN TRIP CITY.

BILLY DOGMA vs The HUMAN BAR-CODE

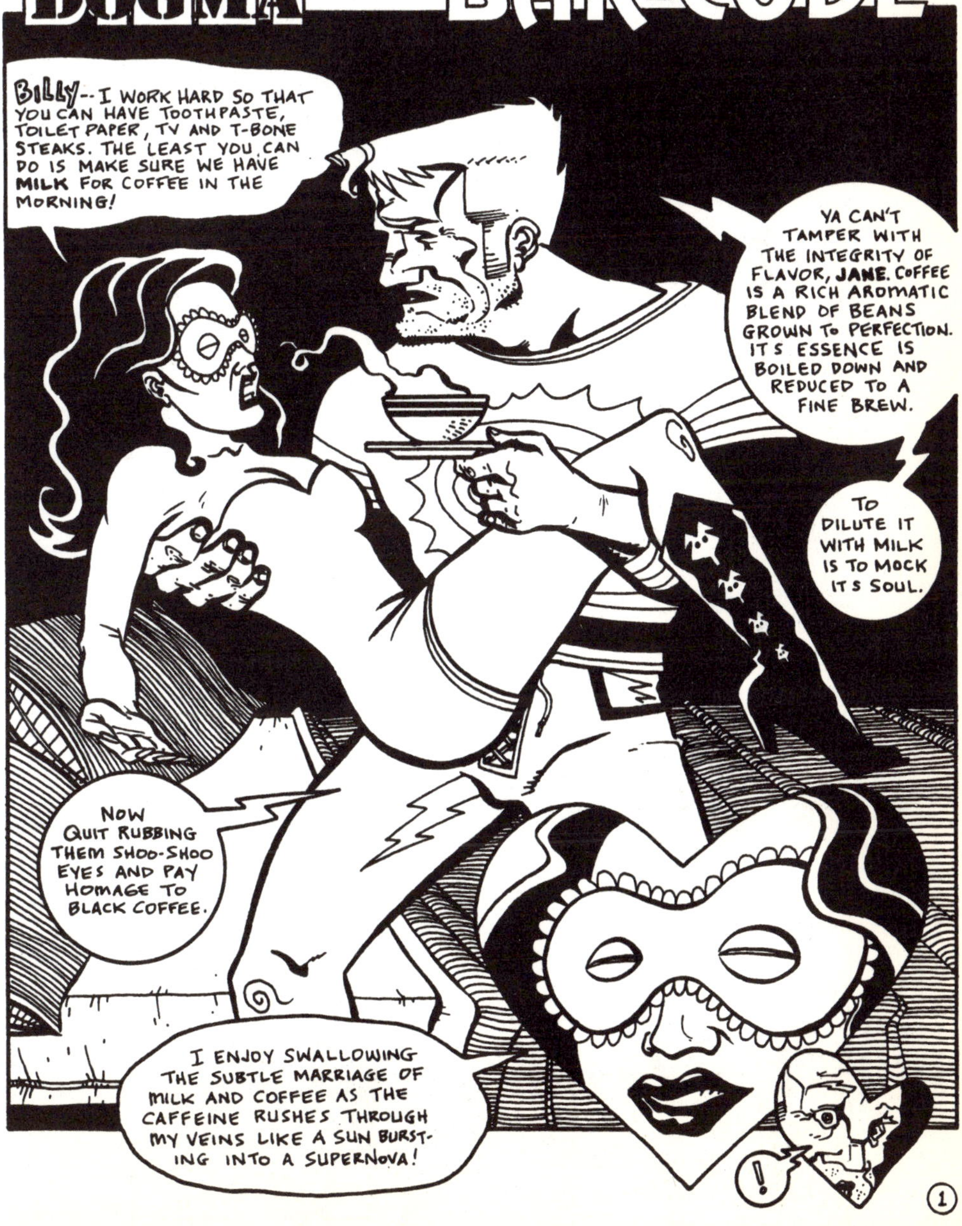
BILLY-- I WORK HARD SO THAT YOU CAN HAVE TOOTHPASTE, TOILET PAPER, TV AND T-BONE STEAKS. THE LEAST YOU CAN DO IS MAKE SURE WE HAVE MILK FOR COFFEE IN THE MORNING!
YA CAN'T TAMPER WITH THE INTEGRITY OF FLAVOR, JANE. COFFEE IS A RICH AROMATIC BLEND OF BEANS GROWN TO PERFECTION. IT'S ESSENCE IS BOILED DOWN AND REDUCED TO A FINE BREW.
TO DILUTE IT WITH MILK IS TO MOCK IT'S SOUL.
NOW QUIT RUBBING THEM SHOO-SHOO EYES AND PAY HOMAGE TO BLACK COFFEE.
I ENJOY SWALLOWING THE SUBTLE MARRIAGE OF MILK AND COFFEE AS THE CAFFEINE RUSHES THROUGH MY VEINS LIKE A SUN BURSTING INTO A SUPERNOVA!
!
1

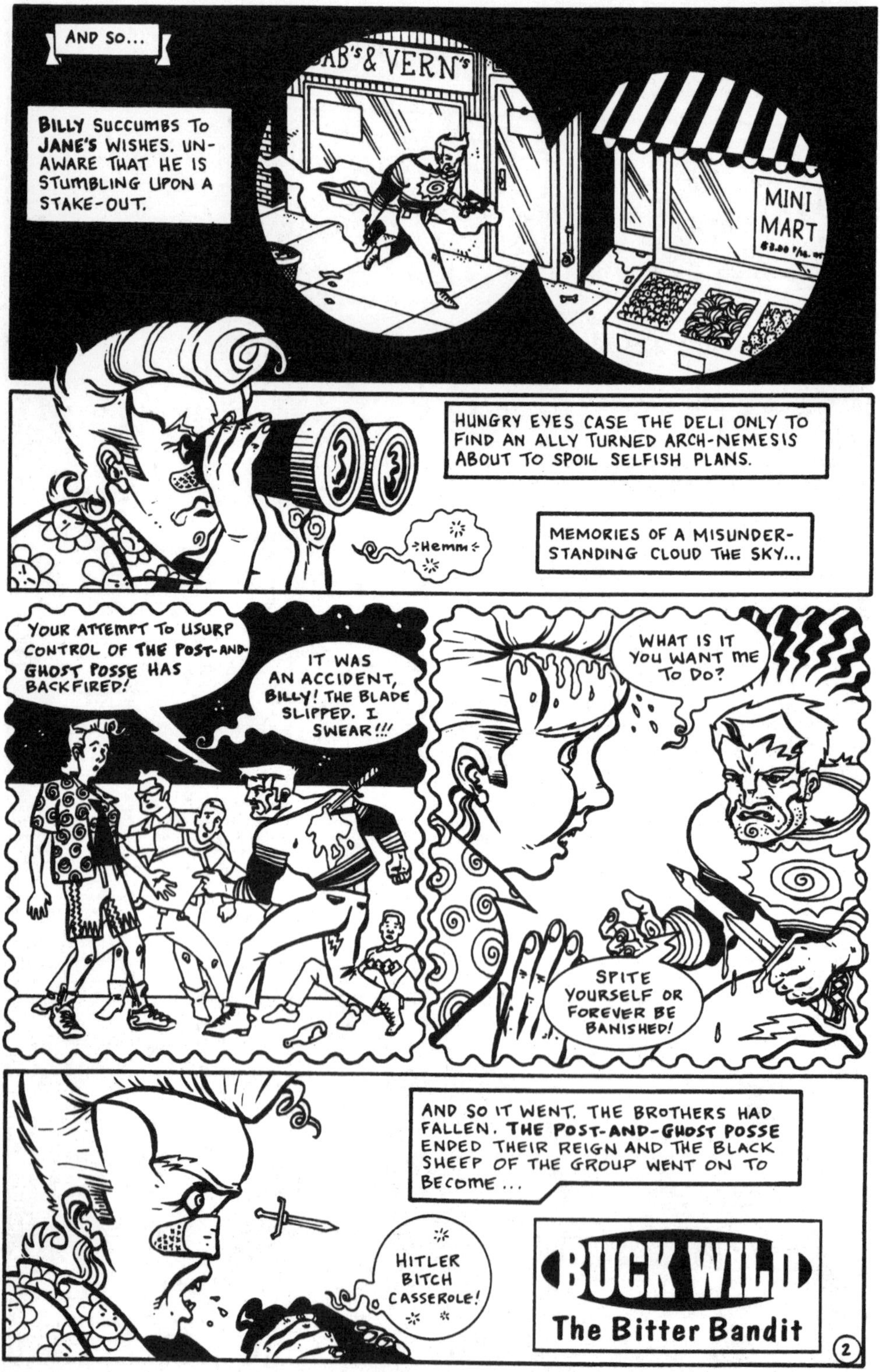
AND SO...
BILLY SUCCUMBS TO JANE'S WISHES. UNAWARE THAT HE IS STUMBLING UPON A STAKE-OUT.
AB'S & VERN'S
MINI MART
HUNGRY EYES CASE THE DELI ONLY TO FIND AN ALLY TURNED ARCH-NEMESIS ABOUT TO SPOIL SELFISH PLANS.
Hemm
MEMORIES OF A MISUNDERSTANDING CLOUD THE SKY...
YOUR ATTEMPT TO USURP CONTROL OF THE POST-AND-GHOST POSSE HAS BACKFIRED!
IT WAS AN ACCIDENT, BILLY! THE BLADE SLIPPED. I SWEAR!!!
WHAT IS IT YOU WANT ME TO DO?
SPITE YOURSELF OR FOREVER BE BANISHED!
AND SO IT WENT. THE BROTHERS HAD FALLEN. THE POST-AND-GHOST POSSE ENDED THEIR REIGN AND THE BLACK SHEEP OF THE GROUP WENT ON TO BECOME...
HITLER BITCH CASSEROLE!
BUCK WILD
The Bitter Bandit
2

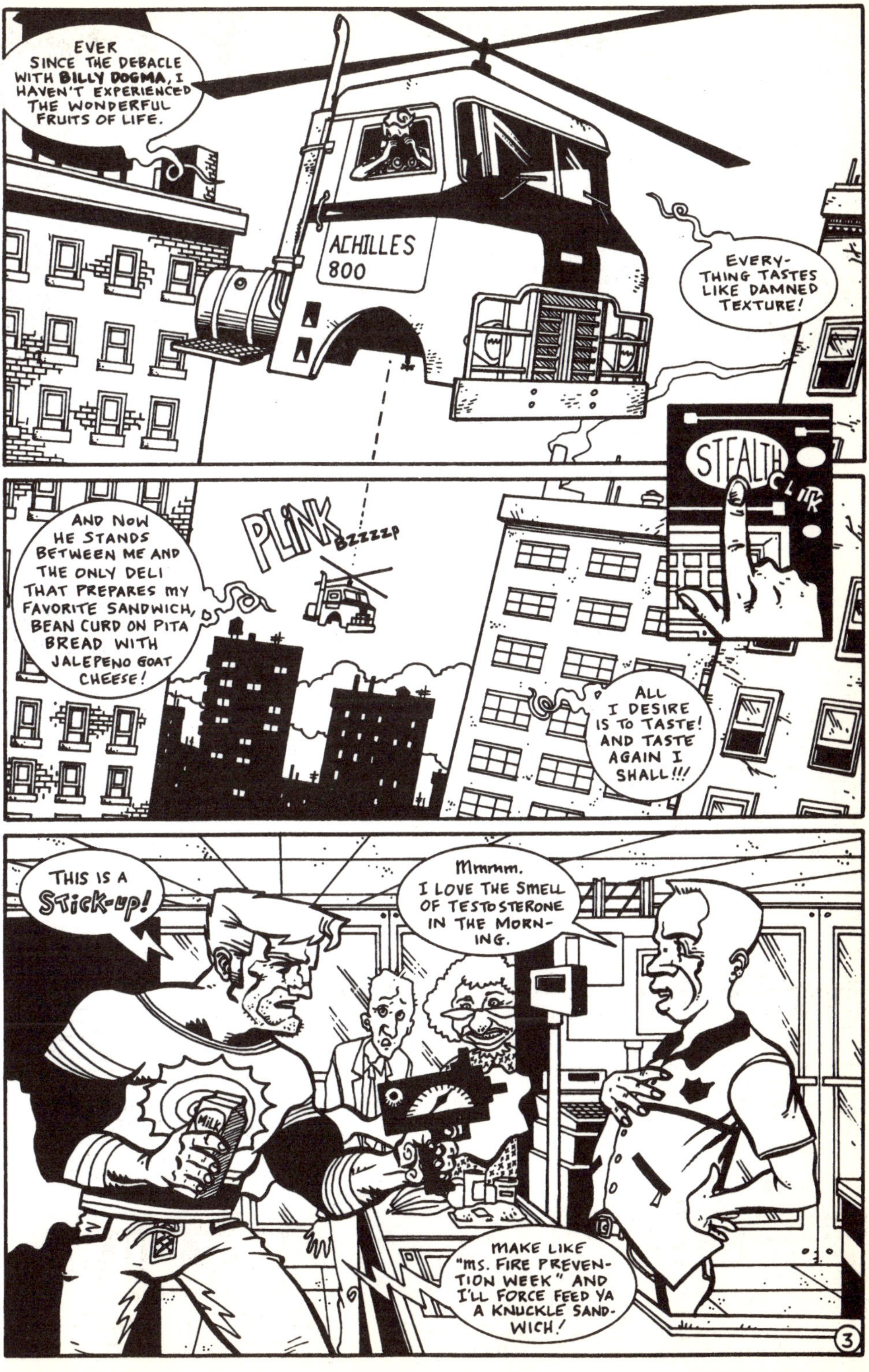
EVER SINCE THE DEBACLE WITH BILLY DOGMA, I HAVEN'T EXPERIENCED THE WONDERFUL FRUITS OF LIFE.
ACHILLES 800
EVERY-THING TASTES LIKE DAMNED TEXTURE!
STEALTH
CLIK
AND NOW HE STANDS BETWEEN ME AND THE ONLY DELI THAT PREPARES MY FAVORITE SANDWICH, BEAN CURD ON PITA BREAD WITH JALEPENO GOAT CHEESE!
PLINK
BZZZZP
ALL I DESIRE IS TO TASTE! AND TASTE AGAIN I SHALL!!!
THIS IS A STICK-UP!
MMMMM. I LOVE THE SMELL OF TESTOSTERONE IN THE MORN-ING.
MILK
MAKE LIKE "MS. FIRE PREVEN-TION WEEK" AND I'LL FORCE FEED YA A KNUCKLE SAND-WICH!
3

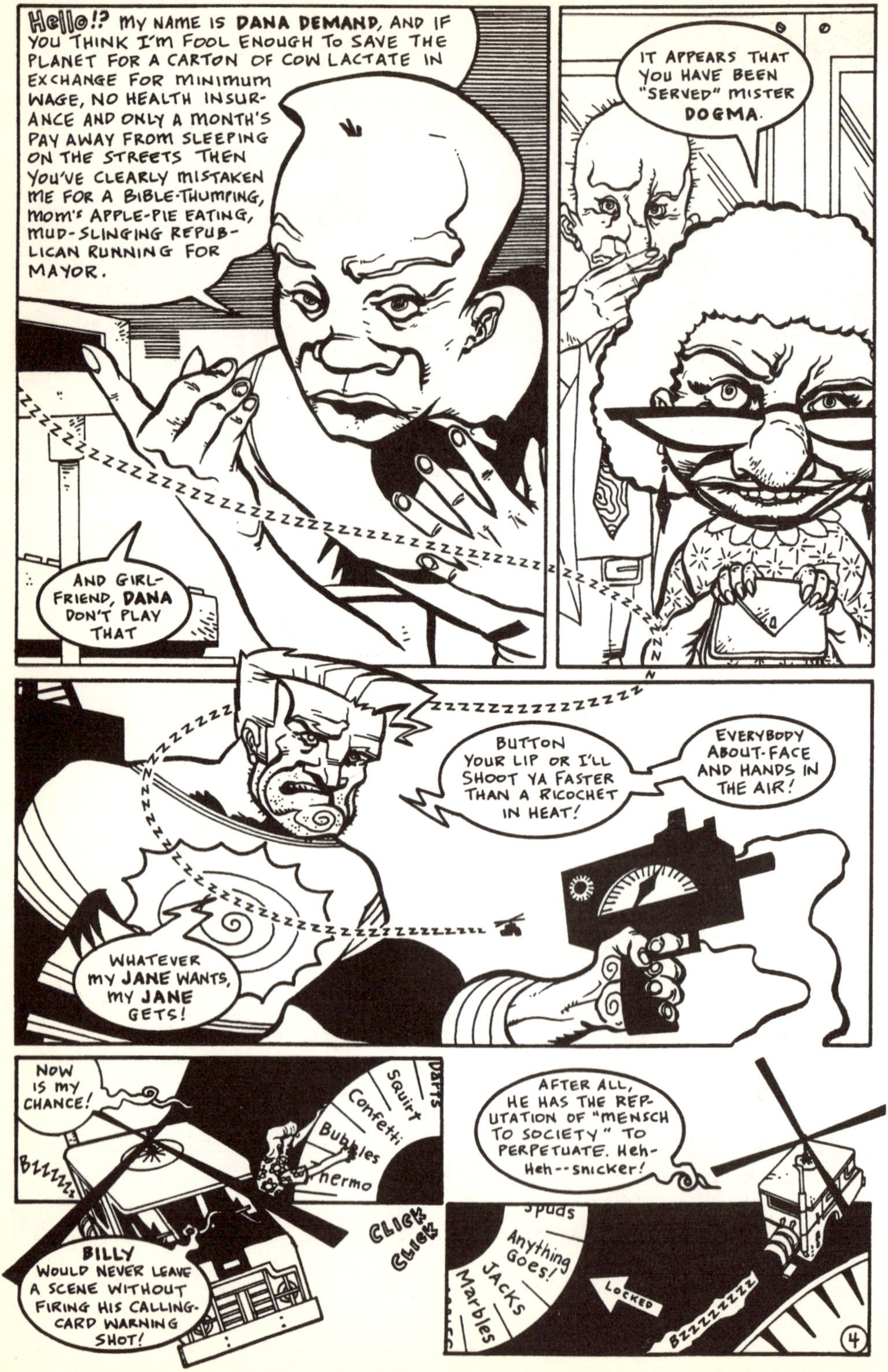
Hello!? My name is DANA DEMAND, and if you think I'm fool enough to save the planet for a carton of cow lactate in exchange for minimum wage, no health insurance and only a month's pay away from sleeping on the streets then you've clearly mistaken me for a Bible-thumping, mom's apple-pie eating, mud-slinging republican running for mayor.
And girlfriend, DANA don't play that
It appears that you have been "served" mister DOGMA.
Button your lip or I'll shoot ya faster than a ricochet in heat!
Everybody about-face and hands in the air!
Whatever my JANE wants, my JANE gets!
Now is my chance!
Darts
Squirt
Confetti
Bubbles
Thermo
BZZZZZZZ
BILLY would never leave a scene without firing his calling-card warning shot!
CLICK CLICK
After all, he has the reputation of "mensch to society" to perpetuate. Heh-heh--snicker!
Spuds
Anything Goes!
Jacks
Marbles
LOCKED
BZZZZZZZZ
4

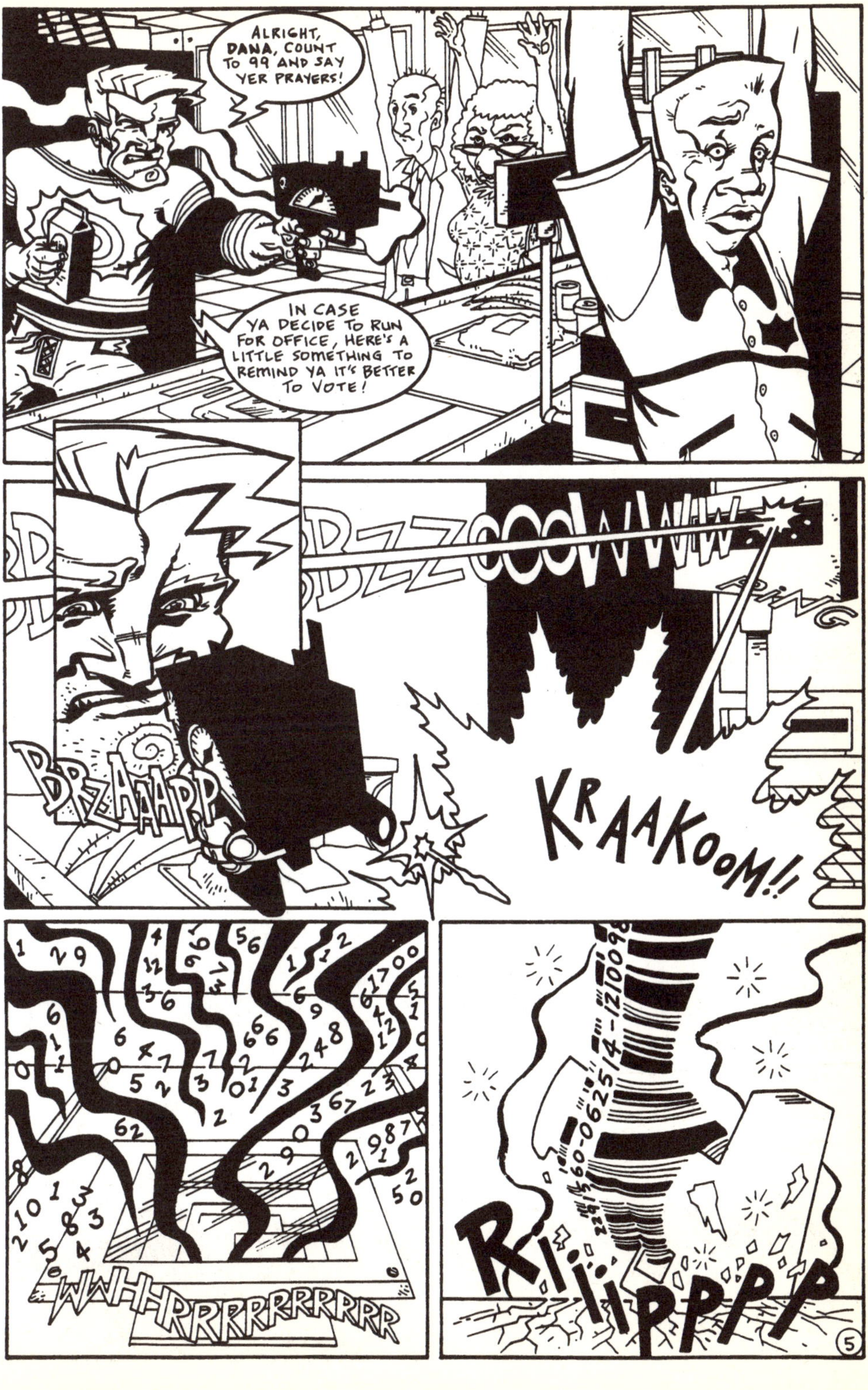

ALRIGHT, DANA, COUNT TO 99 AND SAY YER PRAYERS!
IN CASE YA DECIDE TO RUN FOR OFFICE, HERE'S A LITTLE SOMETHING TO REMIND YA IT'S BETTER TO VOTE!
BZZOOOWWWW
PING
BRZAAAPP
KRAAKOOM!!
WWHHRRRRRRRRRR
RIIIPPPP
5

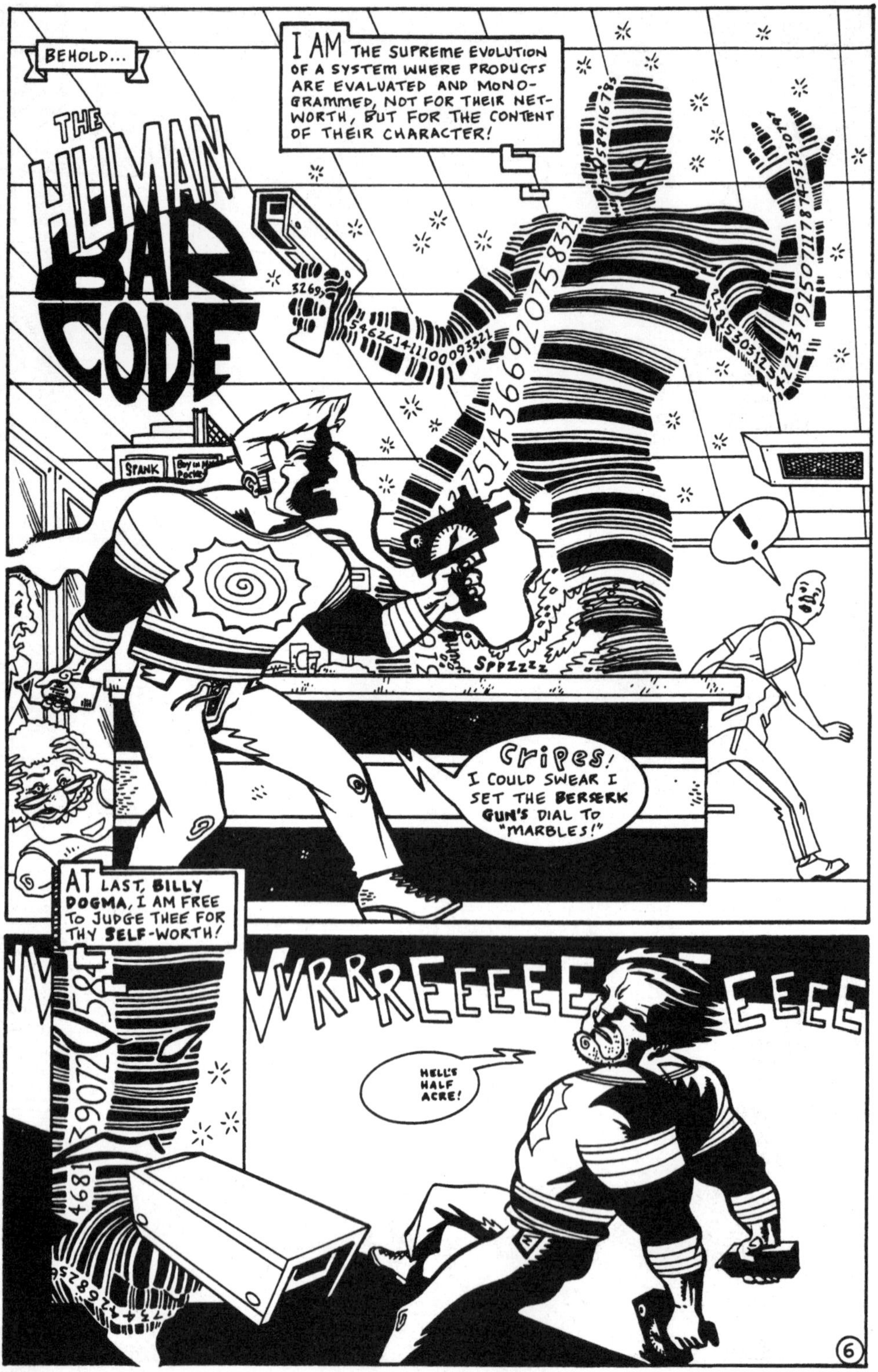
BEHOLD...
THE HUMAN BAR CODE
I AM THE SUPREME EVOLUTION OF A SYSTEM WHERE PRODUCTS ARE EVALUATED AND MONOGRAMMED, NOT FOR THEIR NET-WORTH, BUT FOR THE CONTENT OF THEIR CHARACTER!
SPANK
!
SPPZZZZZ
CRIPES! I COULD SWEAR I SET THE BERSERK GUN'S DIAL TO "MARBLES!"
AT LAST, BILLY DOGMA, I AM FREE TO JUDGE THEE FOR THY SELF-WORTH!
VVRRREEEEEEEEE
HELL'S HALF ACRE!
6

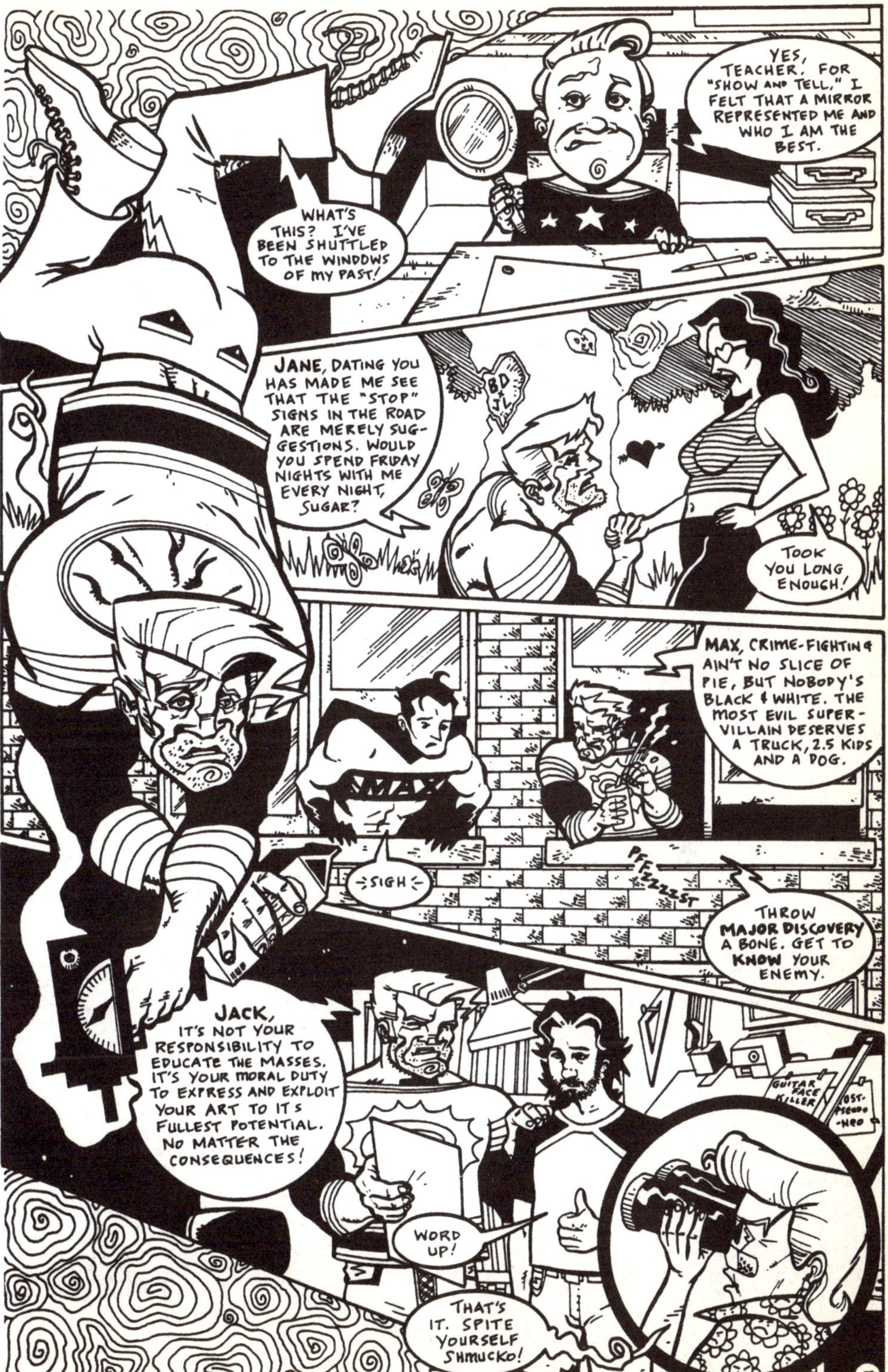
YES, TEACHER. FOR "SHOW AND TELL," I FELT THAT A MIRROR REPRESENTED ME AND WHO I AM THE BEST.
WHAT'S THIS? I'VE BEEN SHUTTLED TO THE WINDOWS OF MY PAST!
BD + JL
JANE, DATING YOU HAS MADE ME SEE THAT THE "STOP" SIGNS IN THE ROAD ARE MERELY SUGGESTIONS. WOULD YOU SPEND FRIDAY NIGHTS WITH ME EVERY NIGHT, SUGAR?
TOOK YOU LONG ENOUGH!
MAX, CRIME-FIGHTING AIN'T NO SLICE OF PIE, BUT NOBODY'S BLACK & WHITE. THE MOST EVIL SUPER-VILLAIN DESERVES A TRUCK, 2.5 KIDS AND A DOG.
MAX
SIGH
PFFZZZZST
THROW MAJOR DISCOVERY A BONE. GET TO KNOW YOUR ENEMY.
JACK, IT'S NOT YOUR RESPONSIBILITY TO EDUCATE THE MASSES. IT'S YOUR MORAL DUTY TO EXPRESS AND EXPLOIT YOUR ART TO ITS FULLEST POTENTIAL. NO MATTER THE CONSEQUENCES!
GUITAR FACE KILLER
POST-PSEUDO-HERO
WORD UP!
THAT'S IT. SPITE YOURSELF SHMUCKO!
7

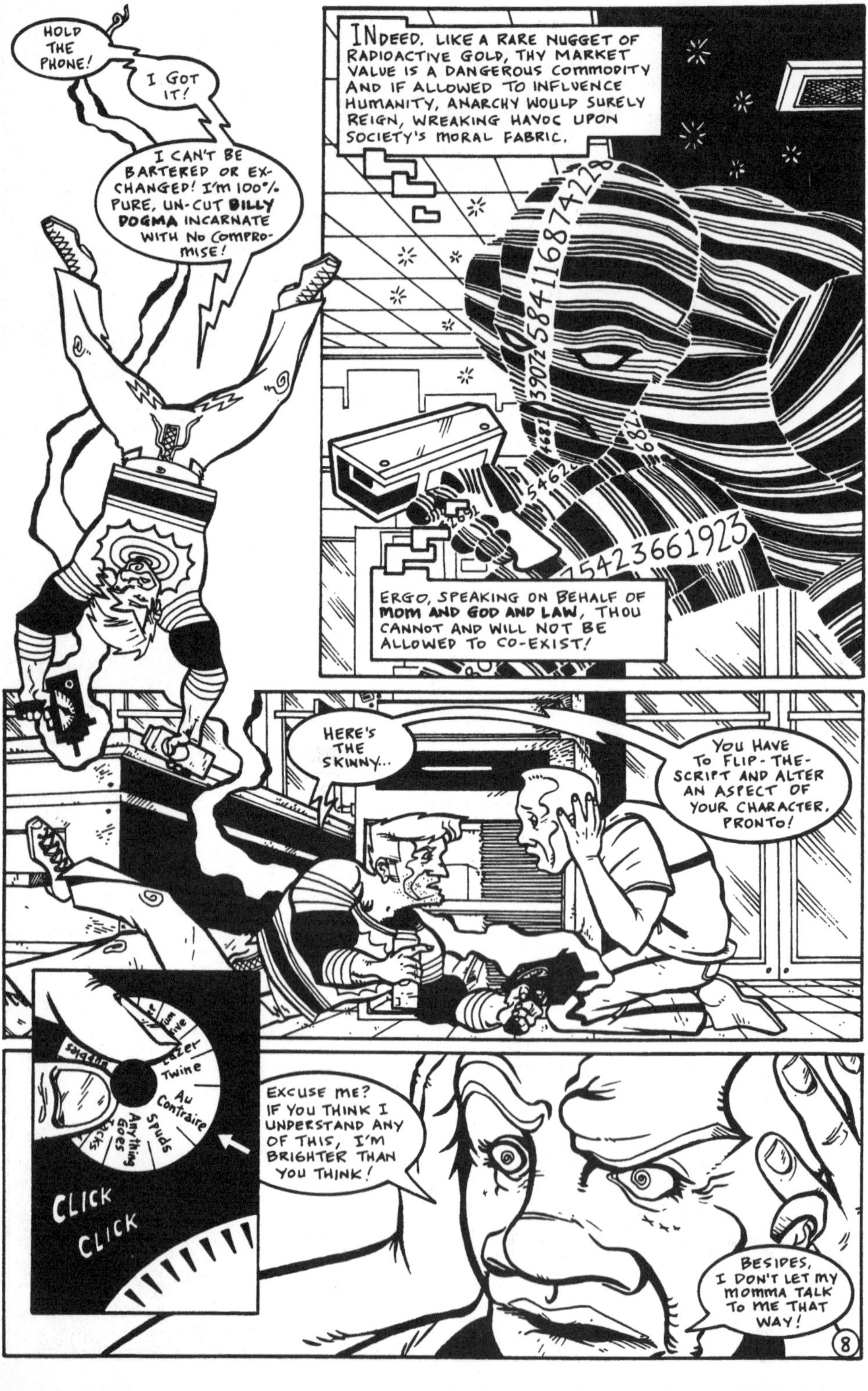
HOLD THE PHONE!
I GOT IT!
I CAN'T BE BARTERED OR EX-CHANGED! I'M 100% PURE, UN-CUT **BILLY DOGMA** INCARNATE WITH NO COMPRO-MISE!
INDEED. LIKE A RARE NUGGET OF RADIOACTIVE GOLD, THY MARKET VALUE IS A DANGEROUS COMMODITY AND IF ALLOWED TO INFLUENCE HUMANITY, ANARCHY WOULD SURELY REIGN, WREAKING HAVOC UPON SOCIETY'S MORAL FABRIC.
ERGO, SPEAKING ON BEHALF OF **MOM AND GOD AND LAW**, THOU CANNOT AND WILL NOT BE ALLOWED TO CO-EXIST!
HERE'S THE SKINNY...
YOU HAVE TO FLIP-THE-SCRIPT AND ALTER AN ASPECT OF YOUR CHARACTER, PRONTO!
Lazer
Twine
Au Contraire
Spuds
Anything Goes
CLICK
CLICK
EXCUSE ME? IF YOU THINK I UNDERSTAND ANY OF THIS, I'M BRIGHTER THAN YOU THINK!
BESIDES, I DON'T LET MY MOMMA TALK TO ME THAT WAY!
8

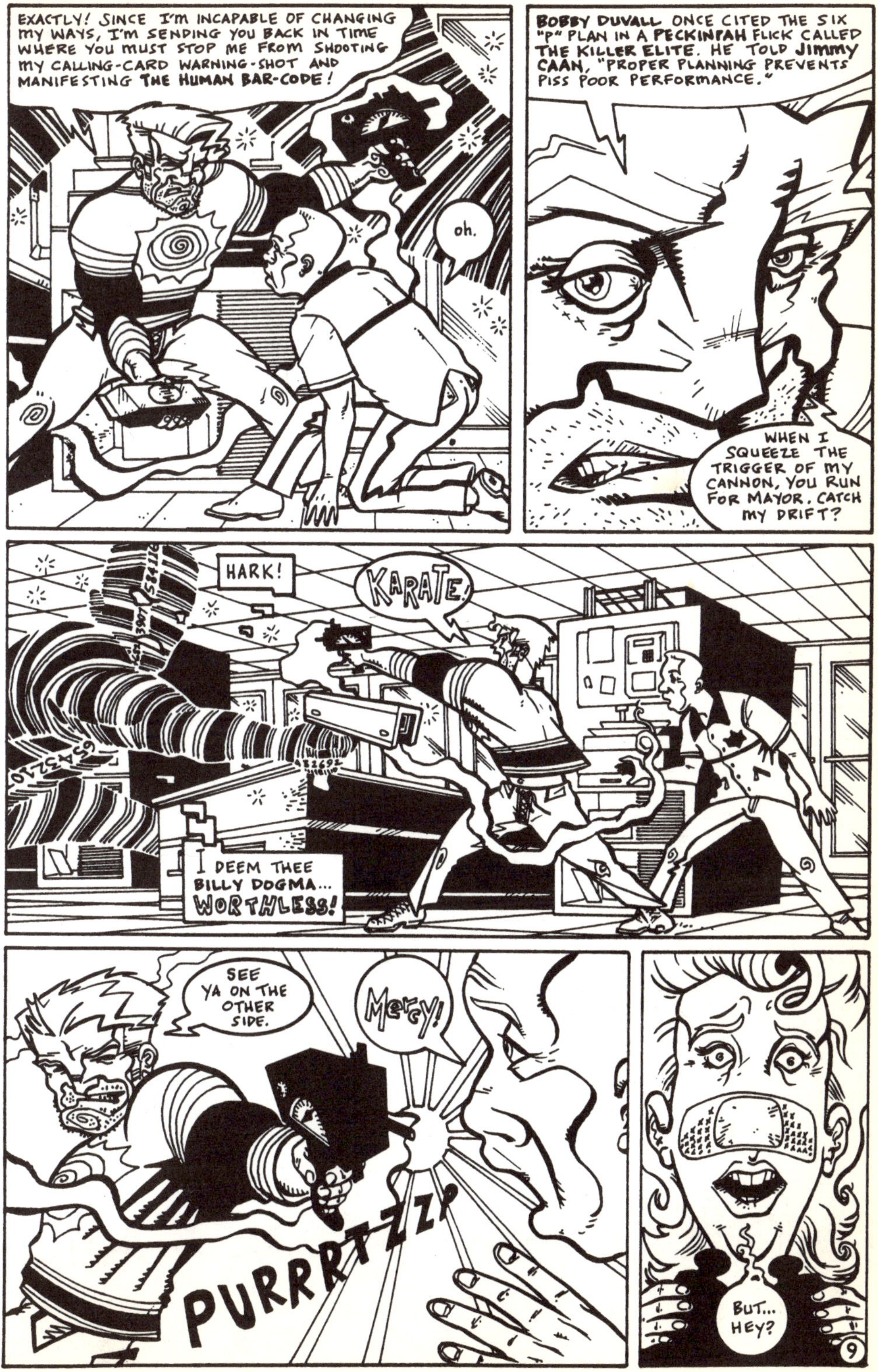
EXACTLY! SINCE I'M INCAPABLE OF CHANGING MY WAYS, I'M SENDING YOU BACK IN TIME WHERE YOU MUST STOP ME FROM SHOOTING MY CALLING-CARD WARNING-SHOT AND MANIFESTING THE HUMAN BAR-CODE!
oh.
BOBBY DUVALL ONCE CITED THE SIX "P" PLAN IN A PECKINPAH FLICK CALLED THE KILLER ELITE. HE TOLD JIMMY CAAN, "PROPER PLANNING PREVENTS PISS POOR PERFORMANCE."
WHEN I SQUEEZE THE TRIGGER OF MY CANNON, YOU RUN FOR MAYOR. CATCH MY DRIFT?
HARK!
KARATE!
I DEEM THEE BILLY DOGMA... WORTHLESS!
SEE YA ON THE OTHER SIDE.
Mercy!
PURRRRTZZZP
BUT... HEY?
9

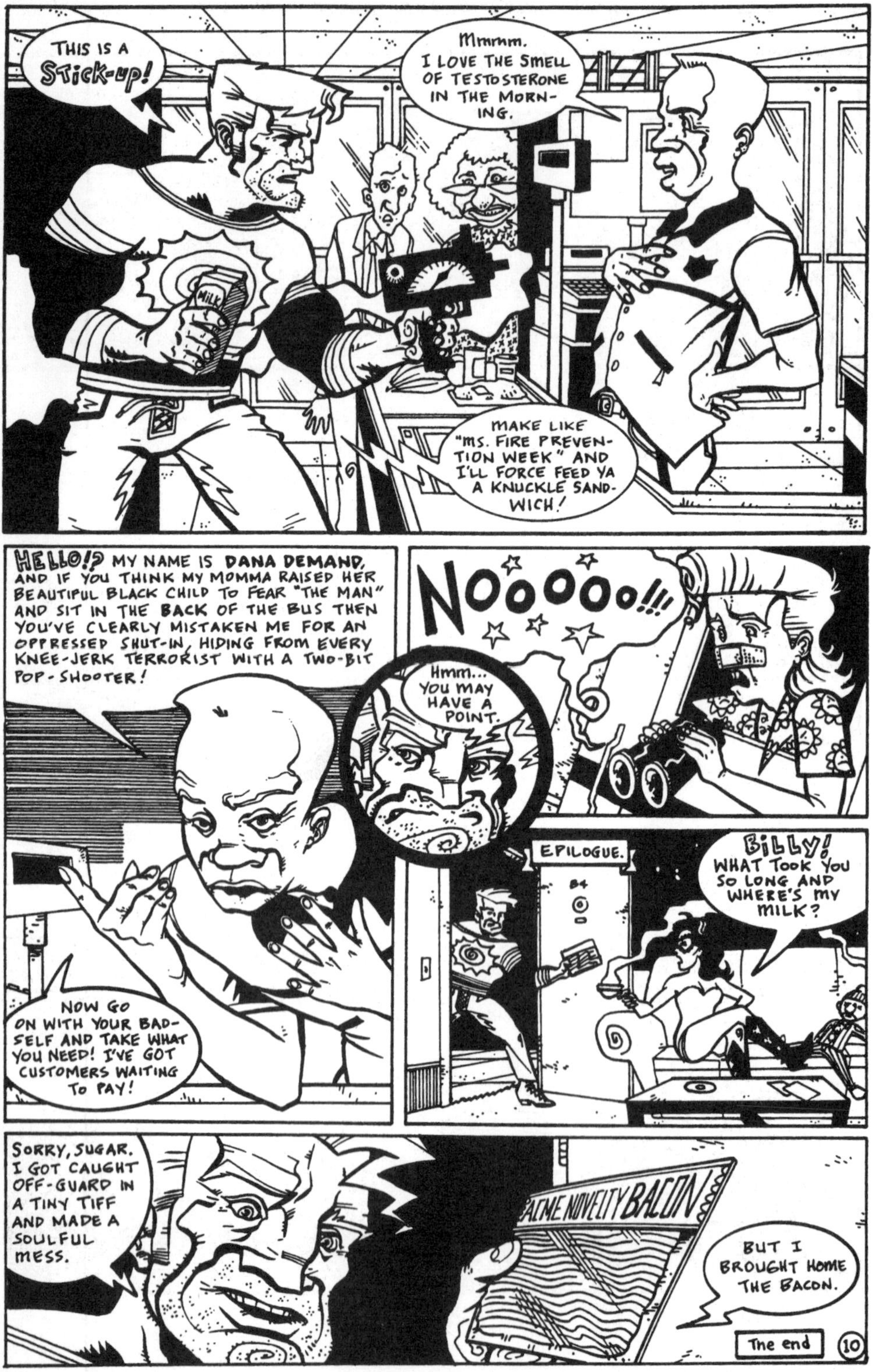
THIS IS A STICK-UP!
Mmmmm. I LOVE THE SMELL OF TESTOSTERONE IN THE MORNING.
MAKE LIKE "MS. FIRE PREVENTION WEEK" AND I'LL FORCE FEED YA A KNUCKLE SANDWICH!
HELLO!? MY NAME IS DANA DEMAND, AND IF YOU THINK MY MOMMA RAISED HER BEAUTIFUL BLACK CHILD TO FEAR "THE MAN" AND SIT IN THE BACK OF THE BUS THEN YOU'VE CLEARLY MISTAKEN ME FOR AN OPPRESSED SHUT-IN, HIDING FROM EVERY KNEE-JERK TERRORIST WITH A TWO-BIT POP-SHOOTER!
Hmm... YOU MAY HAVE A POINT.
NOW GO ON WITH YOUR BAD-SELF AND TAKE WHAT YOU NEED! I'VE GOT CUSTOMERS WAITING TO PAY!
NOOOOO!!!
EPILOGUE.
B4
BILLY! WHAT TOOK YOU SO LONG AND WHERE'S MY MILK?
SORRY, SUGAR. I GOT CAUGHT OFF-GUARD IN A TINY TIFF AND MADE A SOULFUL MESS.
ACME NOVELTY BACON
BUT I BROUGHT HOME THE BACON.
The end
10

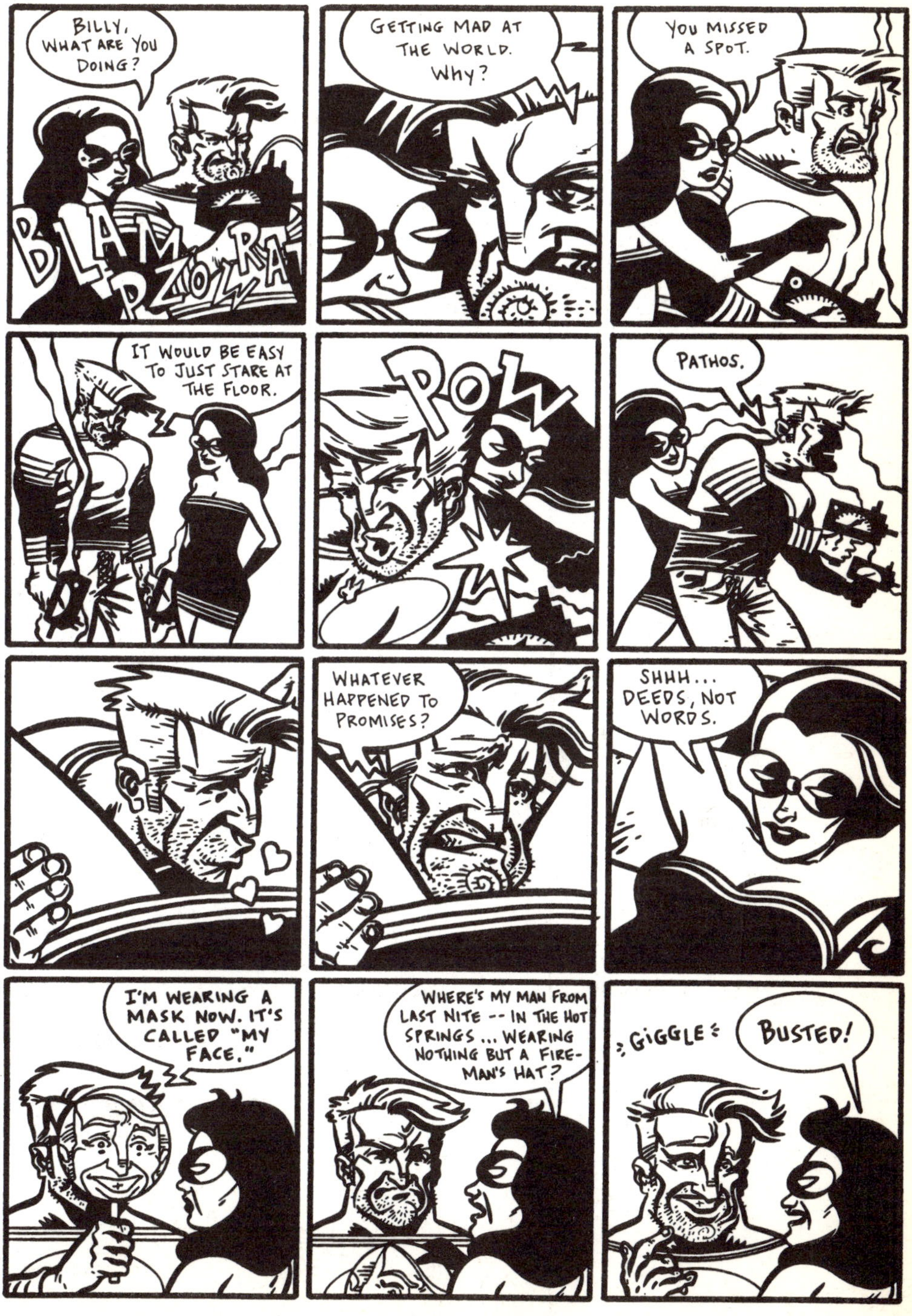
BILLY, WHAT ARE YOU DOING?
BLAM
PZOW
RAT
GETTING MAD AT THE WORLD. Why?
YOU MISSED A SPOT.
IT WOULD BE EASY TO JUST STARE AT THE FLOOR.
POW
PATHOS.
WHATEVER HAPPENED TO PROMISES?
SHHH... DEEDS, NOT WORDS.
I'M WEARING A MASK NOW. IT'S CALLED "MY FACE."
WHERE'S MY MAN FROM LAST NITE -- IN THE HOT SPRINGS... WEARING NOTHING BUT A FIRE-MAN'S HAT?
GIGGLE
BUSTED!

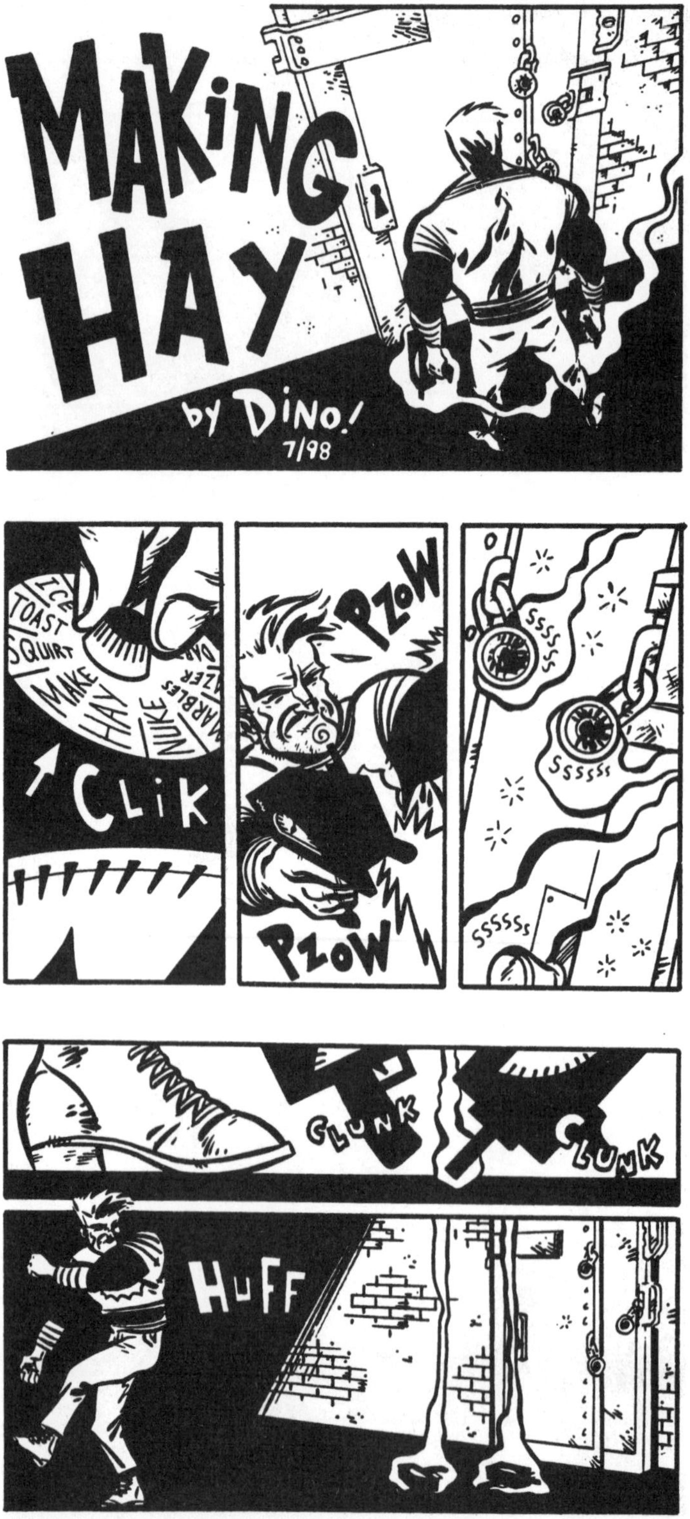
MAKiNG HAY
by DiNO!
7/98
ICE
TOAST
SQUIRT
MAKE HAY
NUKE
MARBLES
CLiK
PZOW
PZOW
SSSSSSS
SSSSSS
SSSSSS
CLUNK
CLUNK
HUFF

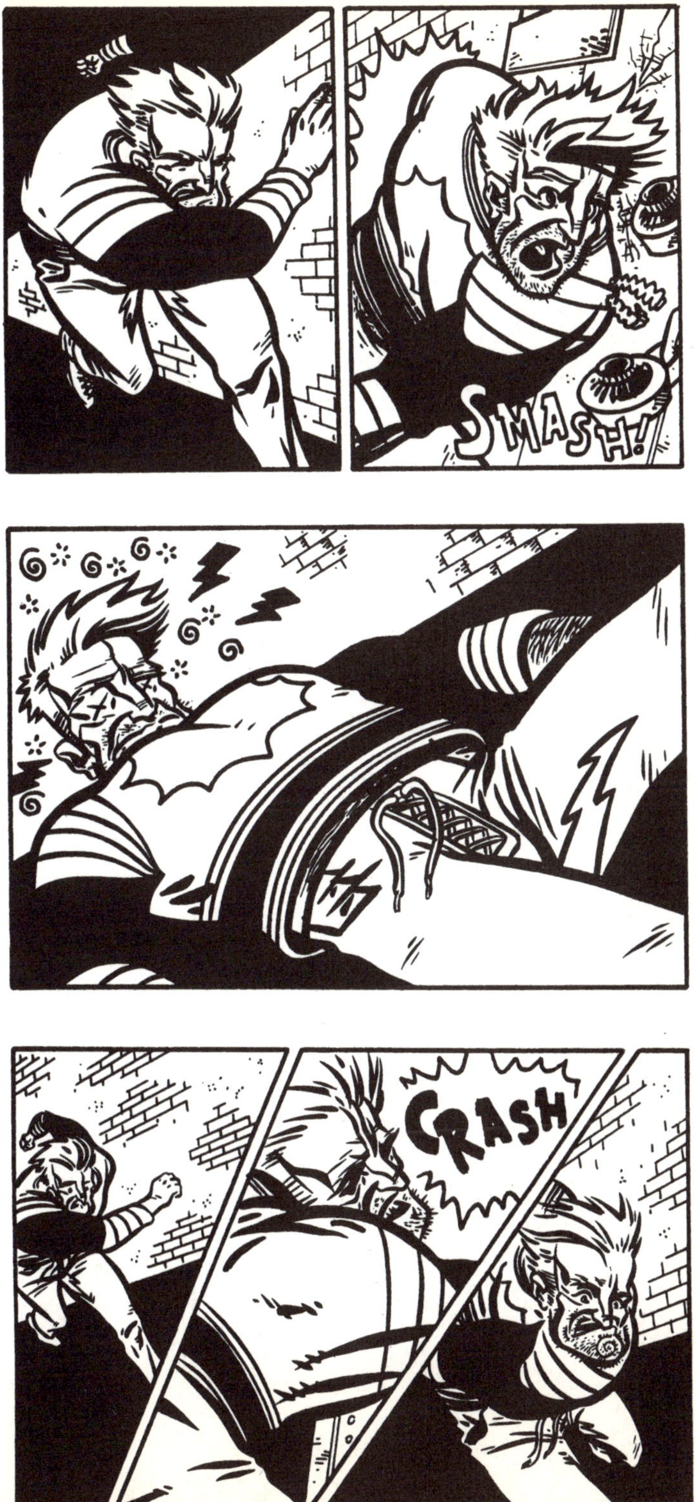
SMASH!
CRASH

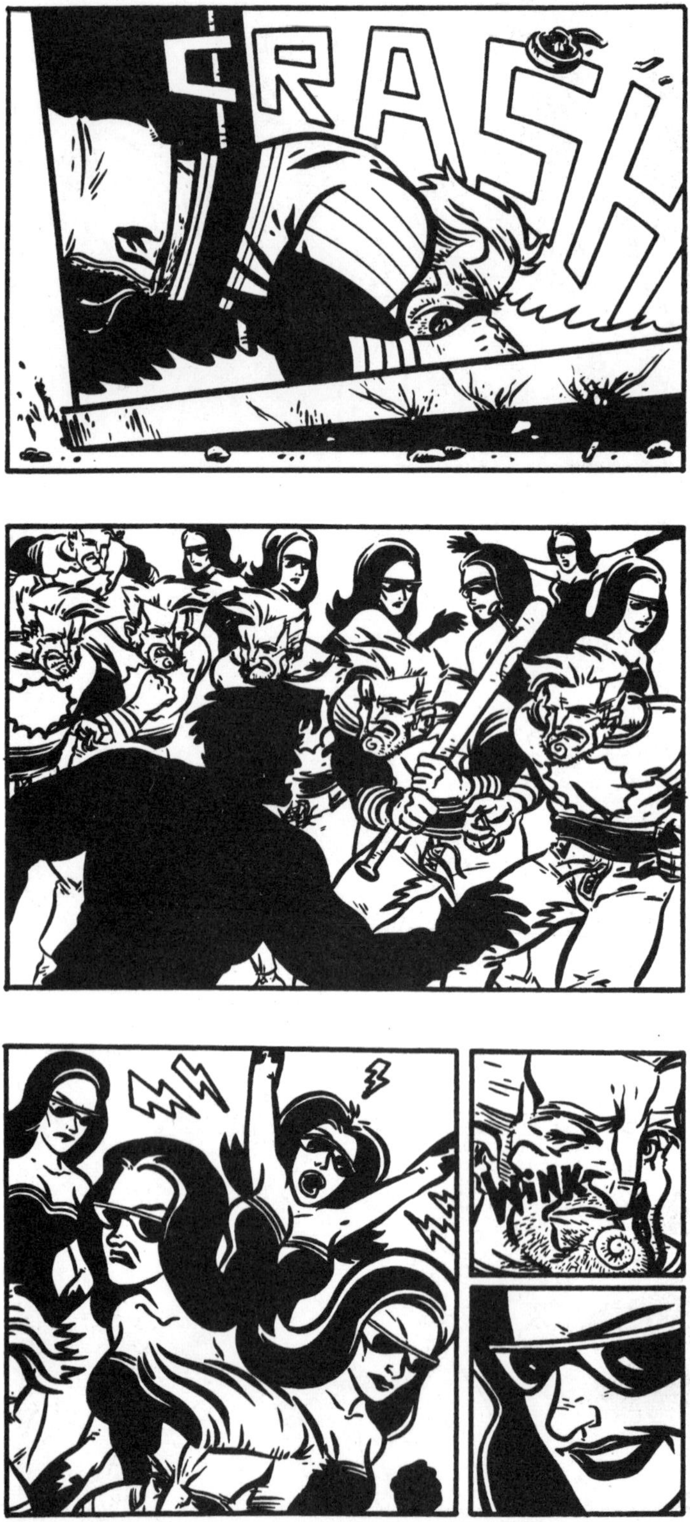
CRASH
WINK

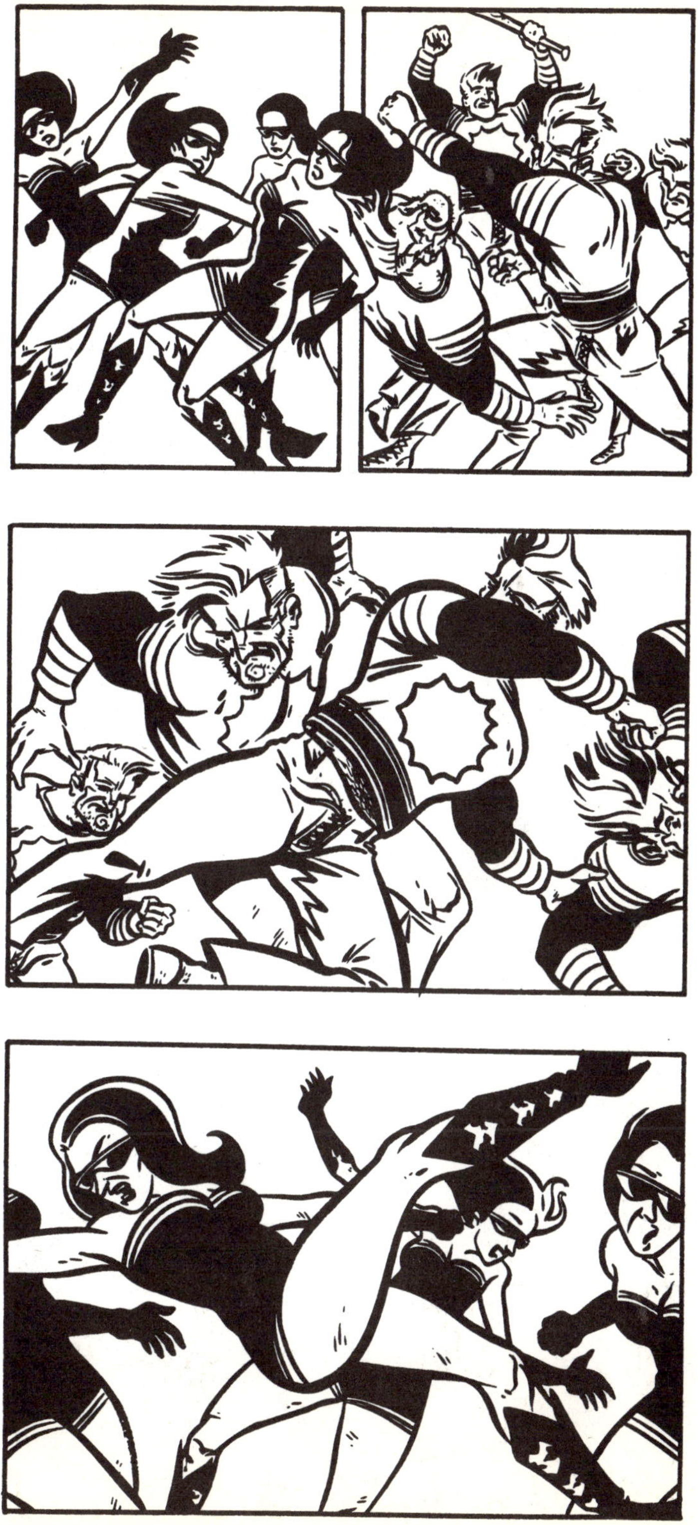

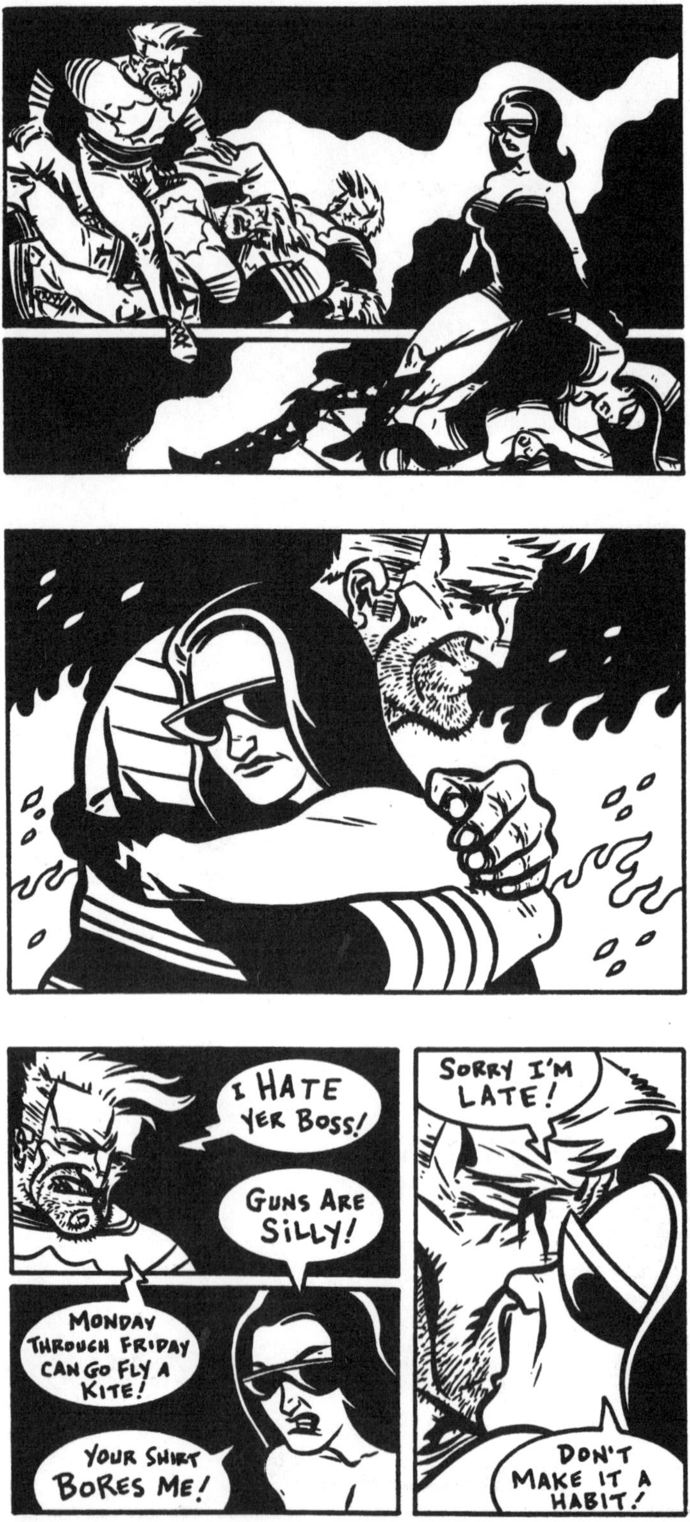
I HATE YER BOSS!
GUNS ARE SILLY!
MONDAY THROUGH FRIDAY CAN GO FLY A KITE!
YOUR SHIRT BORES ME!
SORRY I'M LATE!
DON'T MAKE IT A HABIT!

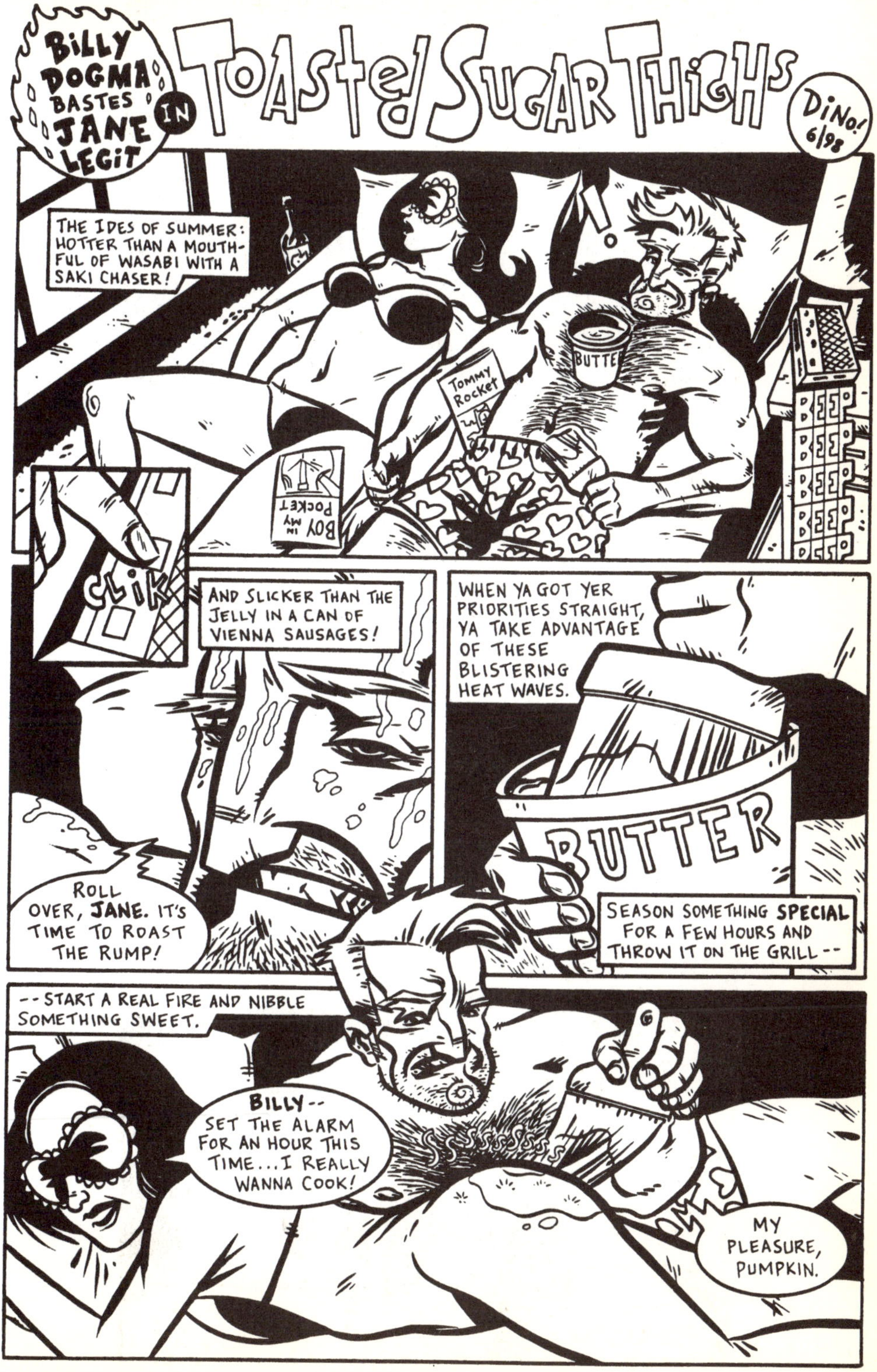
BILLY DOGMA BASTES JANE LEGIT IN
TOASTED SUGAR THIGHS
DiNo! 6/98
THE IDES OF SUMMER: HOTTER THAN A MOUTHFUL OF WASABI WITH A SAKI CHASER!
BUTTE
TOMMY ROCKET
BOY IN MY POCKET
BEEP
BEEP
BEEP
BEEP
BEEP
CLIK
AND SLICKER THAN THE JELLY IN A CAN OF VIENNA SAUSAGES!
WHEN YA GOT YER PRIORITIES STRAIGHT, YA TAKE ADVANTAGE OF THESE BLISTERING HEAT WAVES.
BUTTER
ROLL OVER, JANE. IT'S TIME TO ROAST THE RUMP!
SEASON SOMETHING SPECIAL FOR A FEW HOURS AND THROW IT ON THE GRILL --
-- START A REAL FIRE AND NIBBLE SOMETHING SWEET.
BILLY -- SET THE ALARM FOR AN HOUR THIS TIME... I REALLY WANNA COOK!
SSSSSSSS
MY PLEASURE, PUMPKIN.

Billy Dogma throws speed-knots with The Under-Color Cop in

WHEN AND WHERE I'LL BE THERE

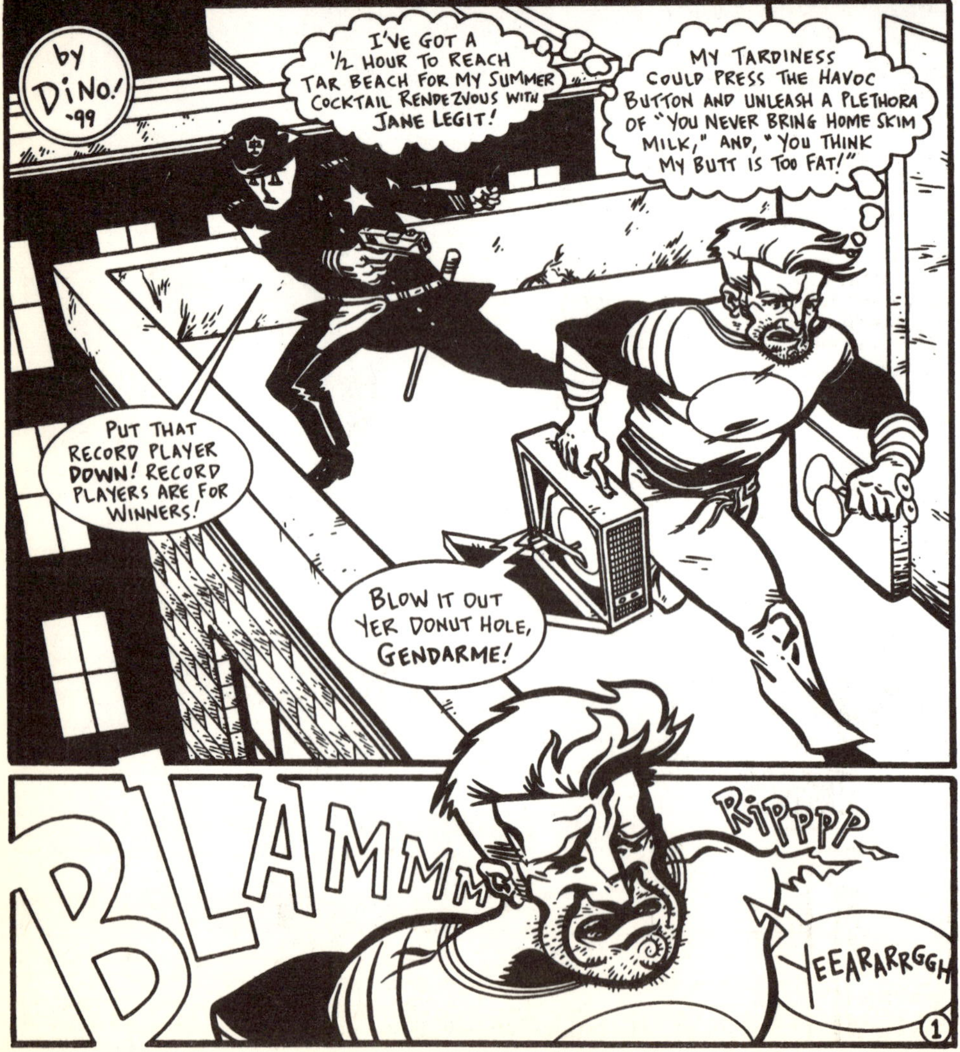

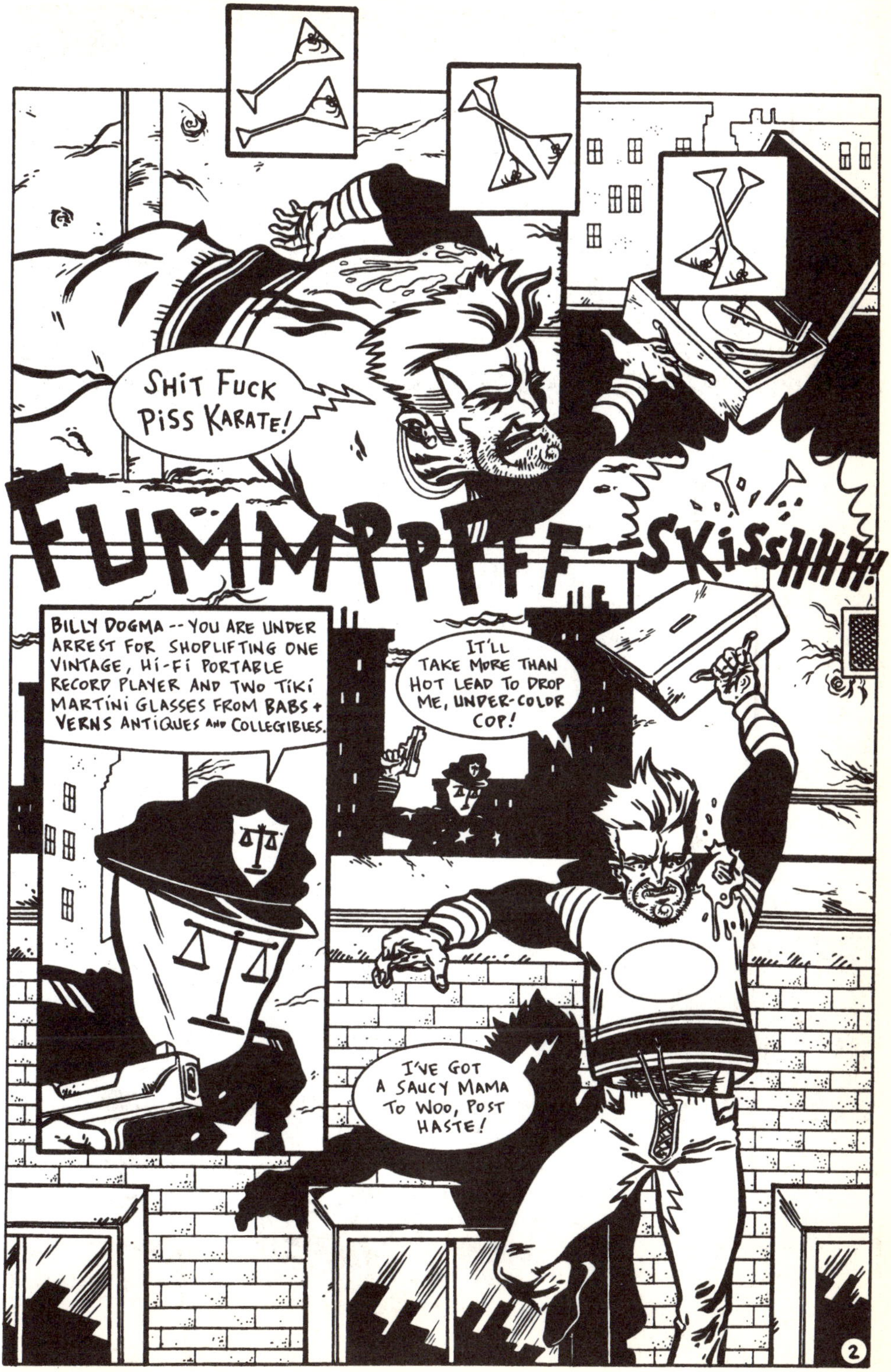
SHIT FUCK PISS KARATE!
FUMMPPFFF-SKISSHHH!
BILLY DOGMA -- YOU ARE UNDER ARREST FOR SHOPLIFTING ONE VINTAGE, HI-FI PORTABLE RECORD PLAYER AND TWO TIKI MARTINI GLASSES FROM BABS + VERNS ANTIQUES AND COLLECTIBLES.
IT'LL TAKE MORE THAN HOT LEAD TO DROP ME, UNDER-COLOR COP!
I'VE GOT A SAUCY MAMA TO WOO, POST HASTE!
2

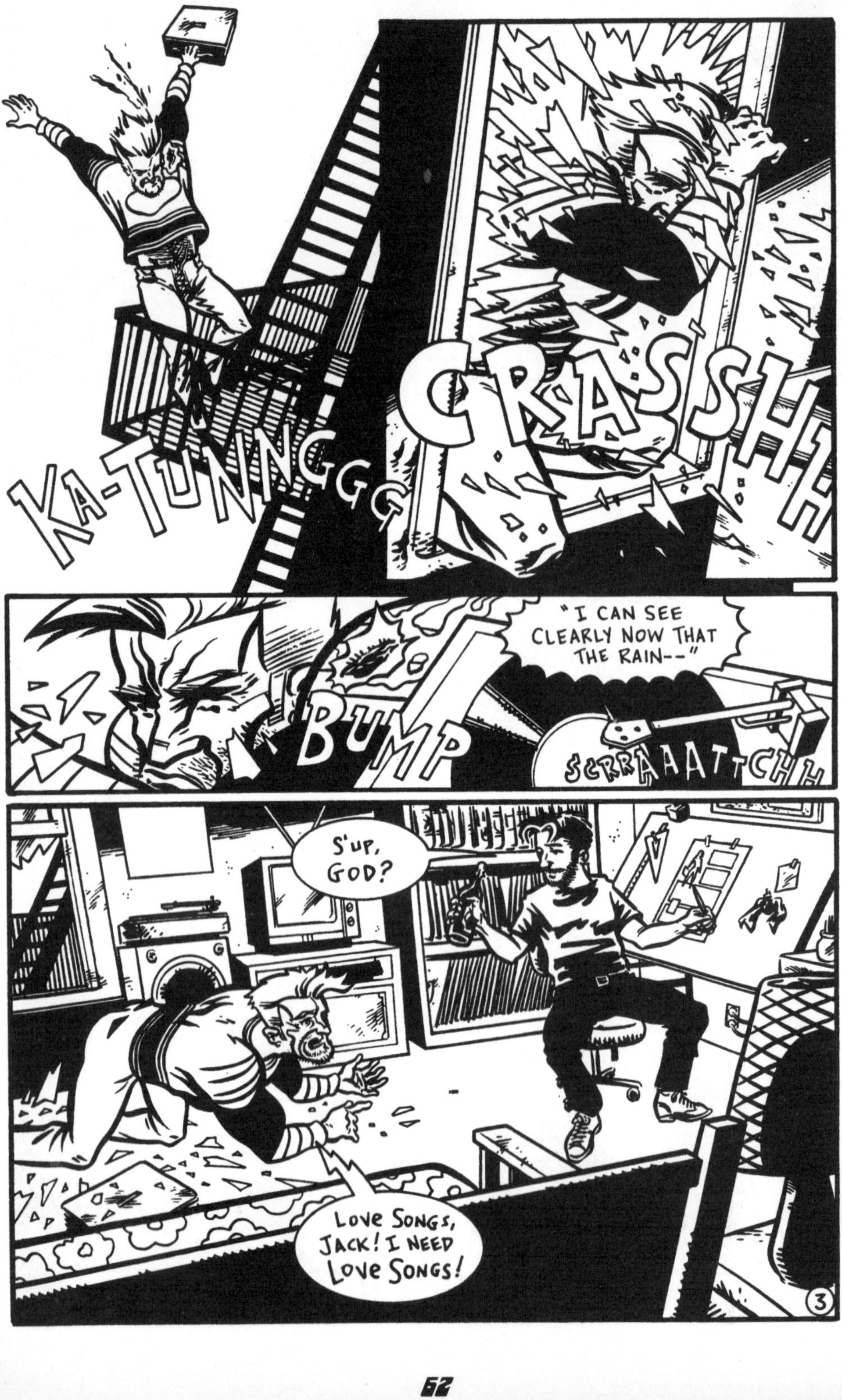
KA-TUNNGGG
CRASSHH
"I CAN SEE CLEARLY NOW THAT THE RAIN--"
BUMP
SCRRAAATTCHH
S'UP, GOD?
Love Songs, JACK! I NEED Love Songs!
3

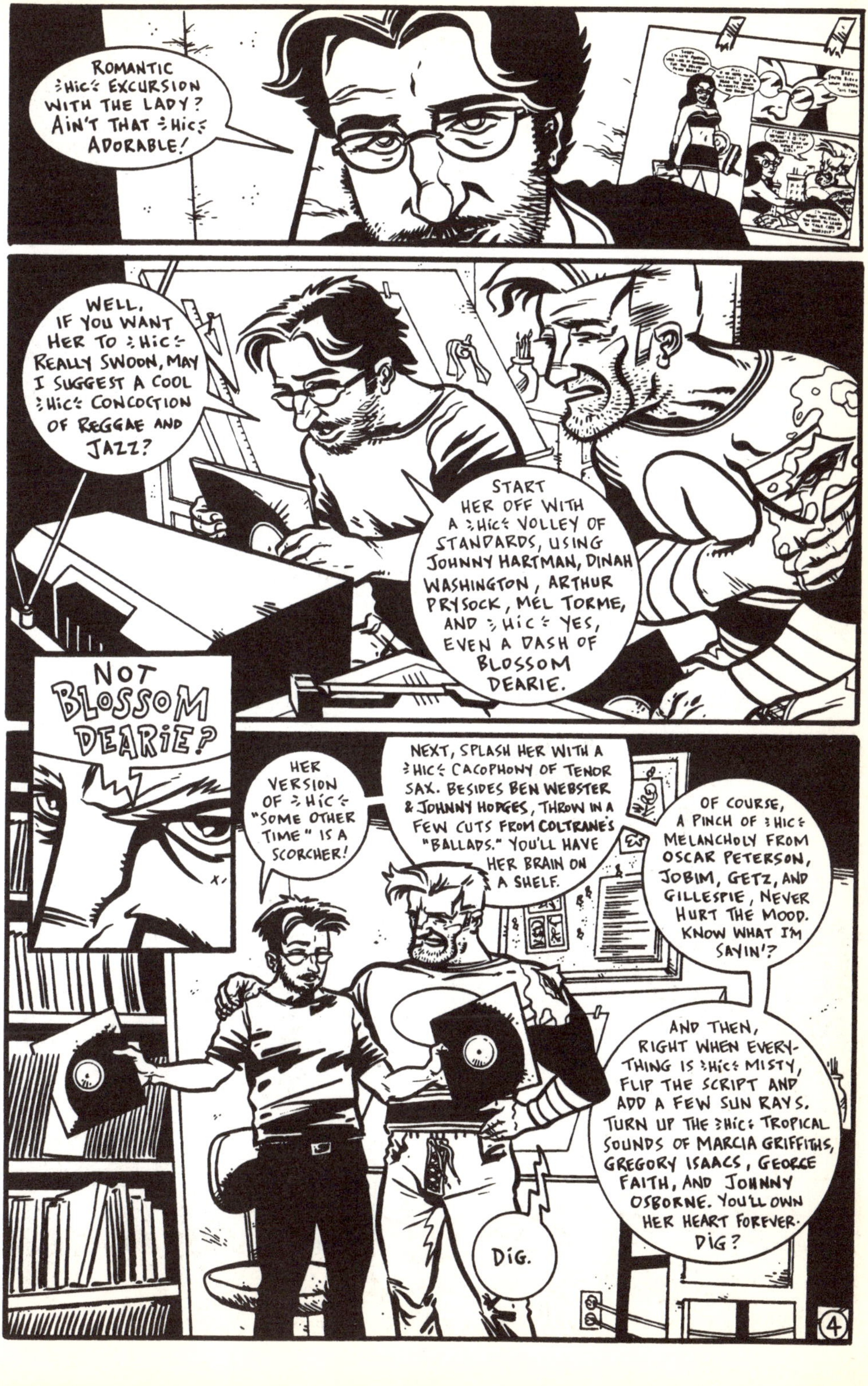
ROMANTIC ❊HIC❊ EXCURSION WITH THE LADY? AIN'T THAT ❊HIC❊ ADORABLE!
WELL, IF YOU WANT HER TO ❊HIC❊ REALLY SWOON, MAY I SUGGEST A COOL ❊HIC❊ CONCOCTION OF REGGAE AND JAZZ?
START HER OFF WITH A ❊HIC❊ VOLLEY OF STANDARDS, USING JOHNNY HARTMAN, DINAH WASHINGTON, ARTHUR PRYSOCK, MEL TORME, AND ❊HIC❊ YES, EVEN A DASH OF BLOSSOM DEARIE.
NOT BLOSSOM DEARIE?
HER VERSION OF ❊HIC❊ "SOME OTHER TIME" IS A SCORCHER!
NEXT, SPLASH HER WITH A ❊HIC❊ CACOPHONY OF TENOR SAX. BESIDES BEN WEBSTER & JOHNNY HODGES, THROW IN A FEW CUTS FROM COLTRANE'S "BALLADS." YOU'LL HAVE HER BRAIN ON A SHELF.
OF COURSE, A PINCH OF ❊HIC❊ MELANCHOLY FROM OSCAR PETERSON, JOBIM, GETZ, AND GILLESPIE, NEVER HURT THE MOOD. KNOW WHAT I'M SAYIN'?
AND THEN, RIGHT WHEN EVERYTHING IS ❊HIC❊ MISTY, FLIP THE SCRIPT AND ADD A FEW SUN RAYS. TURN UP THE ❊HIC❊ TROPICAL SOUNDS OF MARCIA GRIFFITHS, GREGORY ISAACS, GEORGE FAITH, AND JOHNNY OSBORNE. YOU'LL OWN HER HEART FOREVER. DIG?
DIG.
4

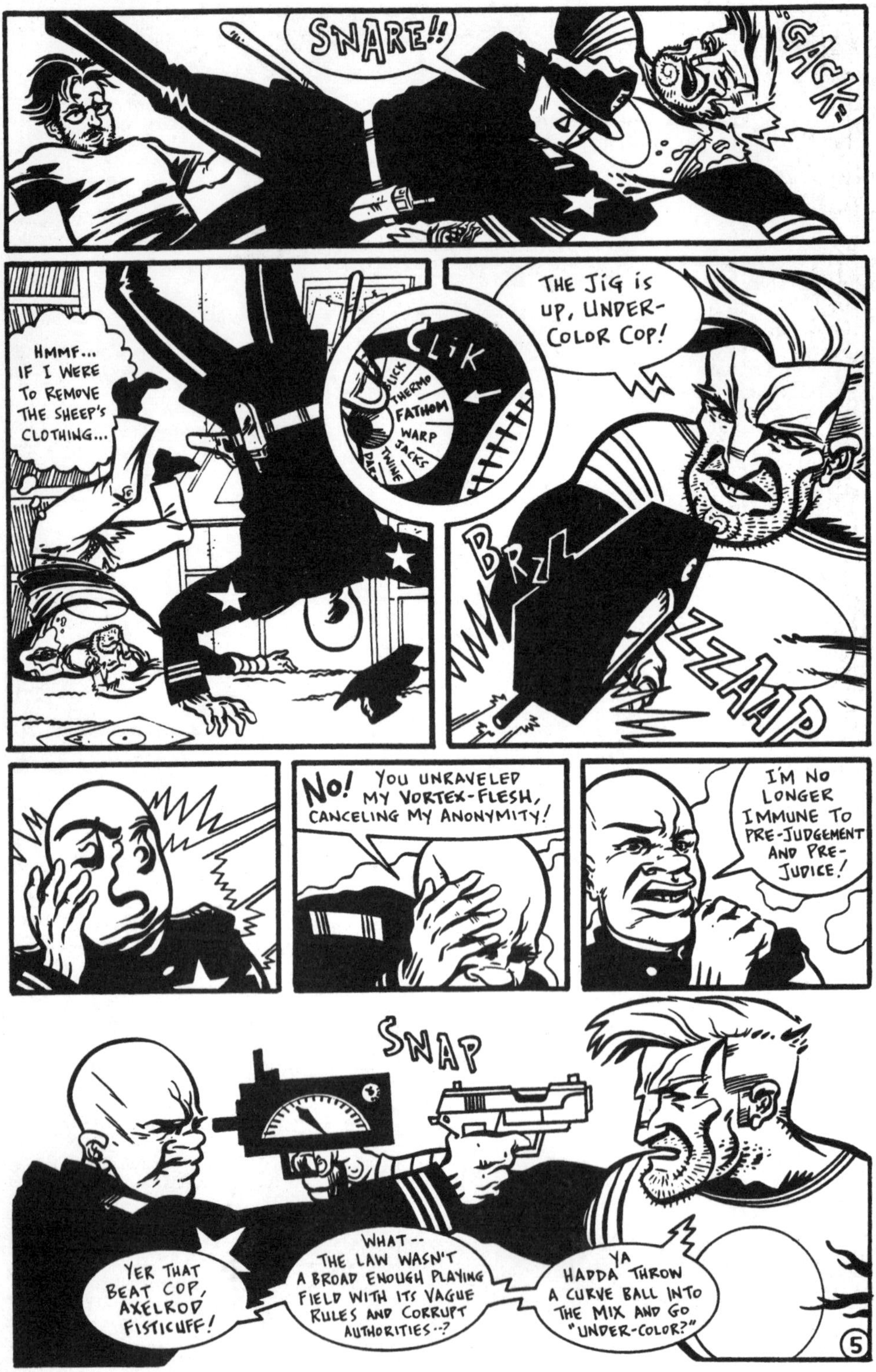
SNARE!!
GACK!
HMMF... IF I WERE TO REMOVE THE SHEEP'S CLOTHING...
CLIK
SLICK
THERMO
FATHOM
WARP
JACKS
TWINE
THE JIG IS UP, UNDER-COLOR COP!
BRZ
ZZZAAP
NO! YOU UNRAVELED MY VORTEX-FLESH, CANCELING MY ANONYMITY!
I'M NO LONGER IMMUNE TO PRE-JUDGEMENT AND PRE-JUDICE!
SNAP
YER THAT BEAT COP, AXELROD FISTICUFF!
WHAT -- THE LAW WASN'T A BROAD ENOUGH PLAYING FIELD WITH ITS VAGUE RULES AND CORRUPT AUTHORITIES --?
YA HADDA THROW A CURVE BALL INTO THE MIX AND GO "UNDER-COLOR?"
5

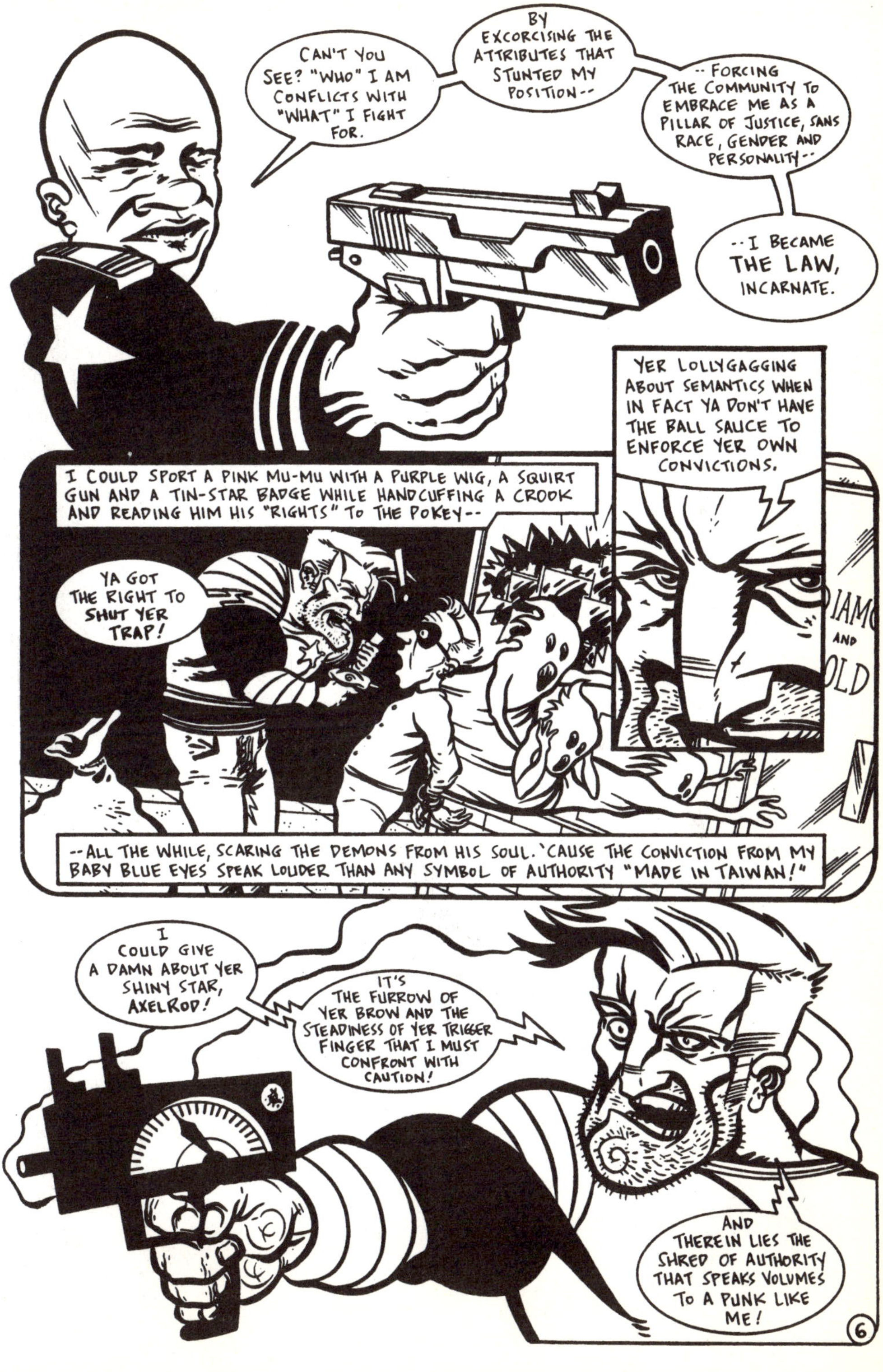

CAN'T YOU SEE? "WHO" I AM CONFLICTS WITH "WHAT" I FIGHT FOR.
BY EXCORCISING THE ATTRIBUTES THAT STUNTED MY POSITION--
--FORCING THE COMMUNITY TO EMBRACE ME AS A PILLAR OF JUSTICE, SANS RACE, GENDER AND PERSONALITY--
--I BECAME THE LAW, INCARNATE.
YER LOLLYGAGGING ABOUT SEMANTICS WHEN IN FACT YA DON'T HAVE THE BALL SAUCE TO ENFORCE YER OWN CONVICTIONS.
I COULD SPORT A PINK MU-MU WITH A PURPLE WIG, A SQUIRT GUN AND A TIN-STAR BADGE WHILE HANDCUFFING A CROOK AND READING HIM HIS "RIGHTS" TO THE POKEY--
YA GOT THE RIGHT TO SHUT YER TRAP!
--ALL THE WHILE, SCARING THE DEMONS FROM HIS SOUL. 'CAUSE THE CONVICTION FROM MY BABY BLUE EYES SPEAK LOUDER THAN ANY SYMBOL OF AUTHORITY "MADE IN TAIWAN!"
I COULD GIVE A DAMN ABOUT YER SHINY STAR, AXELROD!
IT'S THE FURROW OF YER BROW AND THE STEADINESS OF YER TRIGGER FINGER THAT I MUST CONFRONT WITH CAUTION!
AND THEREIN LIES THE SHRED OF AUTHORITY THAT SPEAKS VOLUMES TO A PUNK LIKE ME!
6

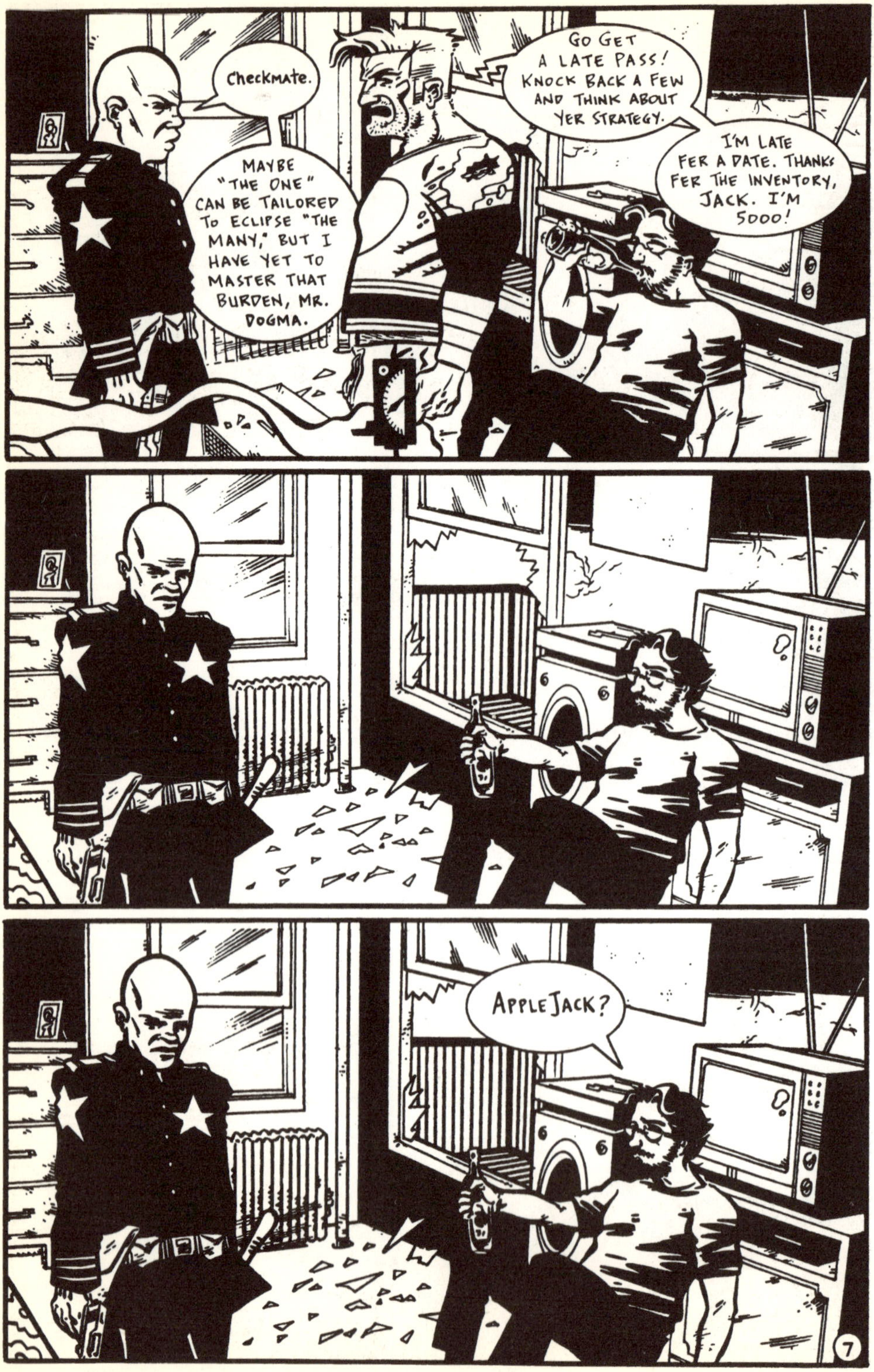
Checkmate.
Go get a late pass! Knock back a few and think about yer strategy.
Maybe "The One" can be tailored to eclipse "The Many," but I have yet to master that burden, Mr. Dogma.
I'm late fer a date. Thanks fer the inventory, Jack. I'm sooo!
AppleJack?
7

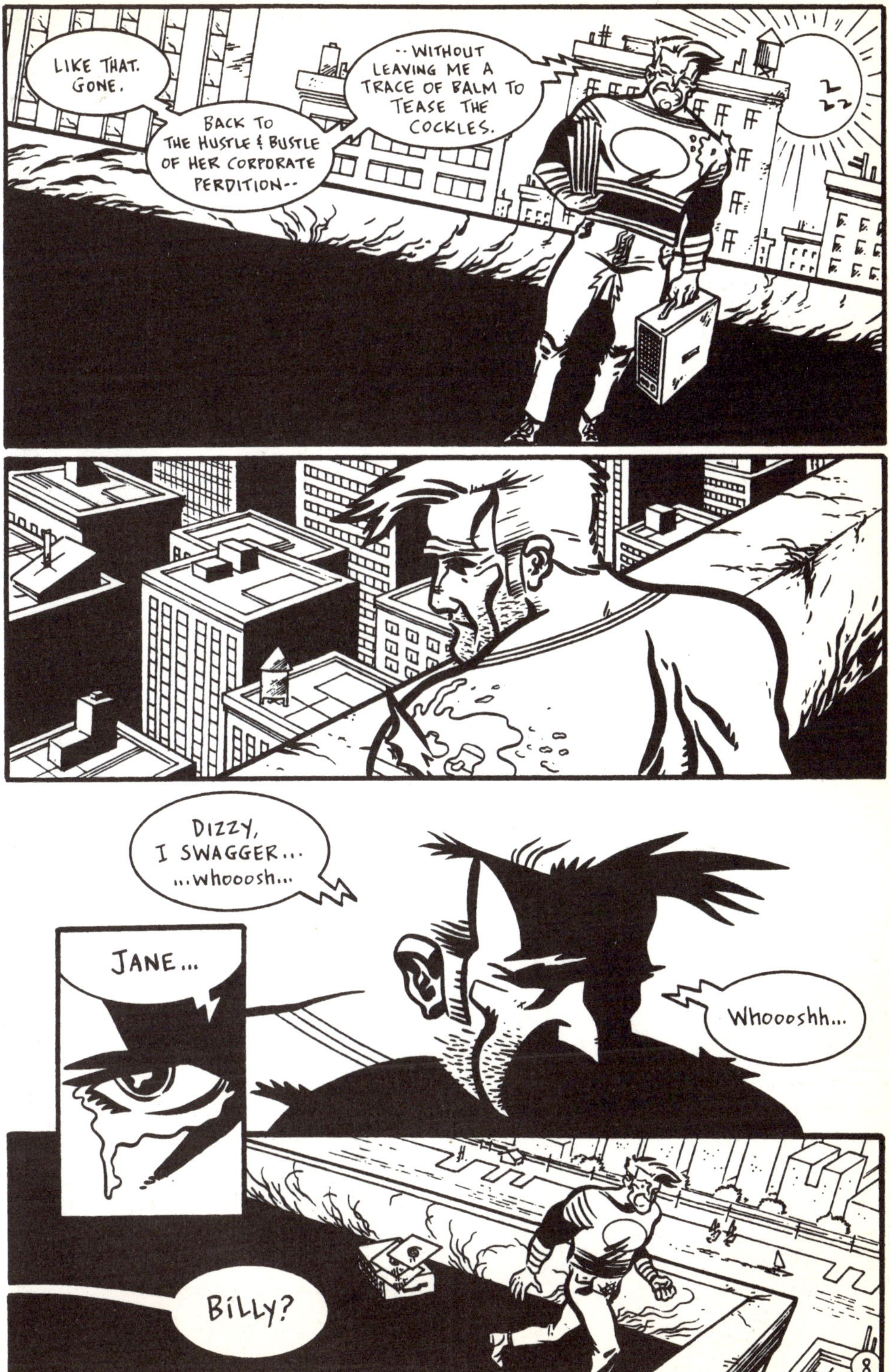
LIKE THAT. GONE.
BACK TO THE HUSTLE & BUSTLE OF HER CORPORATE PERDITION--
--WITHOUT LEAVING ME A TRACE OF BALM TO TEASE THE COCKLES.
DIZZY, I SWAGGER... ...whooosh...
JANE...
Whoooshh...
BILLY?
8

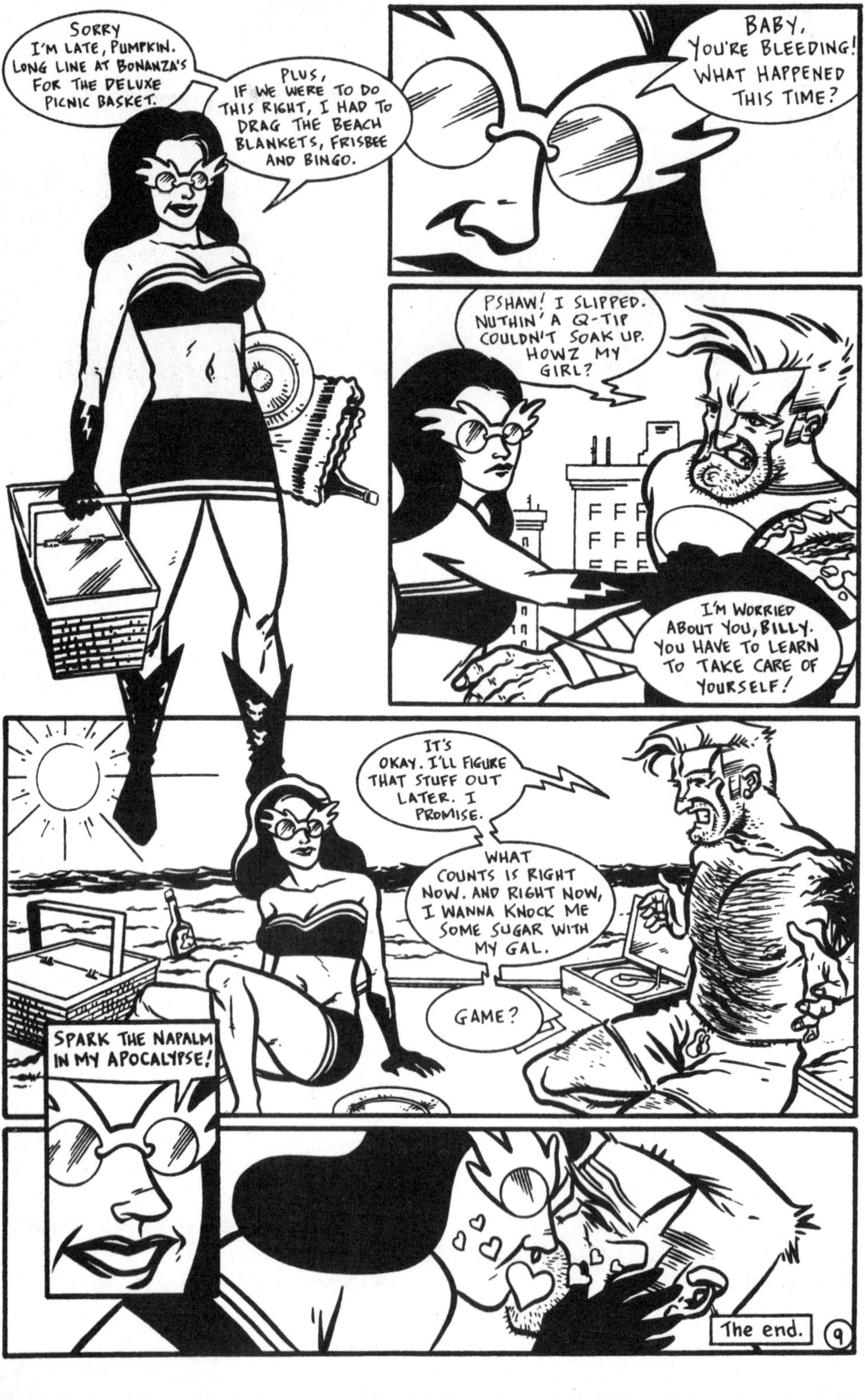
SORRY I'M LATE, PUMPKIN. LONG LINE AT BONANZA'S FOR THE DELUXE PICNIC BASKET.
PLUS, IF WE WERE TO DO THIS RIGHT, I HAD TO DRAG THE BEACH BLANKETS, FRISBEE AND BINGO.
BABY, YOU'RE BLEEDING! WHAT HAPPENED THIS TIME?
PSHAW! I SLIPPED. NUTHIN' A Q-TIP COULDN'T SOAK UP. HOWZ MY GIRL?
I'M WORRIED ABOUT YOU, BILLY. YOU HAVE TO LEARN TO TAKE CARE OF YOURSELF!
IT'S OKAY. I'LL FIGURE THAT STUFF OUT LATER. I PROMISE.
WHAT COUNTS IS RIGHT NOW. AND RIGHT NOW, I WANNA KNOCK ME SOME SUGAR WITH MY GAL.
GAME?
SPARK THE NAPALM IN MY APOCALYPSE!
The end.
9

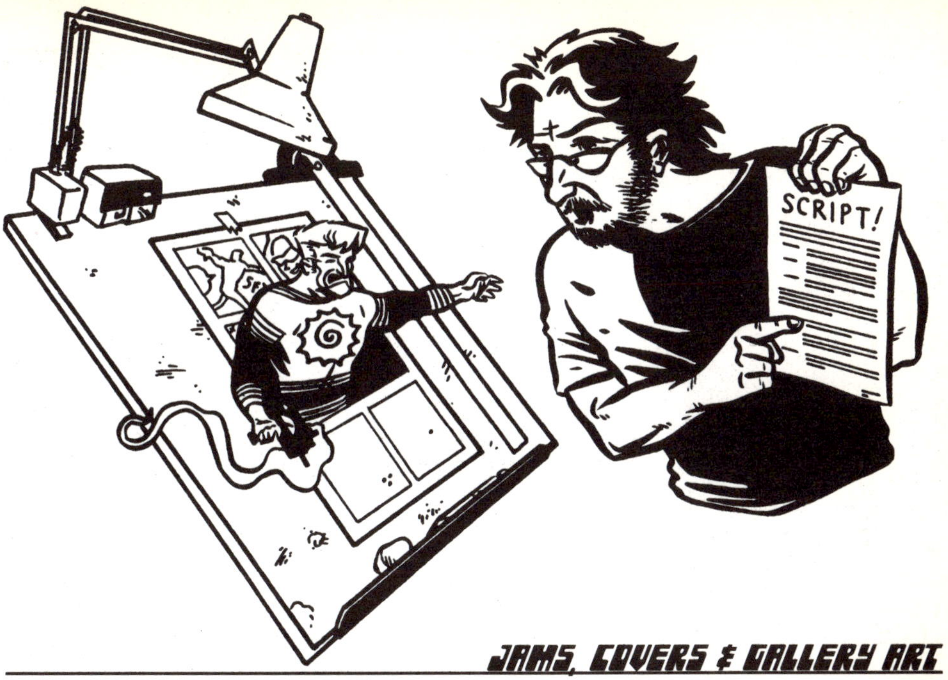
SCRIPT!

JAMS, COVERS & GALLERY ART

As far as I'm concerned, Billy Dogma shares the same alleyways as some of my favorite creator-owned comics characters. Nut jobs like ***The Spirit***, ***Flaming Carrot***, ***Powerhouse Pepper***, ***Mr. Natural***, ***Ed the Happy Clown***, ***Rueben Flagg***, ***Hutch Owen***, ***Marv***, ***Hellboy***, ***Penny Century***, ***Magic Boy***, ***Jimmy Corrigan***, ***Reid Fleming***, ***Harvey Pekar***--the list goes on.

I've been lucky enough to collaborate with some of my favorite cartoonists. The stories that follow are short stabs at bigger ideas wherein *Billy Dogma* gets to vogue with peers in all his knee jerk glory. The mysterious Maze allowed me to borrow his morbid, teenage she-brat, ***Lovely Prudence***, for a quick romp into a suburban mall. The sexy-cyborg ***Viva Muerte*** will probably reappear in Nick Bertozzi's schizophrenic ***Filthy Baby*** series, if he doesn't fix her up with the heartbroken ***Koala*** before hand. Pete Sickman-Garner is busy making folks bust a gut with the hilarity of his cynical trio of unflinching misanthropes in ***Hey, Mister***. The hot and hip ***Courtney Clare*** serves as Jessica Abel's young ace in ***Artbabe***.

I'm also fortunate to have pin-ups drawn by industry veterans of varying tenure. Bob Fingerman is not only talented at writing brutally honest introductions, but he also graces readers with the street savvy of his neo-realistic ***Minimum Wage***. Steve Weissman haunts the racks with his cute monster franchise ***Yikes!*** Matt Madden made an impressive debut last year with his macabre yet viscous ***Black Candy***, as did Jason Little with his revisionist, pop-noir one-shot ***Jack's Luck Runs Out.*** Of course, this collection would not be complete without versions from my own mentors: Howard Chaykin, whose ***American Flagg!*** shined a bright light on where comics could go, and Walter Simonson, whose ***Starslammers*** showed me what comics could look like. Thanks.

--Dino, 1999

LOVELY PRUDENCE MEETS BILLY DOGMA IN:
THE ST. VALENTINE'S DAY MASCARA

WHERE CAN I GET A PAIR OF IMPOSSIBLE PANTIES AND A BULLET-PROOF BRA?

STORY AND ART BY DEAN HASPIEL
PRUDENCE & CO. CREATED BY MAZE
BILLY DOGMA CREATED BY HASPIEL

GOSH! YOU'RE BILLY DOGMA! MY FAVORITE FULMINATED FELON! I'M THE SAURUS BLACK. I HAVE ALL OF YOUR ACTION FIGURES, POGS, REFRIGERATOR MAGNETS AND BUBBLE-GUM CARDS! SAY, WHY ARE YOU MANIACALLY MILLING ABOUT THE MALL?

IT'S SAINT VALENTINE'S DAY, TWERP, WHICH MEANS I NEED TO GET MY GIRL JANE SOMETHING NIFTY. OBVIOUSLY AN ANNIVERSARY THAT DOESN'T CROSS YOUR CALENDAR YEAR.

CLIK

ZOOM

I KNOW! MISS CORSET FACE CAN HELP YOU FIND WHATEVER YOU NEED IN ALL FASHIONS, FITS AND FLAVORS. JUST SLAP HER THIGH AND RIDE THE WAVE IN. SLURP!

VICTORIA'S SECRET
EROTIC CLOTHING & WARES

ZOOM

①

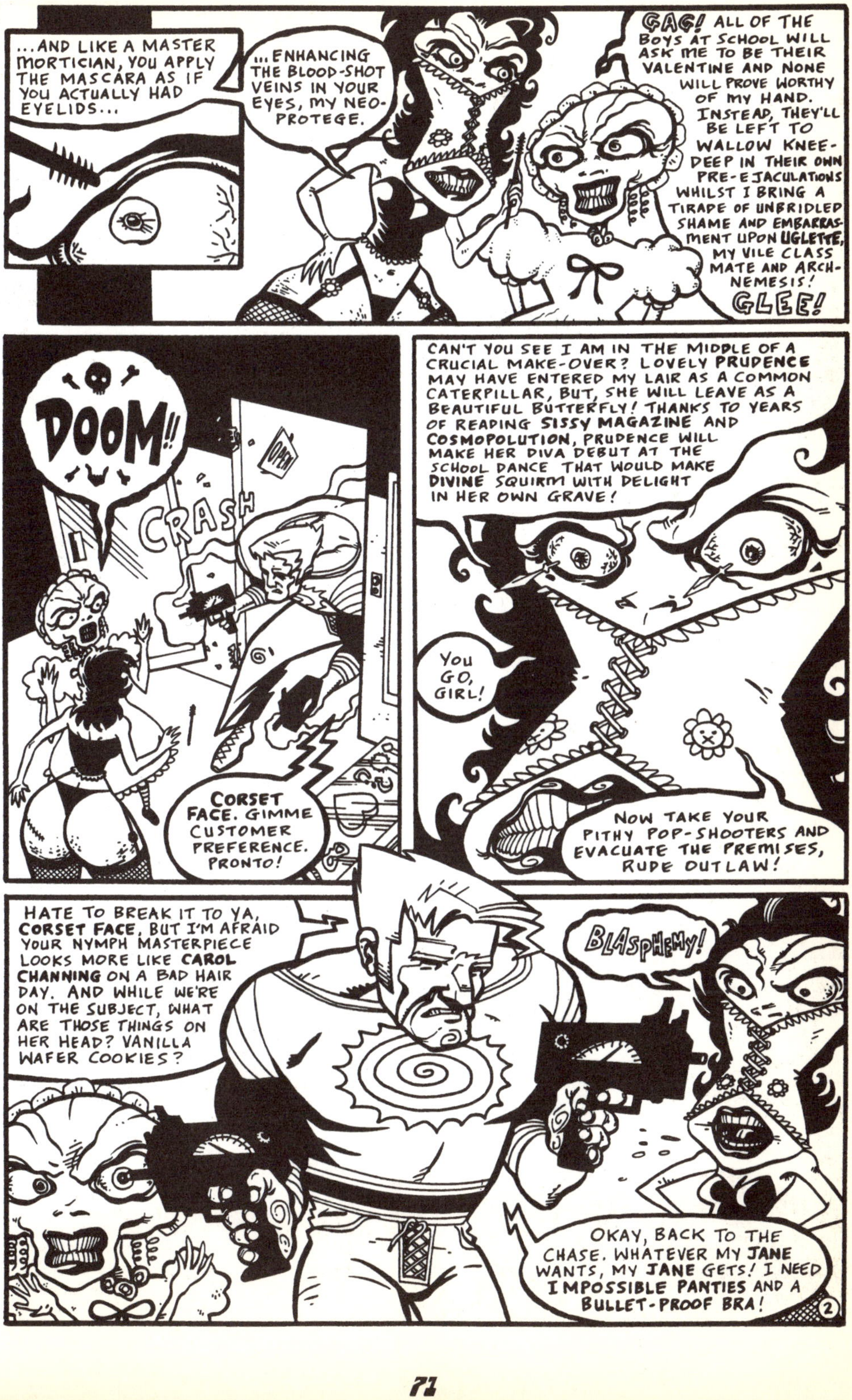
...AND LIKE A MASTER MORTICIAN, YOU APPLY THE MASCARA AS IF YOU ACTUALLY HAD EYELIDS...
...ENHANCING THE BLOOD-SHOT VEINS IN YOUR EYES, MY NEO-PROTEGE.
GAG! ALL OF THE BOYS AT SCHOOL WILL ASK ME TO BE THEIR VALENTINE AND NONE WILL PROVE WORTHY OF MY HAND. INSTEAD, THEY'LL BE LEFT TO WALLOW KNEE-DEEP IN THEIR OWN PRE-EJACULATIONS WHILST I BRING A TIRADE OF UNBRIDLED SHAME AND EMBARRASMENT UPON UGLETTE, MY VILE CLASSMATE AND ARCH-NEMESIS!
GLEE!
DOOM!!
CRASH
OPEN
CORSET FACE. GIMME CUSTOMER PREFERENCE. PRONTO!
CAN'T YOU SEE I AM IN THE MIDDLE OF A CRUCIAL MAKE-OVER? LOVELY PRUDENCE MAY HAVE ENTERED MY LAIR AS A COMMON CATERPILLAR, BUT, SHE WILL LEAVE AS A BEAUTIFUL BUTTERFLY! THANKS TO YEARS OF READING SISSY MAGAZINE AND COSMOPOLUTION, PRUDENCE WILL MAKE HER DIVA DEBUT AT THE SCHOOL DANCE THAT WOULD MAKE DIVINE SQUIRM WITH DELIGHT IN HER OWN GRAVE!
YOU GO, GIRL!
NOW TAKE YOUR PITHY POP-SHOOTERS AND EVACUATE THE PREMISES, RUDE OUTLAW!
HATE TO BREAK IT TO YA, CORSET FACE, BUT I'M AFRAID YOUR NYMPH MASTERPIECE LOOKS MORE LIKE CAROL CHANNING ON A BAD HAIR DAY. AND WHILE WE'RE ON THE SUBJECT, WHAT ARE THOSE THINGS ON HER HEAD? VANILLA WAFER COOKIES?
BLASPHEMY!
OKAY, BACK TO THE CHASE. WHATEVER MY JANE WANTS, MY JANE GETS! I NEED IMPOSSIBLE PANTIES AND A BULLET-PROOF BRA!
2

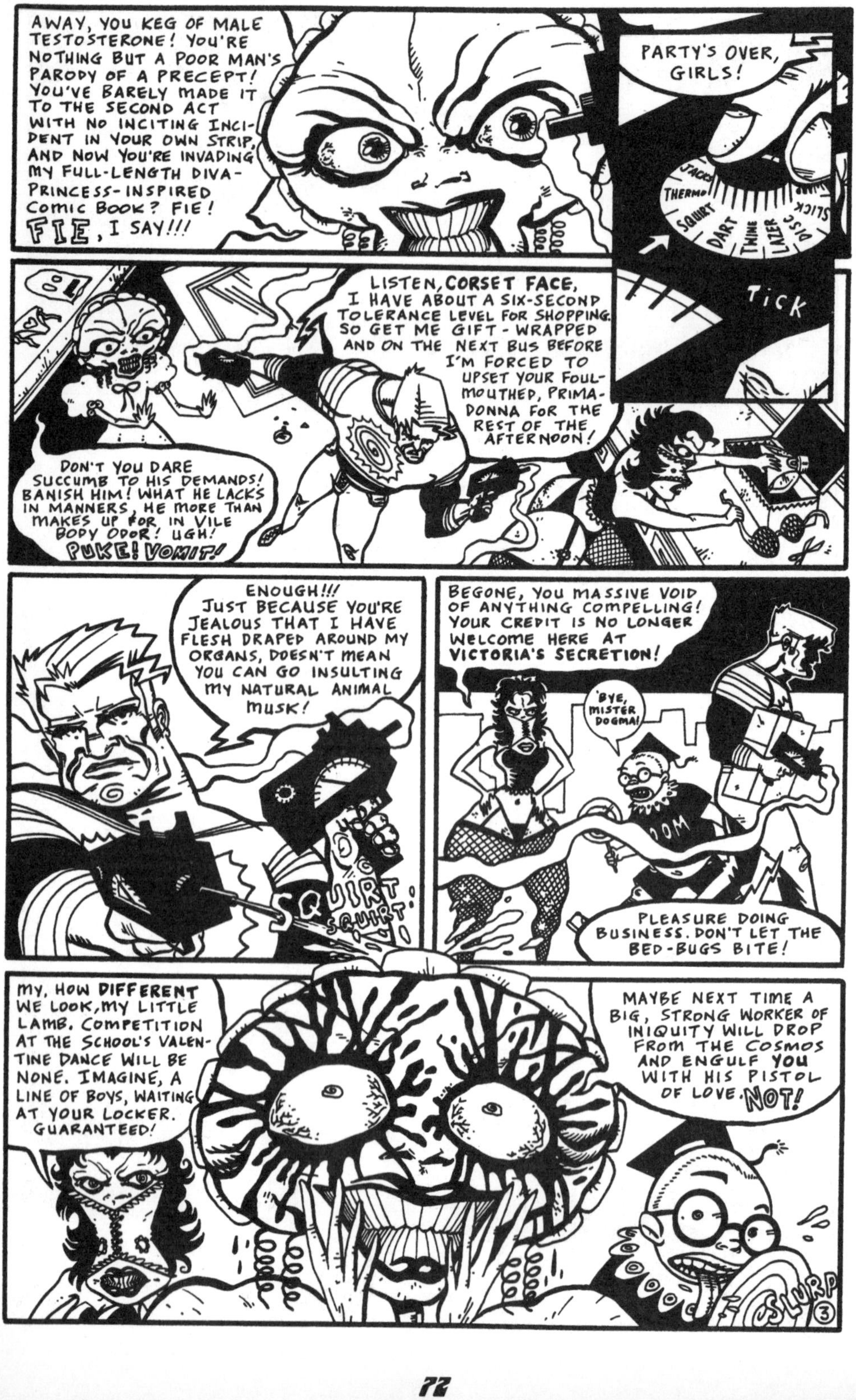

AWAY, YOU KEG OF MALE TESTOSTERONE! YOU'RE NOTHING BUT A POOR MAN'S PARODY OF A PRECEPT! YOU'VE BARELY MADE IT TO THE SECOND ACT WITH NO INCITING INCIDENT IN YOUR OWN STRIP, AND NOW YOU'RE INVADING MY FULL-LENGTH DIVA-PRINCESS-INSPIRED COMIC BOOK? FIE! FIE, I SAY!!!
PARTY'S OVER, GIRLS!
JACKS
THERMO
SQUIRT
DART
TWINE
LAZER
DISC
SLICK
TICK
LISTEN, CORSET FACE, I HAVE ABOUT A SIX-SECOND TOLERANCE LEVEL FOR SHOPPING. SO GET ME GIFT-WRAPPED AND ON THE NEXT BUS BEFORE I'M FORCED TO UPSET YOUR FOUL-MOUTHED, PRIMA-DONNA FOR THE REST OF THE AFTERNOON!
DON'T YOU DARE SUCCUMB TO HIS DEMANDS! BANISH HIM! WHAT HE LACKS IN MANNERS, HE MORE THAN MAKES UP FOR IN VILE BODY ODOR! UGH! PUKE! VOMIT!
ENOUGH!!! JUST BECAUSE YOU'RE JEALOUS THAT I HAVE FLESH DRAPED AROUND MY ORGANS, DOESN'T MEAN YOU CAN GO INSULTING MY NATURAL ANIMAL MUSK!
SQUIRT
SQUIRT
BEGONE, YOU MASSIVE VOID OF ANYTHING COMPELLING! YOUR CREDIT IS NO LONGER WELCOME HERE AT VICTORIA'S SECRETION!
'BYE, MISTER DOGMA!
PLEASURE DOING BUSINESS. DON'T LET THE BED-BUGS BITE!
MY, HOW DIFFERENT WE LOOK, MY LITTLE LAMB. COMPETITION AT THE SCHOOL'S VALENTINE DANCE WILL BE NONE. IMAGINE, A LINE OF BOYS, WAITING AT YOUR LOCKER. GUARANTEED!
MAYBE NEXT TIME A BIG, STRONG WORKER OF INIQUITY WILL DROP FROM THE COSMOS AND ENGULF YOU WITH HIS PISTOL OF LOVE. NOT!
SLURP
3

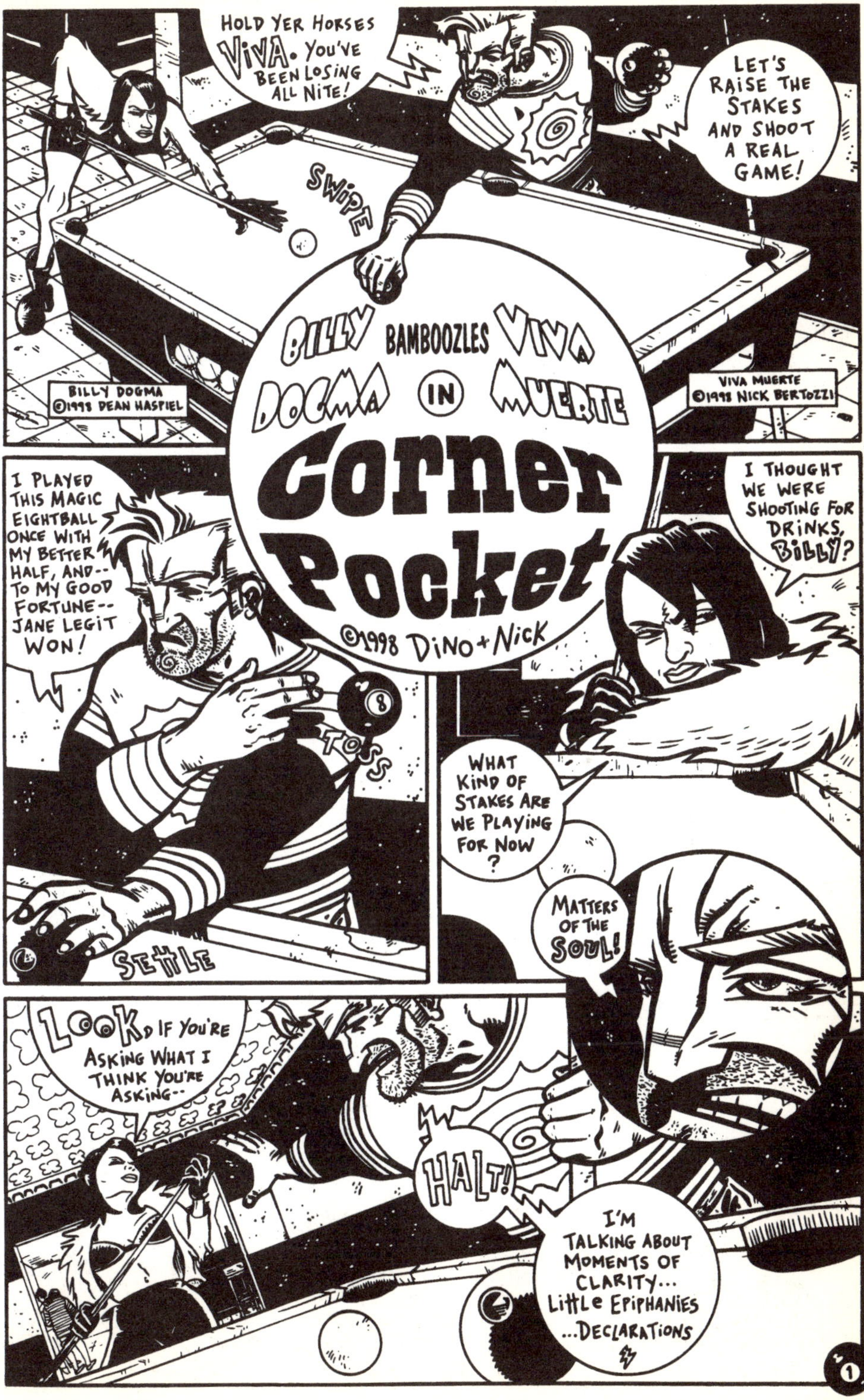

HOLD YER HORSES VIVA. YOU'VE BEEN LOSING ALL NITE!
LET'S RAISE THE STAKES AND SHOOT A REAL GAME!
SWIPE
BILLY BAMBOOZLES VIVA DOGMA IN MUERTE
Corner Pocket
©1998 DINO + NICK
BILLY DOGMA ©1998 DEAN HASPIEL
VIVA MUERTE ©1998 NICK BERTOZZI
I PLAYED THIS MAGIC EIGHTBALL ONCE WITH MY BETTER HALF, AND-- TO MY GOOD FORTUNE-- JANE LEGIT WON!
TOSS
SETTLE
I THOUGHT WE WERE SHOOTING FOR DRINKS, BILLY?
WHAT KIND OF STAKES ARE WE PLAYING FOR NOW ?
MATTERS OF THE SOUL!
LOOK, IF YOU'RE ASKING WHAT I THINK YOU'RE ASKING--
HALT!
I'M TALKING ABOUT MOMENTS OF CLARITY... LITTLE EPIPHANIES ...DECLARATIONS
1

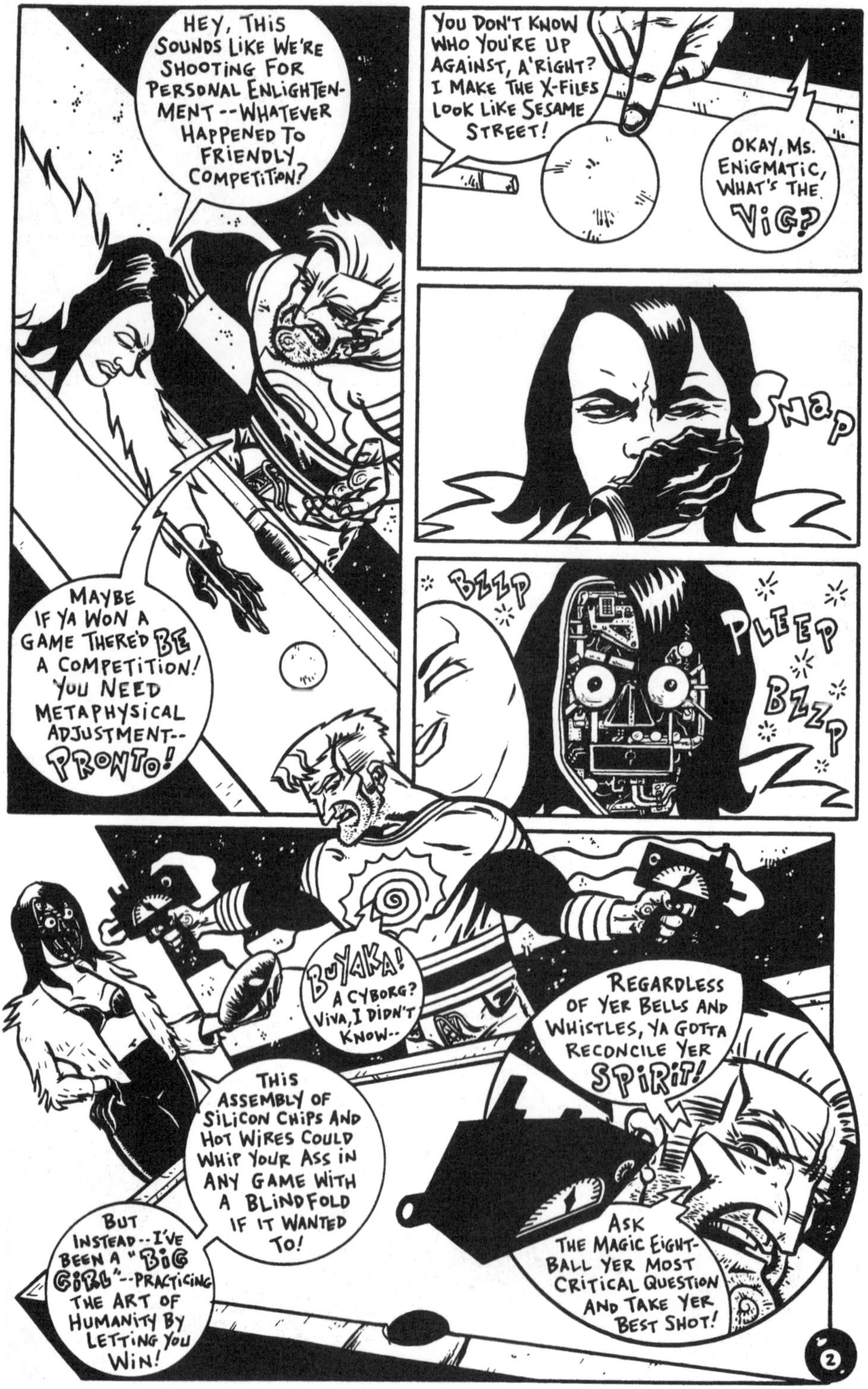

HEY, THIS SOUNDS LIKE WE'RE SHOOTING FOR PERSONAL ENLIGHTEN-MENT --WHATEVER HAPPENED TO FRIENDLY COMPETITION?
MAYBE IF YA WON A GAME THERE'D BE A COMPETITION! YOU NEED METAPHYSICAL ADJUSTMENT-- PRONTO!
YOU DON'T KNOW WHO YOU'RE UP AGAINST, A'RIGHT? I MAKE THE X-FILES LOOK LIKE SESAME STREET!
OKAY, MS. ENIGMATIC, WHAT'S THE VIG?
SNAP
BZZP
PLEEP
BZZP
BUYAKA! A CYBORG? VIVA, I DIDN'T KNOW--
REGARDLESS OF YER BELLS AND WHISTLES, YA GOTTA RECONCILE YER SPIRIT!
THIS ASSEMBLY OF SILICON CHIPS AND HOT WIRES COULD WHIP YOUR ASS IN ANY GAME WITH A BLINDFOLD IF IT WANTED TO!
BUT INSTEAD--I'VE BEEN A "BIG GIRL"--PRACTICING THE ART OF HUMANITY BY LETTING YOU WIN!
ASK THE MAGIC EIGHT-BALL YER MOST CRITICAL QUESTION AND TAKE YER BEST SHOT!
2

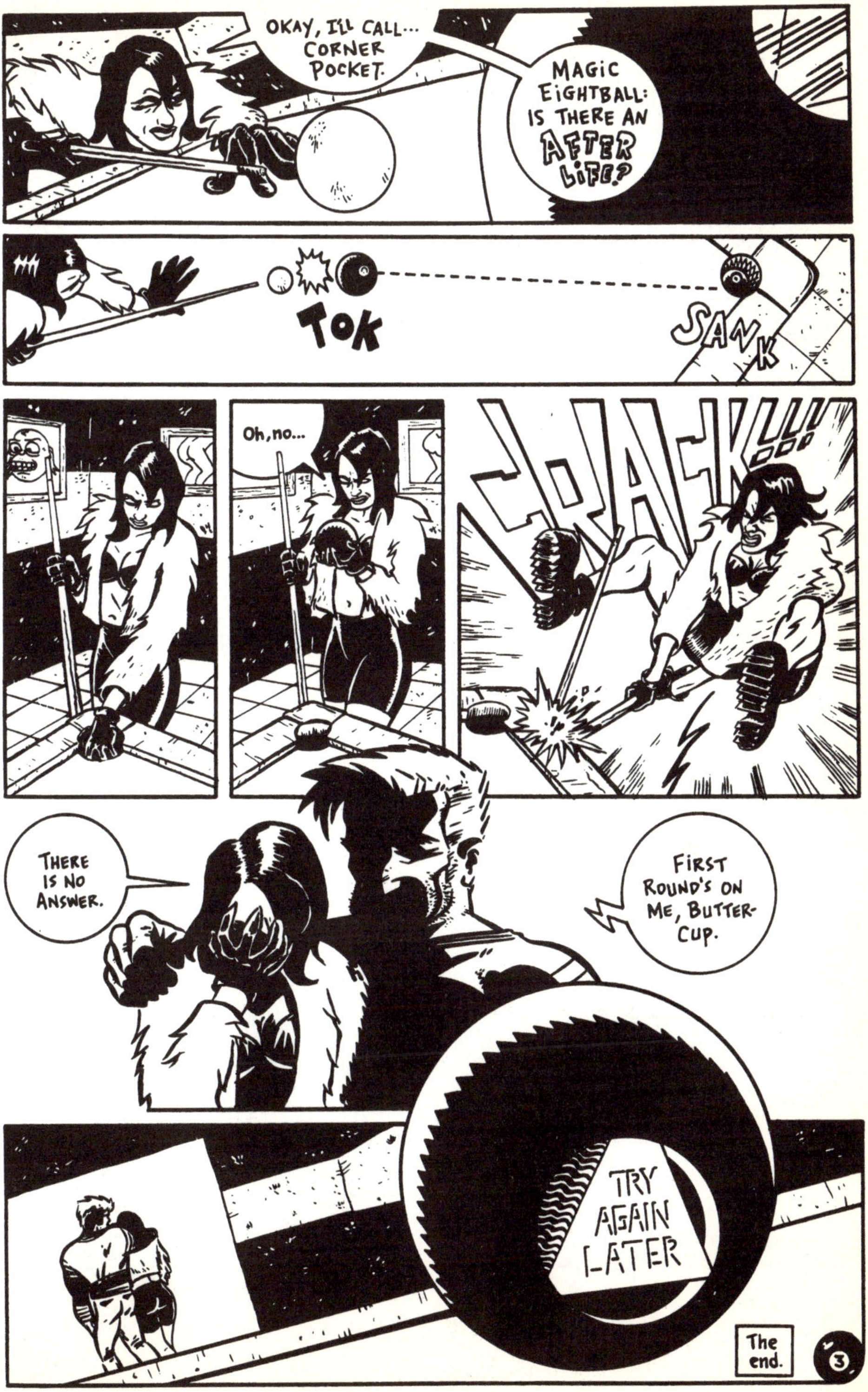
OKAY, I'LL CALL... CORNER POCKET.
MAGIC EIGHTBALL: IS THERE AN AFTER LIFE?
TOK
SANK
Oh, no...
CRACK!!!
THERE IS NO ANSWER.
FIRST ROUND'S ON ME, BUTTER-CUP.
TRY AGAIN LATER
The end.
3

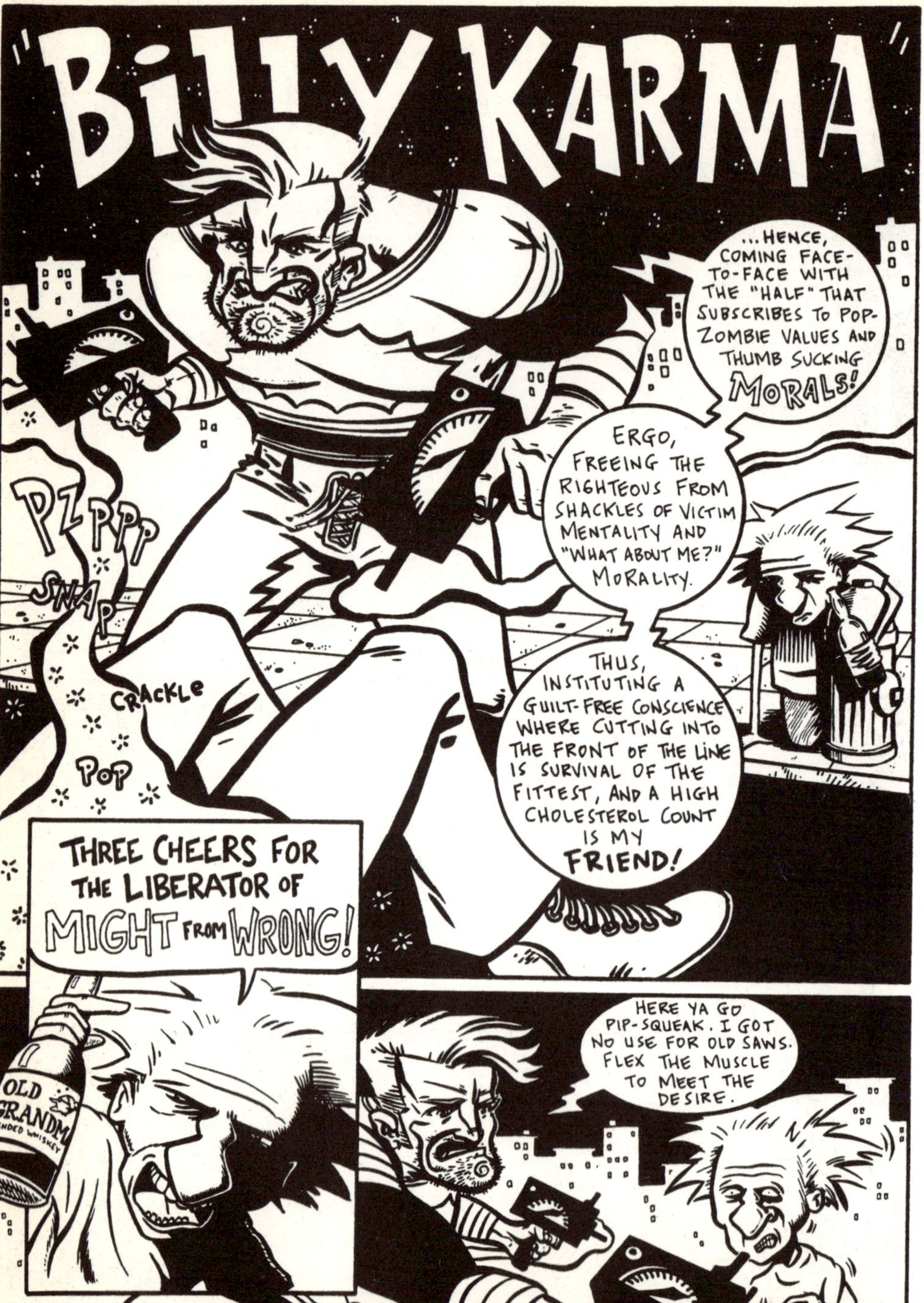
"BILLY KARMA"
...HENCE, COMING FACE-TO-FACE WITH THE "HALF" THAT SUBSCRIBES TO POP-ZOMBIE VALUES AND THUMB SUCKING MORALS!
ERGO, FREEING THE RIGHTEOUS FROM SHACKLES OF VICTIM MENTALITY AND "WHAT ABOUT ME?" MORALITY.
THUS, INSTITUTING A GUILT-FREE CONSCIENCE WHERE CUTTING INTO THE FRONT OF THE LINE IS SURVIVAL OF THE FITTEST, AND A HIGH CHOLESTEROL COUNT IS MY FRIEND!
PZPPP
SNAP
CRACKLE
POP
THREE CHEERS FOR THE LIBERATOR OF MIGHT FROM WRONG!
OLD GRANDM BLENDED WHISKEY
HERE YA GO PIP-SQUEAK. I GOT NO USE FOR OLD SAWS. FLEX THE MUSCLE TO MEET THE DESIRE.
1

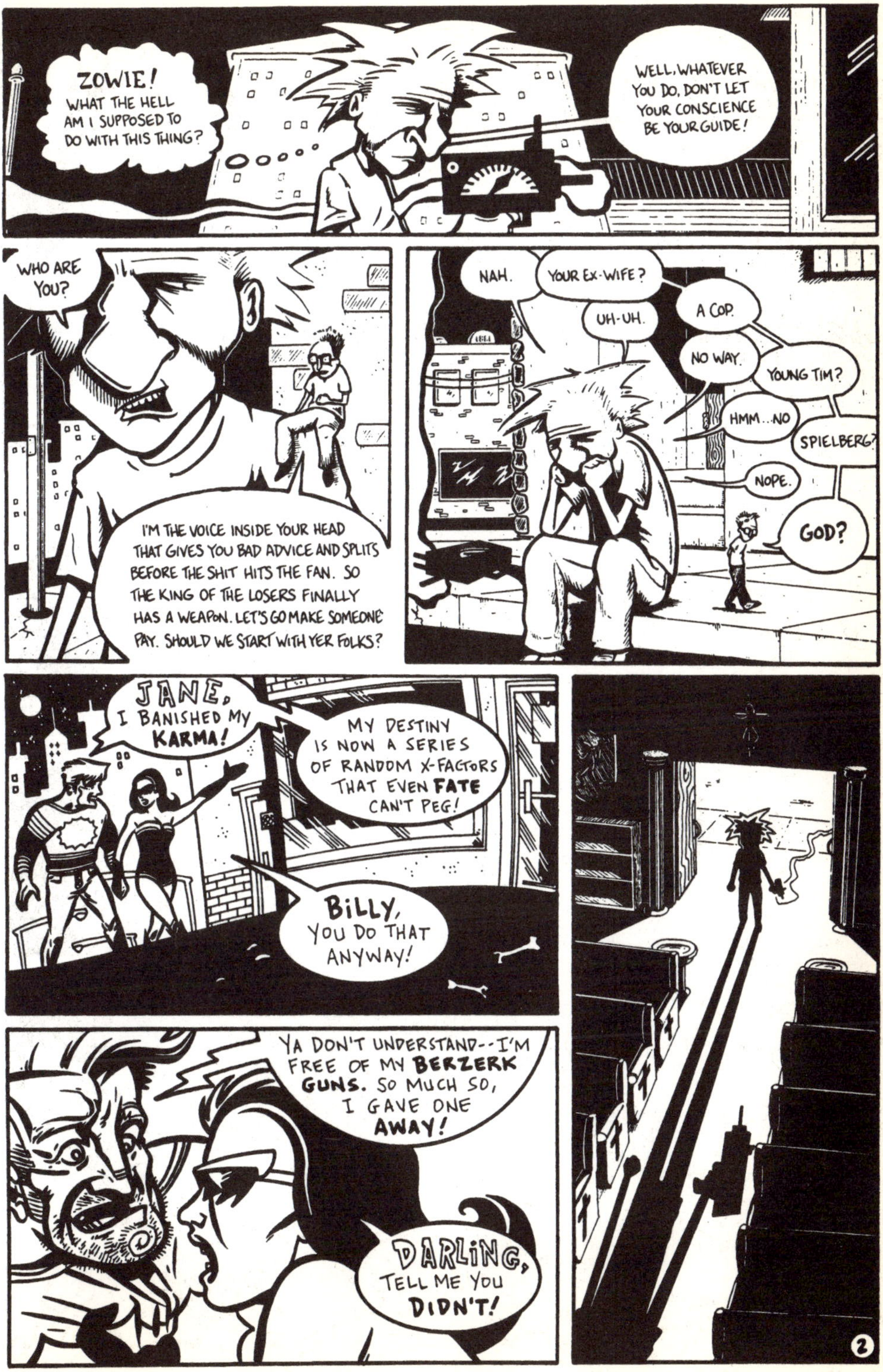
ZOWIE! WHAT THE HELL AM I SUPPOSED TO DO WITH THIS THING?
WELL, WHATEVER YOU DO, DON'T LET YOUR CONSCIENCE BE YOUR GUIDE!
WHO ARE YOU?
I'M THE VOICE INSIDE YOUR HEAD THAT GIVES YOU BAD ADVICE AND SPLITS BEFORE THE SHIT HITS THE FAN. SO THE KING OF THE LOSERS FINALLY HAS A WEAPON. LET'S GO MAKE SOMEONE PAY. SHOULD WE START WITH YER FOLKS?
NAH.
YOUR EX-WIFE?
UH-UH.
A COP.
NO WAY.
YOUNG TIM?
HMM...NO
SPIELBERG?
NOPE.
GOD?
JANE, I BANISHED MY KARMA!
MY DESTINY IS NOW A SERIES OF RANDOM X-FACTORS THAT EVEN FATE CAN'T PEG!
BILLY, YOU DO THAT ANYWAY!
YA DON'T UNDERSTAND--I'M FREE OF MY BERZERK GUNS. SO MUCH SO, I GAVE ONE AWAY!
DARLING, TELL ME YOU DIDN'T!
2

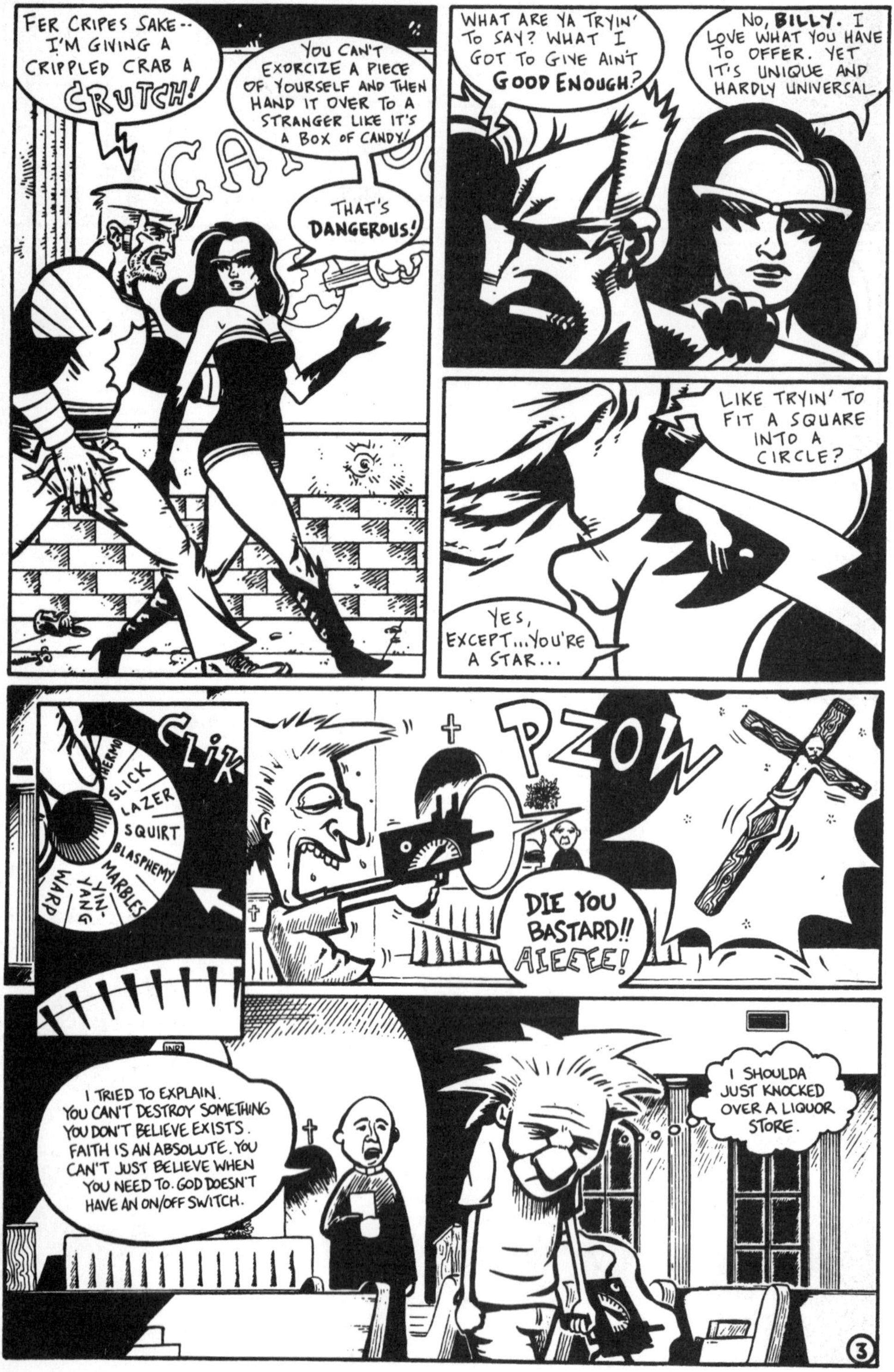
FER CRIPES SAKE-- I'M GIVING A CRIPPLED CRAB A CRUTCH!
YOU CAN'T EXORCIZE A PIECE OF YOURSELF AND THEN HAND IT OVER TO A STRANGER LIKE IT'S A BOX OF CANDY!
THAT'S DANGEROUS!
WHAT ARE YA TRYIN' TO SAY? WHAT I GOT TO GIVE AIN'T GOOD ENOUGH?
NO, BILLY. I LOVE WHAT YOU HAVE TO OFFER. YET IT'S UNIQUE AND HARDLY UNIVERSAL.
LIKE TRYIN' TO FIT A SQUARE INTO A CIRCLE?
YES, EXCEPT... YOU'RE A STAR...
CLIK
THERMO
SLICK
LAZER
SQUIRT
BLASPHEMY
MARBLES
YIN-YANG
WARP
PZOW
DIE YOU BASTARD!!
AIEEEE!
I TRIED TO EXPLAIN. YOU CAN'T DESTROY SOMETHING YOU DON'T BELIEVE EXISTS. FAITH IS AN ABSOLUTE. YOU CAN'T JUST BELIEVE WHEN YOU NEED TO. GOD DOESN'T HAVE AN ON/OFF SWITCH.
I SHOULDA JUST KNOCKED OVER A LIQUOR STORE.
3

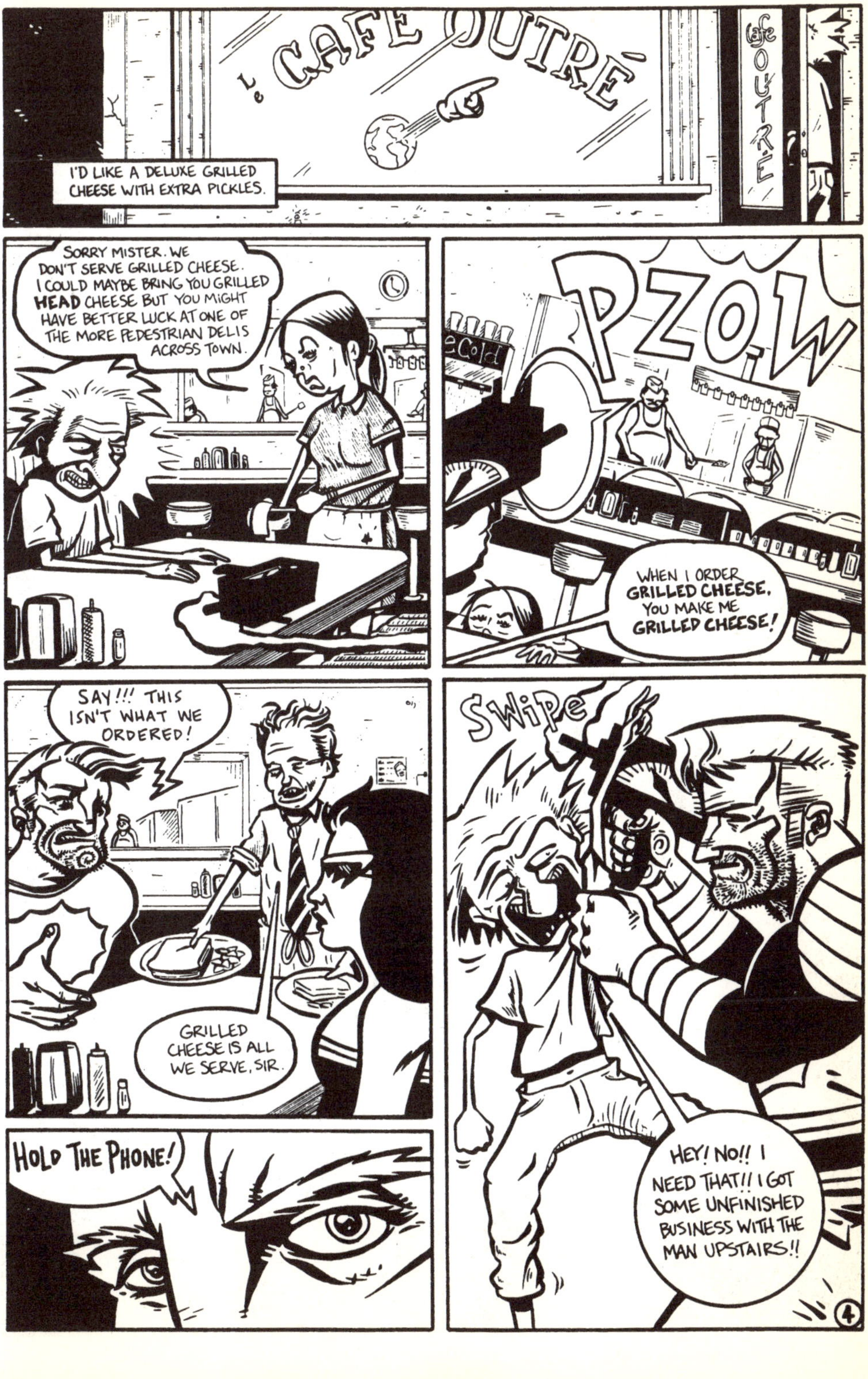
Le CAFE OUTRÉ
Cafe OUTRÉ
I'D LIKE A DELUXE GRILLED CHEESE WITH EXTRA PICKLES.
SORRY MISTER. WE DON'T SERVE GRILLED CHEESE. I COULD MAYBE BRING YOU GRILLED HEAD CHEESE BUT YOU MIGHT HAVE BETTER LUCK AT ONE OF THE MORE PEDESTRIAN DELIS ACROSS TOWN.
PZOW
WHEN I ORDER GRILLED CHEESE, YOU MAKE ME GRILLED CHEESE!
SAY!!! THIS ISN'T WHAT WE ORDERED!
GRILLED CHEESE IS ALL WE SERVE, SIR.
HOLD THE PHONE!
SWIPE
HEY! NO!! I NEED THAT!! I GOT SOME UNFINISHED BUSINESS WITH THE MAN UPSTAIRS!!
4

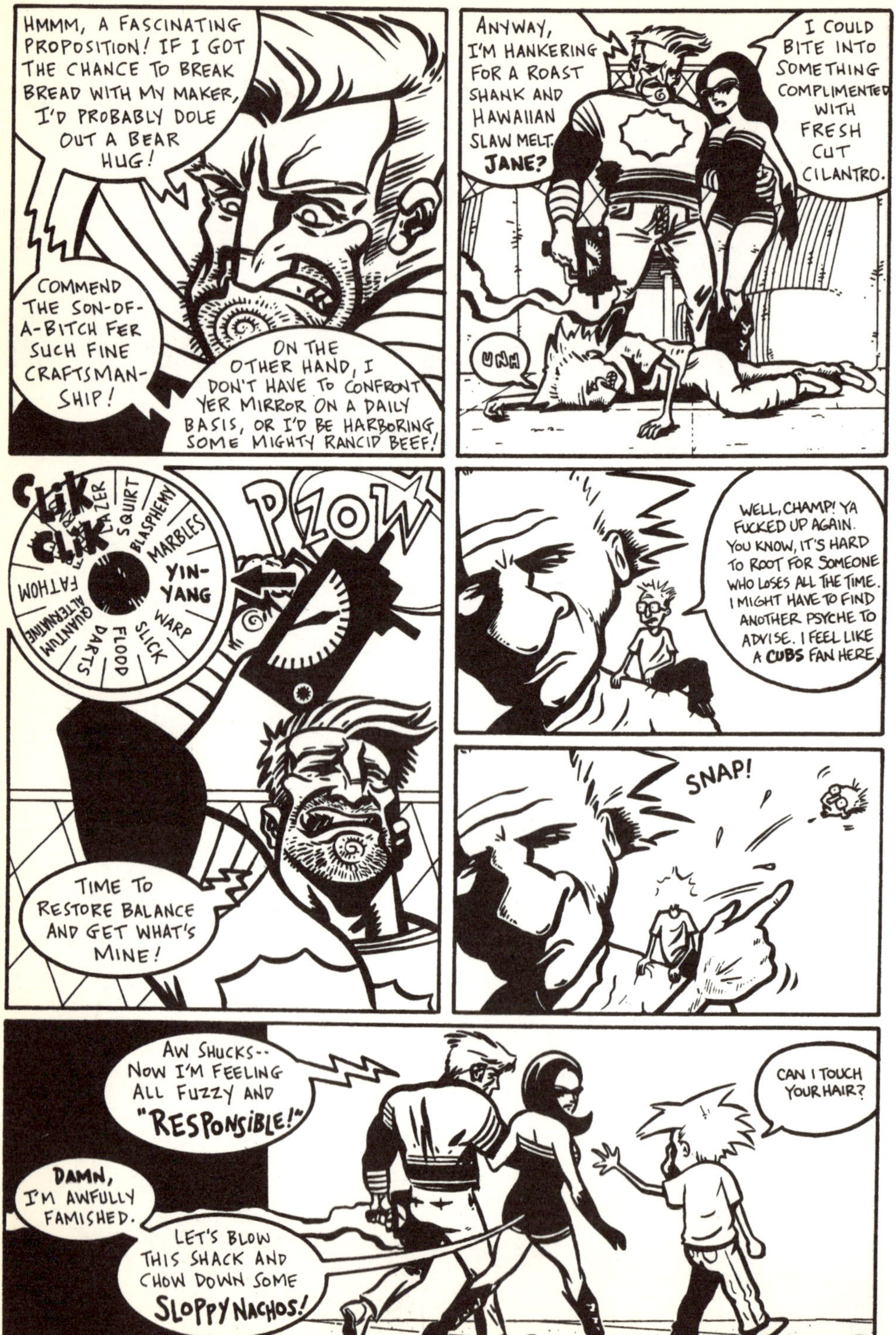
HMMM, A FASCINATING PROPOSITION! IF I GOT THE CHANCE TO BREAK BREAD WITH MY MAKER, I'D PROBABLY DOLE OUT A BEAR HUG!
COMMEND THE SON-OF-A-BITCH FER SUCH FINE CRAFTSMANSHIP!
ON THE OTHER HAND, I DON'T HAVE TO CONFRONT YER MIRROR ON A DAILY BASIS, OR I'D BE HARBORING SOME MIGHTY RANCID BEEF!
ANYWAY, I'M HANKERING FOR A ROAST SHANK AND HAWAIIAN SLAW MELT. JANE?
I COULD BITE INTO SOMETHING COMPLIMENTED WITH FRESH CUT CILANTRO.
UNH
CLIK CLIK
LAZER
SQUIRT
BLASPHEMY
MARBLES
YIN-YANG
WARP
SLICK
FLOOD
DARTS
QUANTUM ALTERNATIVE
FATHOM
PZOW
TIME TO RESTORE BALANCE AND GET WHAT'S MINE!
WELL, CHAMP! YA FUCKED UP AGAIN. YOU KNOW, IT'S HARD TO ROOT FOR SOMEONE WHO LOSES ALL THE TIME. I MIGHT HAVE TO FIND ANOTHER PSYCHE TO ADVISE. I FEEL LIKE A CUBS FAN HERE.
SNAP!
AW SHUCKS-- NOW I'M FEELING ALL FUZZY AND "RESPONSIBLE!"
DAMN, I'M AWFULLY FAMISHED.
LET'S BLOW THIS SHACK AND CHOW DOWN SOME SLOPPY NACHOS!
CAN I TOUCH YOUR HAIR?
5

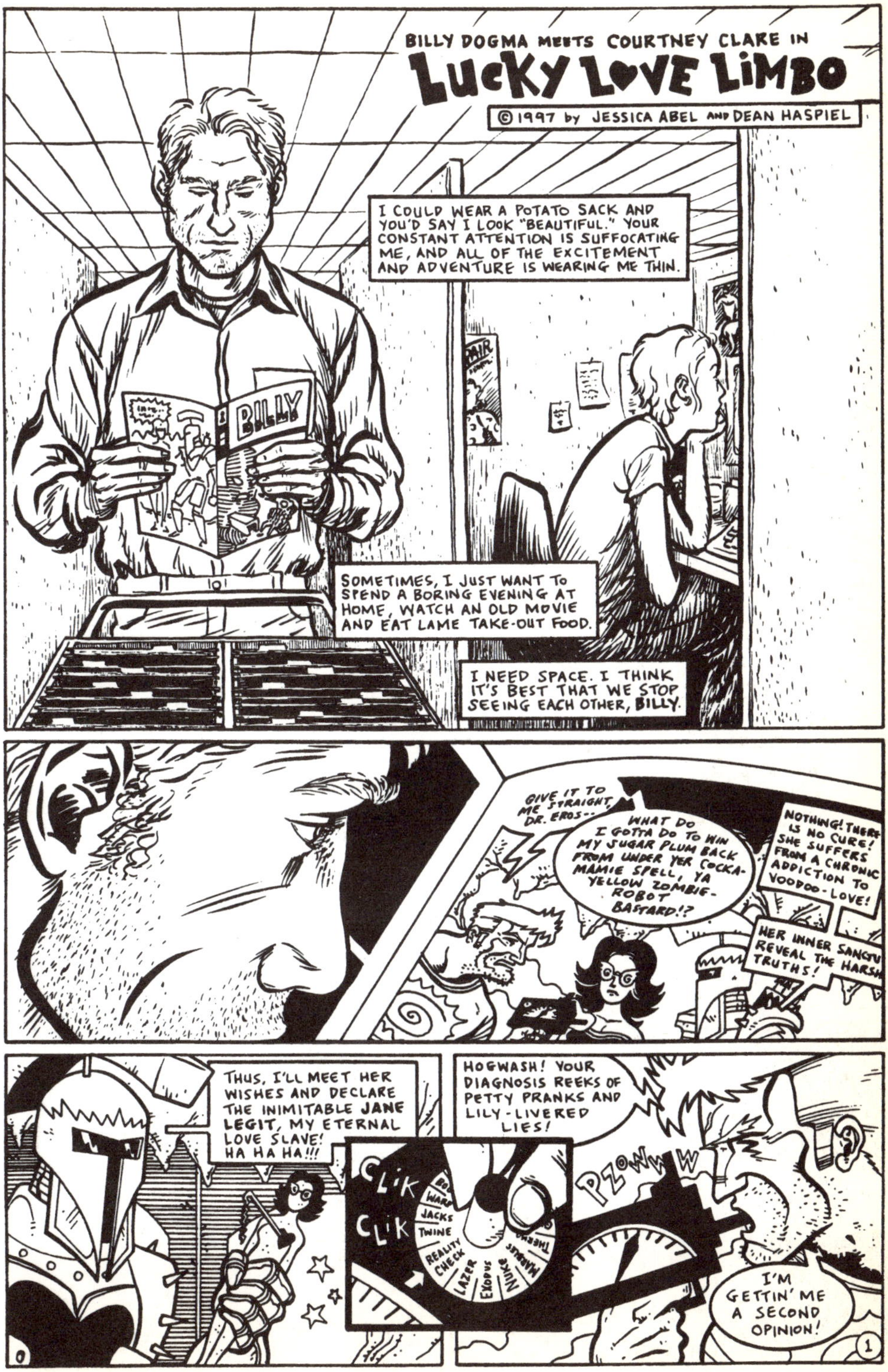
BILLY DOGMA MEETS COURTNEY CLARE IN
LUCKY LOVE LIMBO
© 1997 by JESSICA ABEL AND DEAN HASPIEL
I COULD WEAR A POTATO SACK AND YOU'D SAY I LOOK "BEAUTIFUL." YOUR CONSTANT ATTENTION IS SUFFOCATING ME, AND ALL OF THE EXCITEMENT AND ADVENTURE IS WEARING ME THIN.
SOMETIMES, I JUST WANT TO SPEND A BORING EVENING AT HOME, WATCH AN OLD MOVIE AND EAT LAME TAKE-OUT FOOD.
I NEED SPACE. I THINK IT'S BEST THAT WE STOP SEEING EACH OTHER, BILLY.
BILLY
GIVE IT TO ME STRAIGHT, DR. EROS--
WHAT DO I GOTTA DO TO WIN MY SUGAR PLUM BACK FROM UNDER YER COCKAMAMIE SPELL, YA YELLOW ZOMBIE-ROBOT BASTARD!?
NOTHING! THERE IS NO CURE! SHE SUFFERS FROM A CHRONIC ADDICTION TO VOODOO-LOVE!
HER INNER SANCTU REVEAL THE HARSH TRUTHS!
THUS, I'LL MEET HER WISHES AND DECLARE THE INIMITABLE JANE LEGIT, MY ETERNAL LOVE SLAVE! HA HA HA!!!
HOGWASH! YOUR DIAGNOSIS REEKS OF PETTY PRANKS AND LILY-LIVERED LIES!
CLIK
CLIK
JACKS
TWINE
REALITY CHECK
LAZER
EXODUS
NUKE
MARBLES
THERMO
PZOWWW
I'M GETTIN' ME A SECOND OPINION!
1

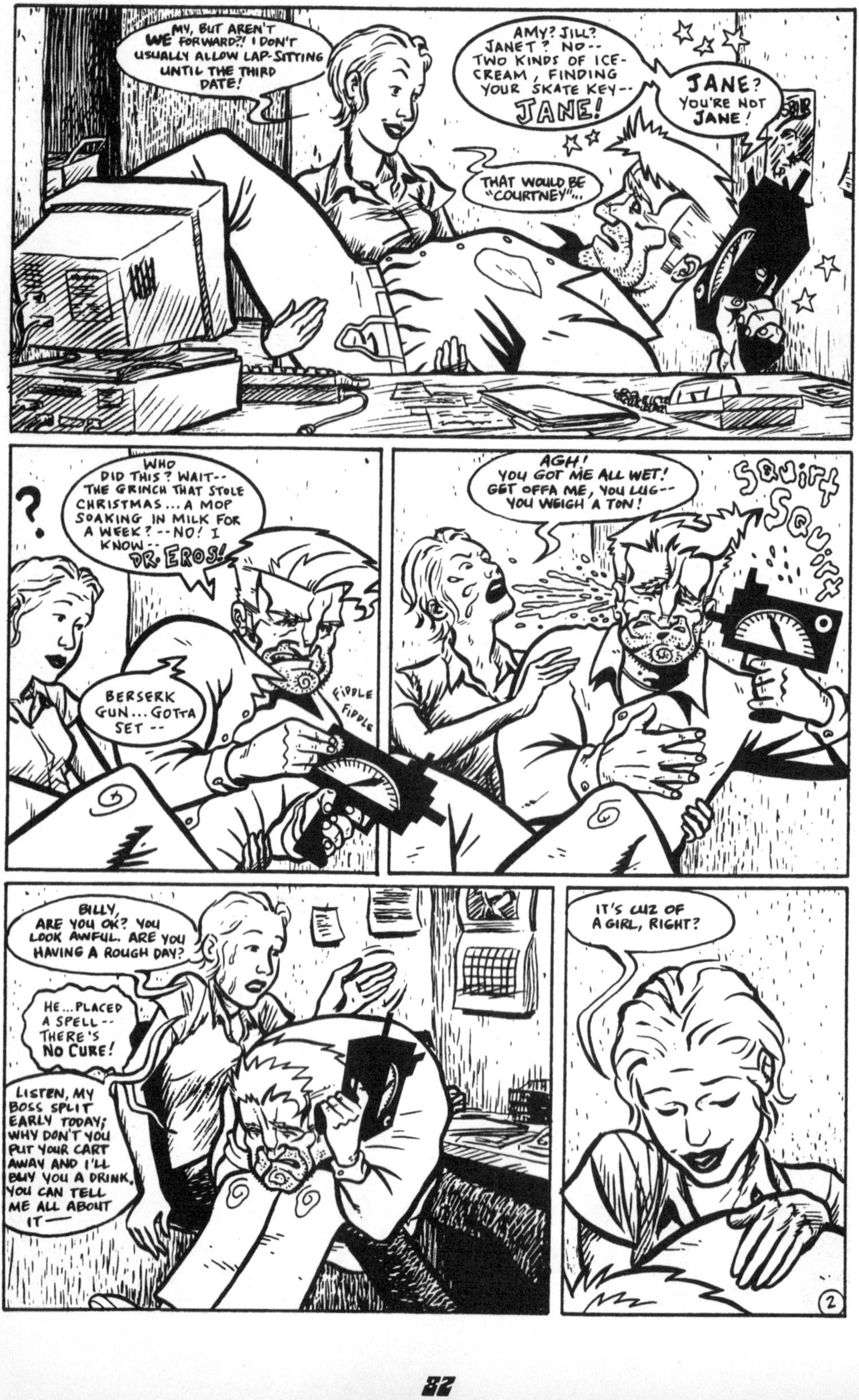
MY, BUT AREN'T WE FORWARD?! I DON'T USUALLY ALLOW LAP-SITTING UNTIL THE THIRD DATE!
AMY? JILL? JANET? NO-- TWO KINDS OF ICE-CREAM, FINDING YOUR SKATE KEY-- JANE!
JANE? YOU'RE NOT JANE!
THAT WOULD BE "COURTNEY"...
WHO DID THIS? WAIT-- THE GRINCH THAT STOLE CHRISTMAS... A MOP SOAKING IN MILK FOR A WEEK? --NO! I KNOW-- DR. EROS!
BERSERK GUN... GOTTA SET --
FIDDLE FIDDLE
AGH! YOU GOT ME ALL WET! GET OFFA ME, YOU LUG-- YOU WEIGH A TON!
SQUIRT SQUIRT
BILLY, ARE YOU OK? YOU LOOK AWFUL. ARE YOU HAVING A ROUGH DAY?
HE... PLACED A SPELL-- THERE'S NO CURE!
LISTEN, MY BOSS SPLIT EARLY TODAY; WHY DON'T YOU PUT YOUR CART AWAY AND I'LL BUY YOU A DRINK. YOU CAN TELL ME ALL ABOUT IT—
IT'S CUZ OF A GIRL, RIGHT?
2

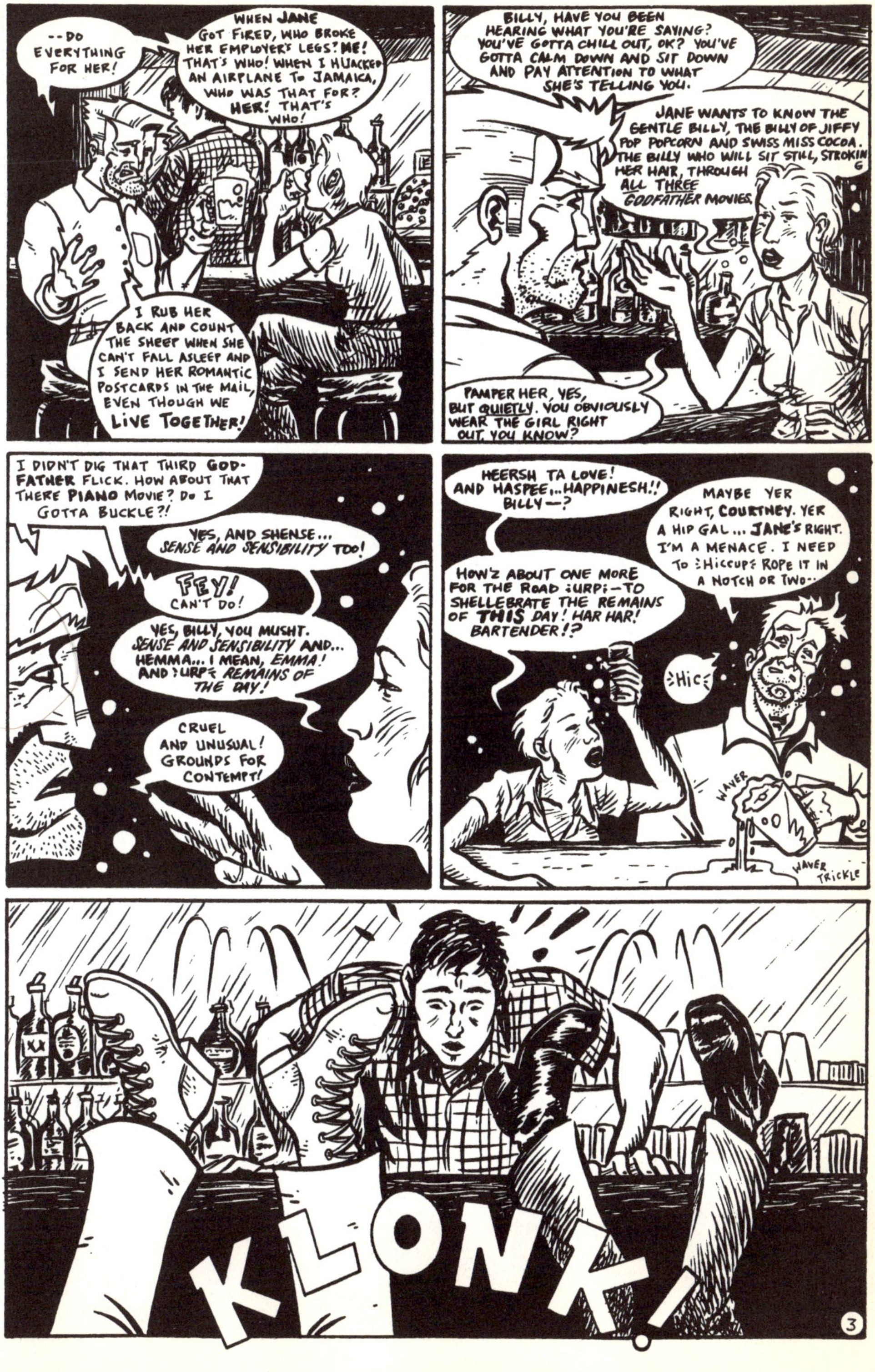
--DO EVERYTHING FOR HER!
WHEN JANE GOT FIRED, WHO BROKE HER EMPLOYER'S LEGS? ME! THAT'S WHO! WHEN I HIJACKED AN AIRPLANE TO JAMAICA, WHO WAS THAT FOR? HER! THAT'S WHO!
I RUB HER BACK AND COUNT THE SHEEP WHEN SHE CAN'T FALL ASLEEP AND I SEND HER ROMANTIC POSTCARDS IN THE MAIL, EVEN THOUGH WE LIVE TOGETHER!
BILLY, HAVE YOU BEEN HEARING WHAT YOU'RE SAYING? YOU'VE GOTTA CHILL OUT, OK? YOU'VE GOTTA CALM DOWN AND SIT DOWN AND PAY ATTENTION TO WHAT SHE'S TELLING YOU.
JANE WANTS TO KNOW THE GENTLE BILLY, THE BILLY OF JIFFY POP POPCORN AND SWISS MISS COCOA. THE BILLY WHO WILL SIT STILL, STROKING HER HAIR, THROUGH ALL THREE GODFATHER MOVIES.
PAMPER HER, YES, BUT QUIETLY. YOU OBVIOUSLY WEAR THE GIRL RIGHT OUT, YOU KNOW?
I DIDN'T DIG THAT THIRD GODFATHER FLICK. HOW ABOUT THAT THERE PIANO MOVIE? DO I GOTTA BUCKLE?!
YES, AND SHENSE... SENSE AND SENSIBILITY TOO!
FEY! CAN'T DO!
YES, BILLY, YOU MUSHT. SENSE AND SENSIBILITY AND... HEMMA... I MEAN, EMMA! AND ¡URP¡ REMAINS OF THE DAY!
CRUEL AND UNUSUAL! GROUNDS FOR CONTEMPT!
HEERSH TA LOVE! AND HASPEE...HAPPINESH!! BILLY—?
MAYBE YER RIGHT, COURTNEY. YER A HIP GAL... JANE'S RIGHT. I'M A MENACE. I NEED TO ¡HICCUP¡ ROPE IT IN A NOTCH OR TWO..
HOW'Z ABOUT ONE MORE FOR THE ROAD ¡URP¡—TO SHELLEBRATE THE REMAINS OF THIS DAY! HAR HAR! BARTENDER!?
HIC
WAVER
WAVER
TRICKLE
!!
KLONK!
3

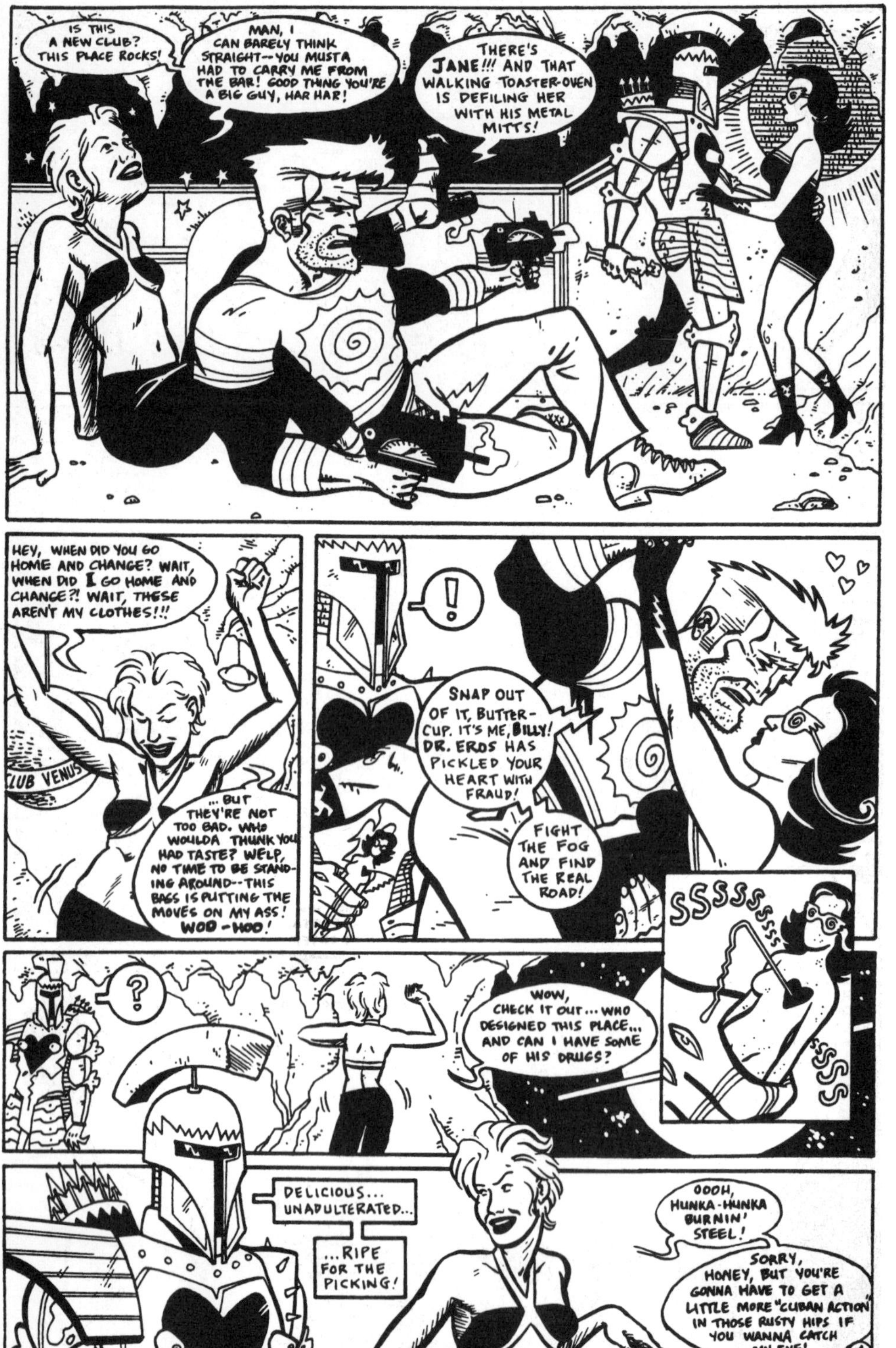
IS THIS A NEW CLUB? THIS PLACE ROCKS!
MAN, I CAN BARELY THINK STRAIGHT--YOU MUSTA HAD TO CARRY ME FROM THE BAR! GOOD THING YOU'RE A BIG GUY, HAR HAR!
THERE'S JANE!!! AND THAT WALKING TOASTER-OVEN IS DEFILING HER WITH HIS METAL MITTS!
HEY, WHEN DID YOU GO HOME AND CHANGE? WAIT, WHEN DID I GO HOME AND CHANGE?! WAIT, THESE AREN'T MY CLOTHES!!!
CLUB VENUS
...BUT THEY'RE NOT TOO BAD. WHO WOULDA THUNK YOU HAD TASTE? WELP, NO TIME TO BE STANDING AROUND--THIS BASS IS PUTTING THE MOVES ON MY ASS! WOO-HOO!
!
SNAP OUT OF IT, BUTTERCUP. IT'S ME, BILLY! DR. EROS HAS PICKLED YOUR HEART WITH FRAUD!
FIGHT THE FOG AND FIND THE REAL ROAD!
SSSSSSSSS
SSSS
?
WOW, CHECK IT OUT... WHO DESIGNED THIS PLACE... AND CAN I HAVE SOME OF HIS DRUGS?
DELICIOUS... UNADULTERATED...
...RIPE FOR THE PICKING!
OOOH, HUNKA-HUNKA BURNIN' STEEL!
SORRY, HONEY, BUT YOU'RE GONNA HAVE TO GET A LITTLE MORE "CUBAN ACTION" IN THOSE RUSTY HIPS IF YOU WANNA CATCH MY EYE!
4

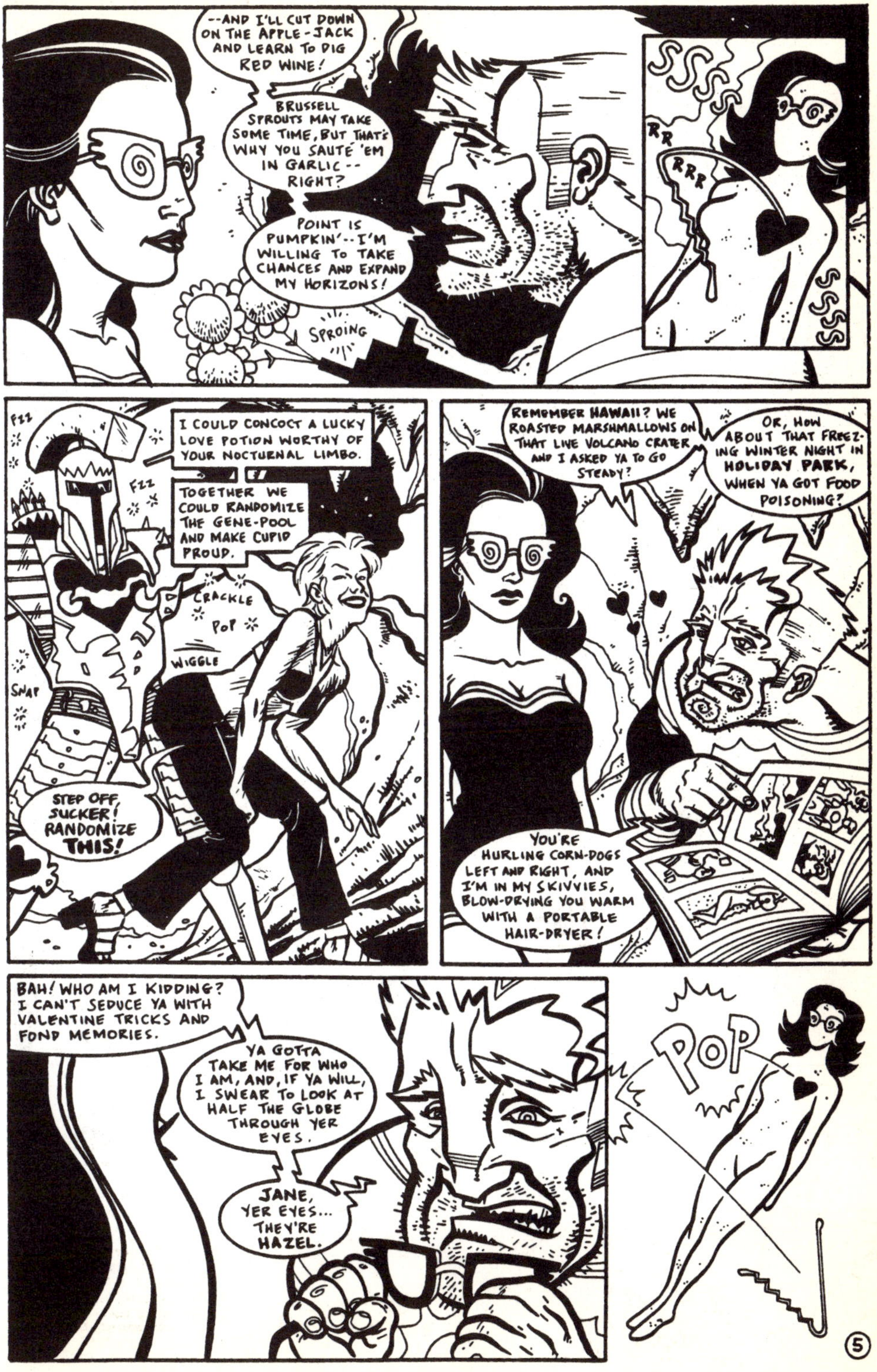
--AND I'LL CUT DOWN ON THE APPLE-JACK AND LEARN TO DIG RED WINE!
BRUSSELL SPROUTS MAY TAKE SOME TIME, BUT THAT'S WHY YOU SAUTÉ 'EM IN GARLIC -- RIGHT?
POINT IS PUMPKIN'-- I'M WILLING TO TAKE CHANCES AND EXPAND MY HORIZONS!
SPROING
SSSS
RR
RRR
SSSS
I COULD CONCOCT A LUCKY LOVE POTION WORTHY OF YOUR NOCTURNAL LIMBO.
TOGETHER WE COULD RANDOMIZE THE GENE-POOL AND MAKE CUPID PROUD.
FZZ
FZZ
CRACKLE
POP
WIGGLE
SNAP
STEP OFF, SUCKER! RANDOMIZE THIS!
REMEMBER HAWAII? WE ROASTED MARSHMALLOWS ON THAT LIVE VOLCANO CRATER AND I ASKED YA TO GO STEADY?
OR, HOW ABOUT THAT FREEZING WINTER NIGHT IN HOLIDAY PARK, WHEN YA GOT FOOD POISONING?
YOU'RE HURLING CORN-DOGS LEFT AND RIGHT, AND I'M IN MY SKIVVIES, BLOW-DRYING YOU WARM WITH A PORTABLE HAIR-DRYER!
BAH! WHO AM I KIDDING? I CAN'T SEDUCE YA WITH VALENTINE TRICKS AND FOND MEMORIES.
YA GOTTA TAKE ME FOR WHO I AM, AND, IF YA WILL, I SWEAR TO LOOK AT HALF THE GLOBE THROUGH YER EYES.
JANE, YER EYES... THEY'RE HAZEL.
POP
5

OH, BILLY! YOU NOTICED!
SMOOCH
SMOOCH
OH, WHAT THE HELL, ONLY ACTION OFFERING IN THIS DUMP-- HEY METAL HEAD! COME ON, I WAS ONLY KIDDING!
SSSSSSSSSS
FZZ
SSSSSSSSS
FZZ
FZZ
DON'T CHA WANNA C'MERE AND--
BA
BOOOMM
DON'T YOU THINK WE SHOULD GO ON A FEW DATES FIRST?!
BILLY
The end?
6

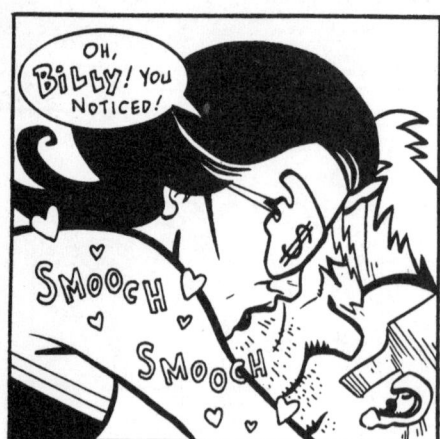

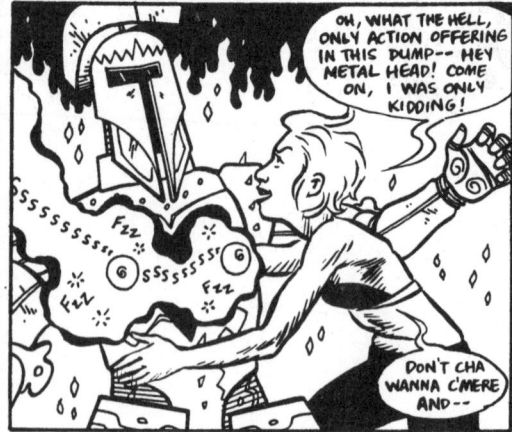

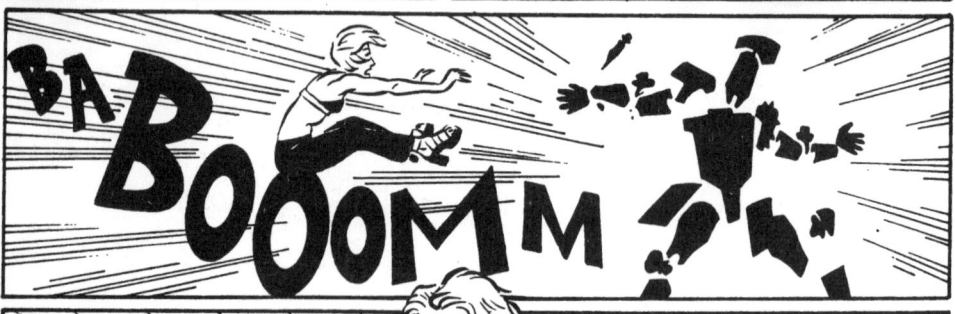

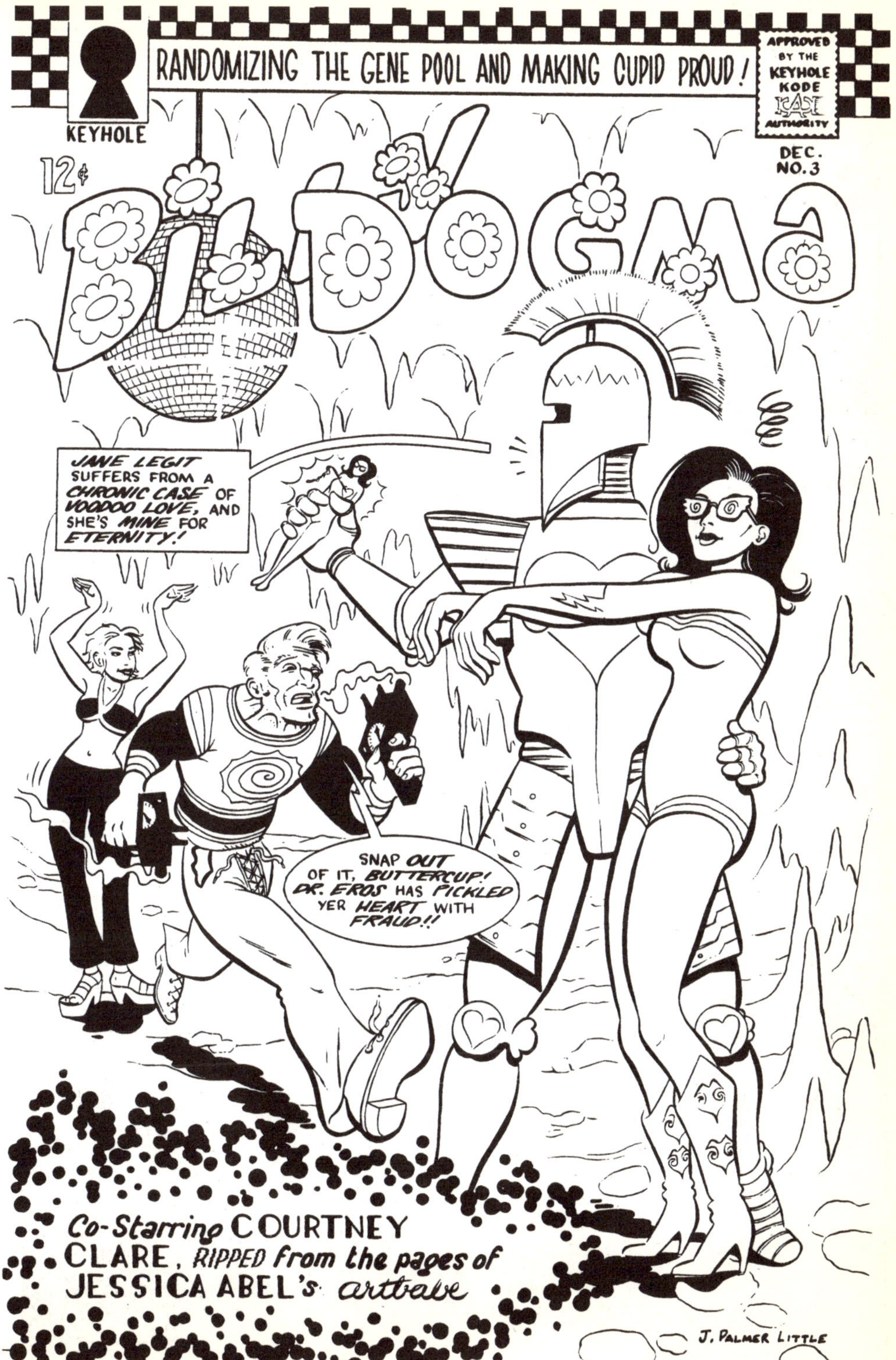
RANDOMIZING THE GENE POOL AND MAKING CUPID PROUD!
KEYHOLE
APPROVED BY THE KEYHOLE KODE AUTHORITY
12¢
DEC. NO. 3
BILDOGMA
JANE LEGIT SUFFERS FROM A CHRONIC CASE OF VOODOO LOVE, AND SHE'S MINE FOR ETERNITY!
SNAP OUT OF IT, BUTTERCUP! DR. EROS HAS PICKLED YER HEART WITH FRAUD!!
Co-Starring COURTNEY CLARE, RIPPED from the pages of JESSICA ABEL's artbabe
J. PALMER LITTLE

Jason Little

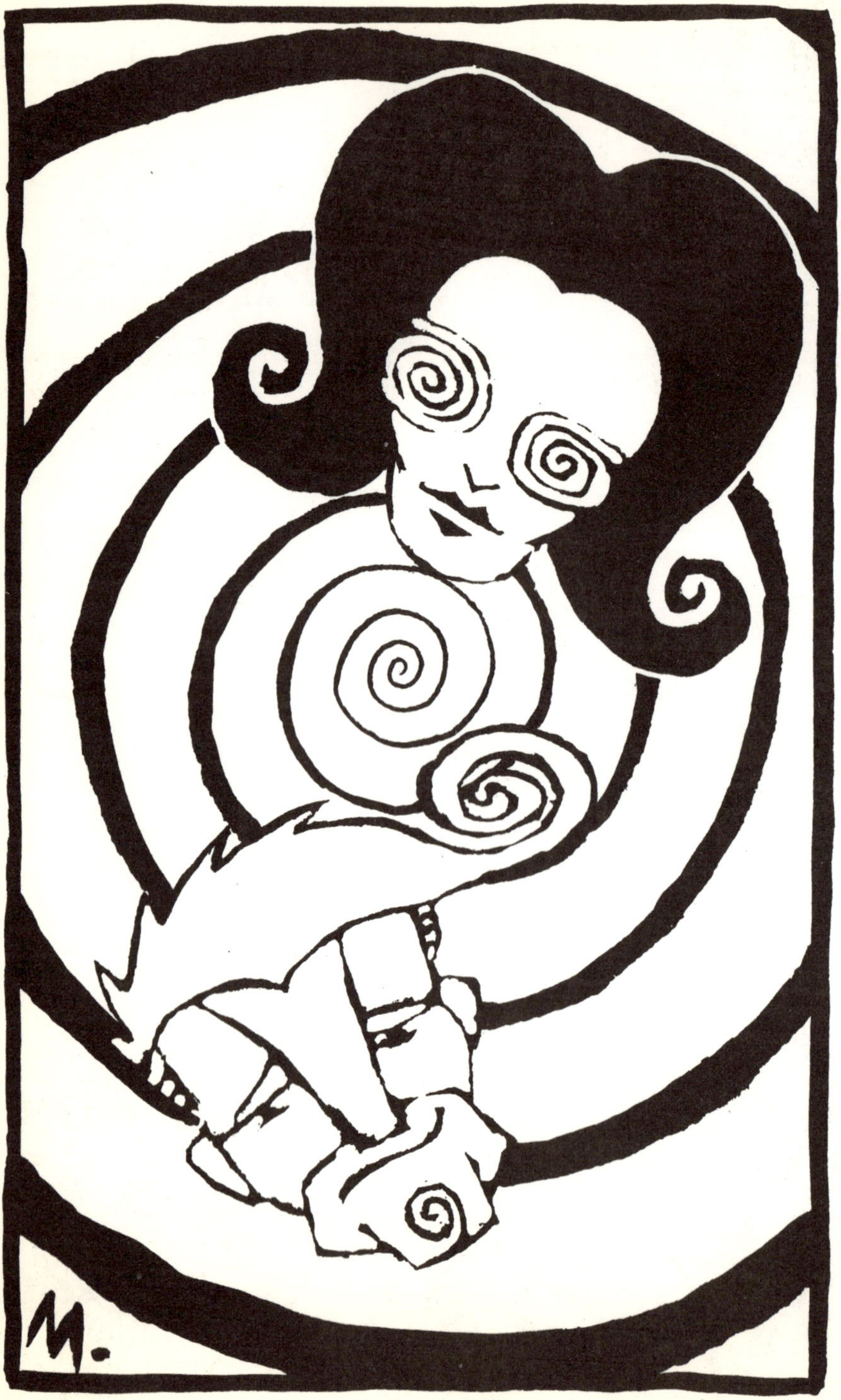
M.

Matt Madden

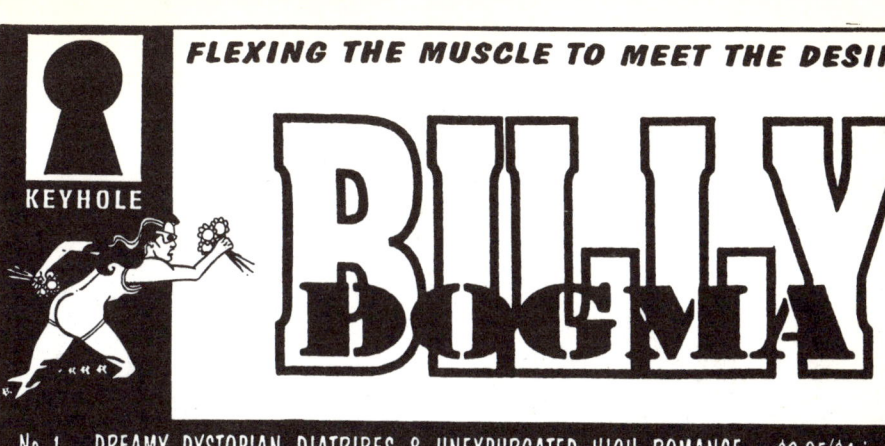

FLEXING THE MUSCLE TO MEET THE DESIRE!

KEYHOLE

BILLY DOGMA

No. 1   DREAMY DYSTOPIAN DIATRIBES & UNEXPURGATED HIGH ROMANCE $2.95/$4 in CAN.

THE EXTREME VIOLENCE IN MY HEAD IS A WARNING OF THINGS TO COME

DiNO 3/96

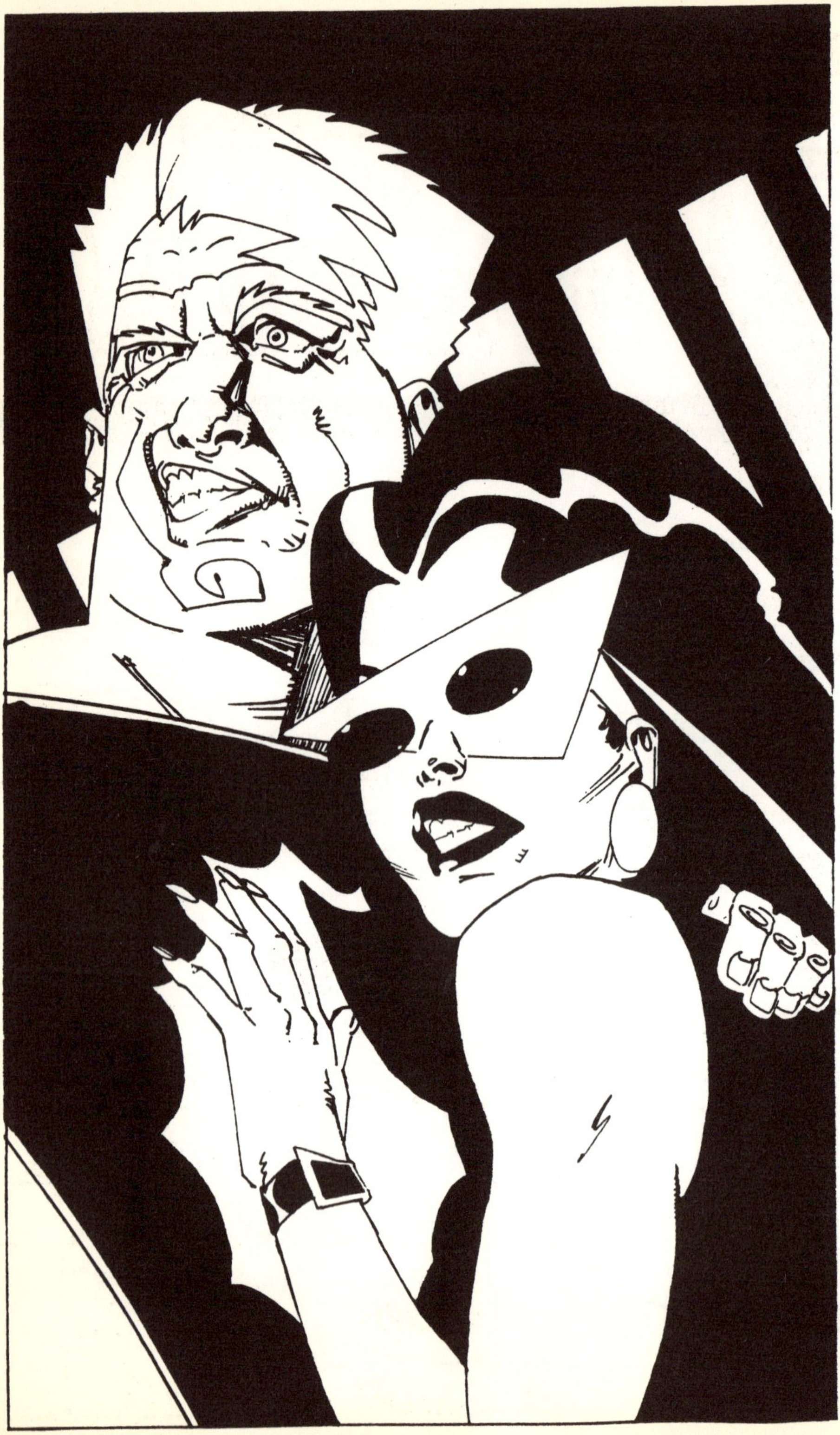

Howard Chaykin

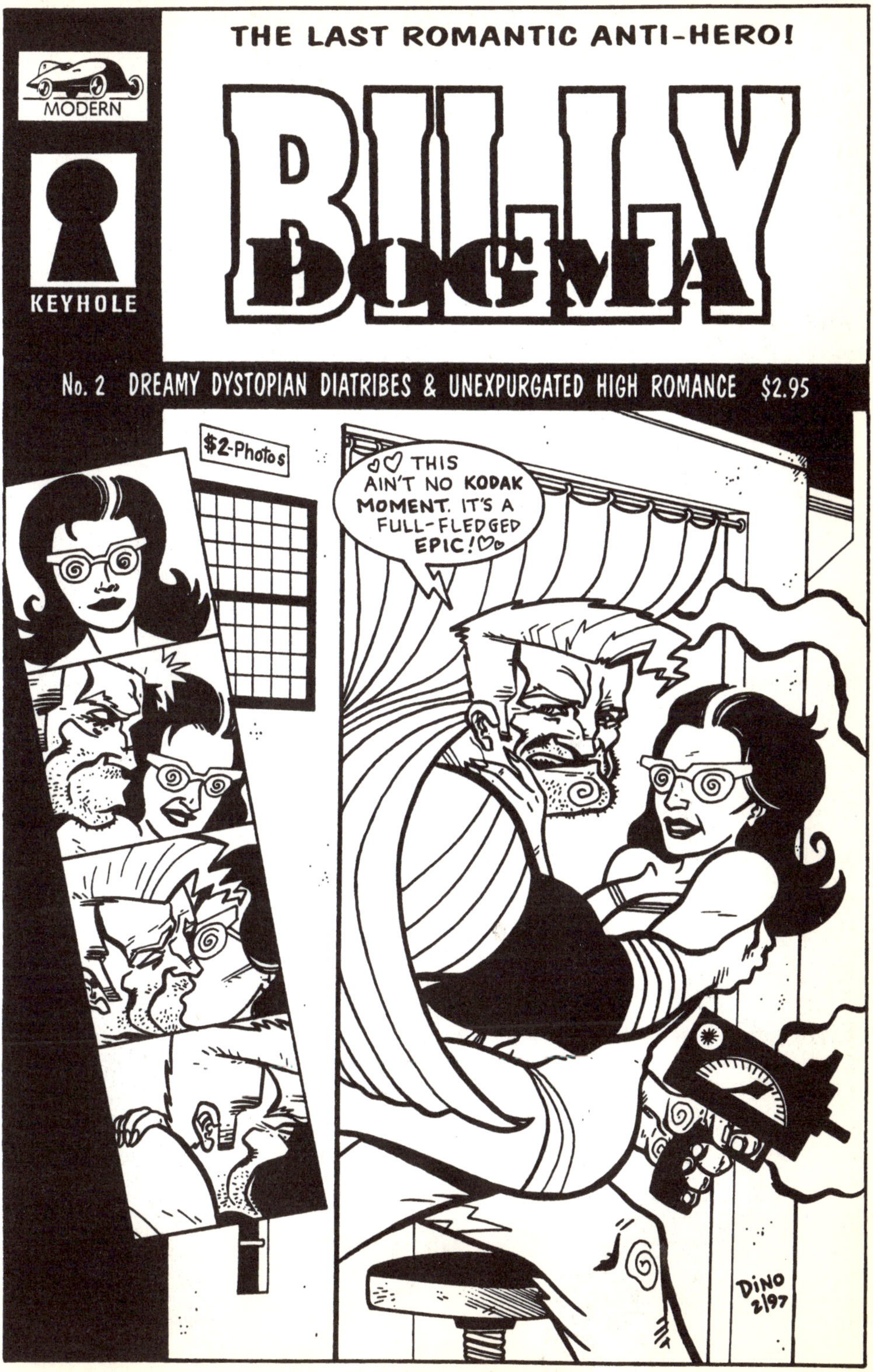

THE LAST ROMANTIC ANTI-HERO!
MODERN
KEYHOLE
BILLY DOGMA
No. 2 DREAMY DYSTOPIAN DIATRIBES & UNEXPURGATED HIGH ROMANCE $2.95
$2-Photos
THIS AIN'T NO KODAK MOMENT. IT'S A FULL-FLEDGED EPIC!
DINO 2/97

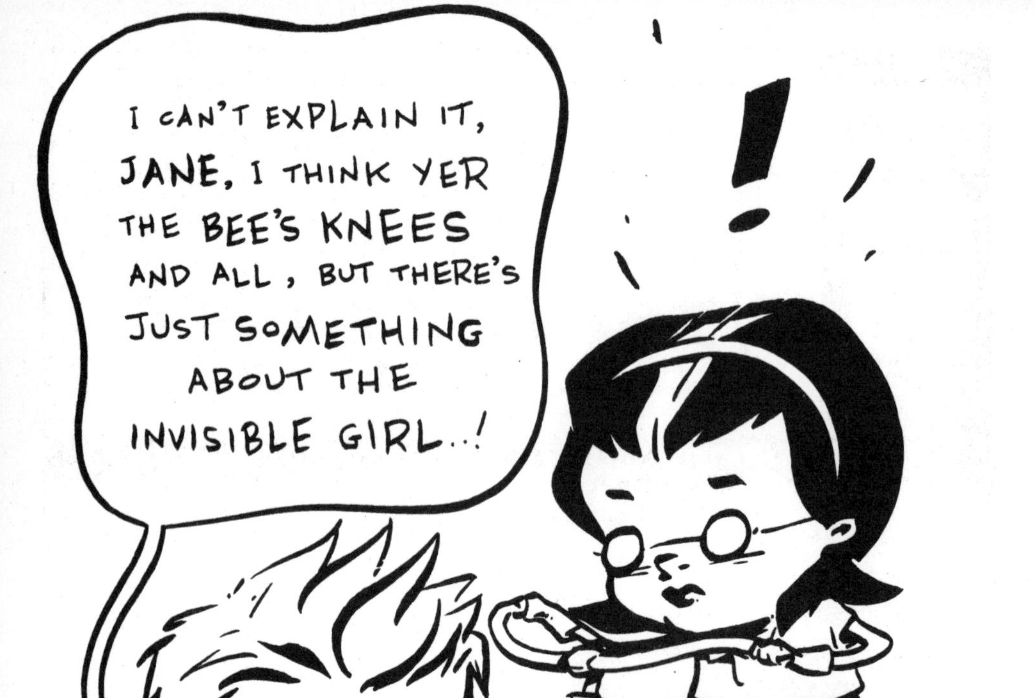
I CAN'T EXPLAIN IT, JANE, I THINK YER THE BEE'S KNEES AND ALL, BUT THERE'S JUST SOMETHING ABOUT THE INVISIBLE GIRL..!
!
Fantastic Four
PIN-UP BY-Ribs 99

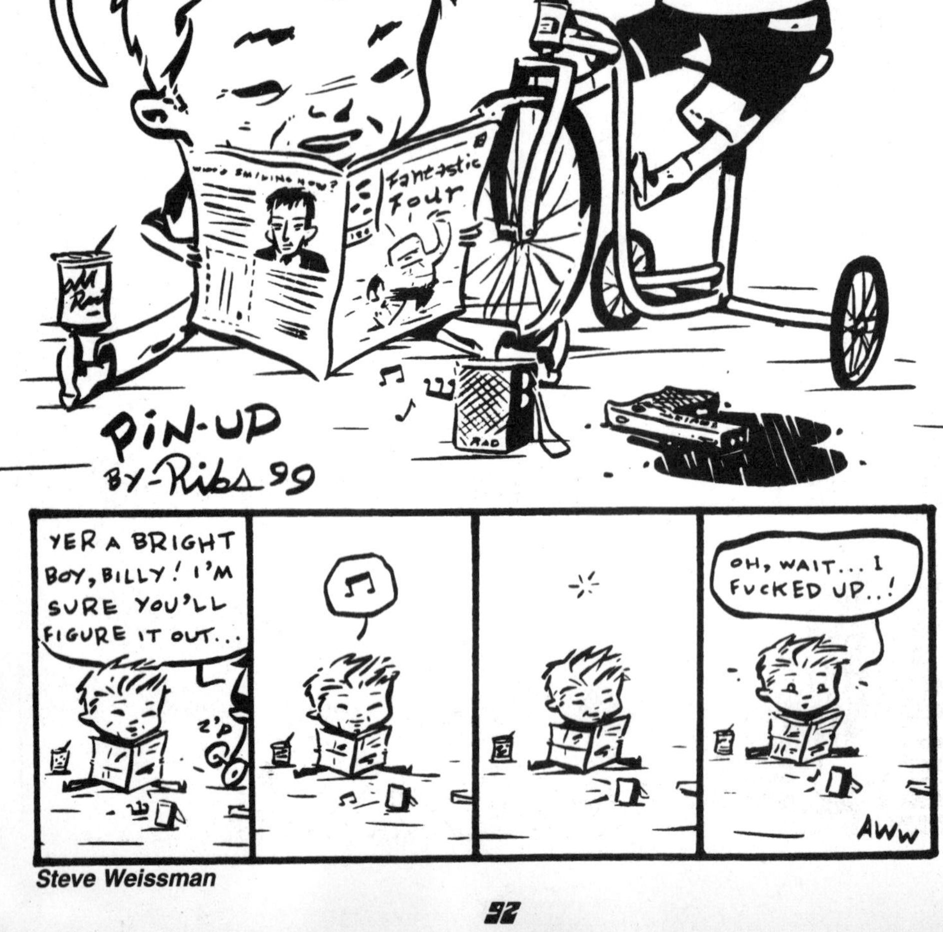
YER A BRIGHT BOY, BILLY! I'M SURE YOU'LL FIGURE IT OUT...
OH, WAIT... I FUCKED UP..!
AWW

Steve Weissman

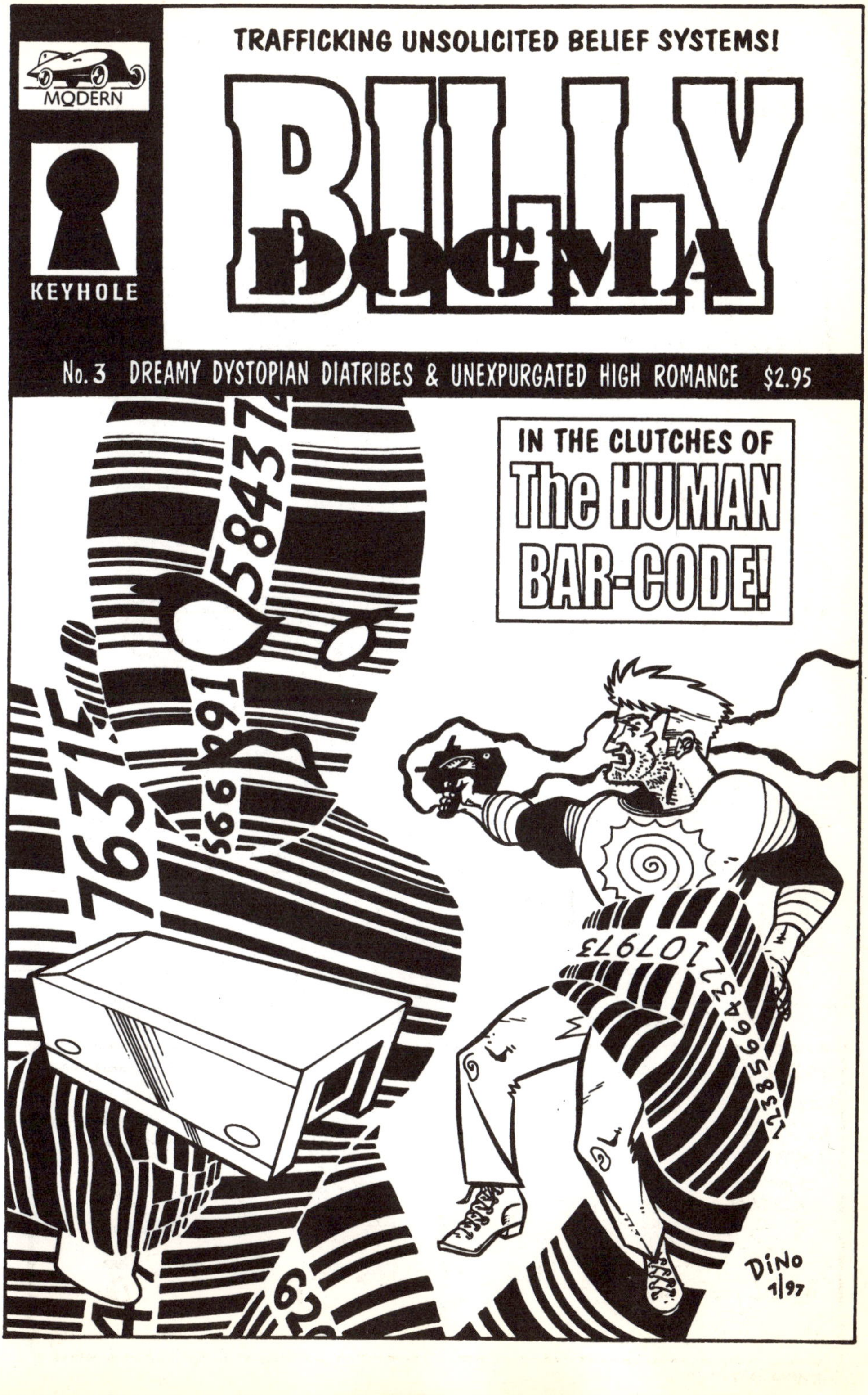
TRAFFICKING UNSOLICITED BELIEF SYSTEMS!
MODERN
KEYHOLE
BILLY DOGMA
No. 3 DREAMY DYSTOPIAN DIATRIBES & UNEXPURGATED HIGH ROMANCE $2.95
IN THE CLUTCHES OF The HUMAN BAR-CODE!
DiNo 1/97

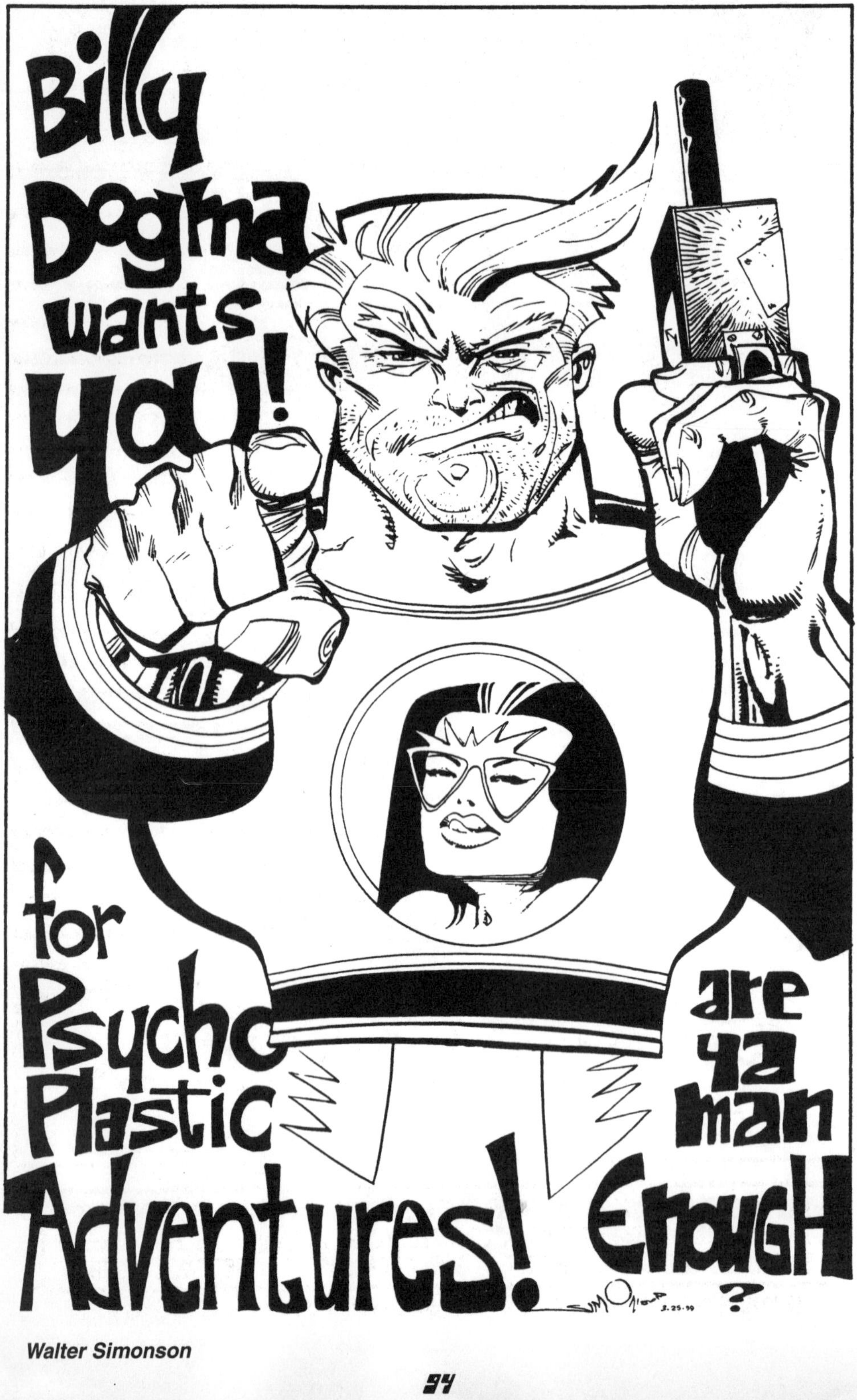
Billy Dogma wants YOU!
for Psycho Plastic Adventures!
are ya man Enough?
SIMONSON
3.25.99

Walter Simonson

WANTED

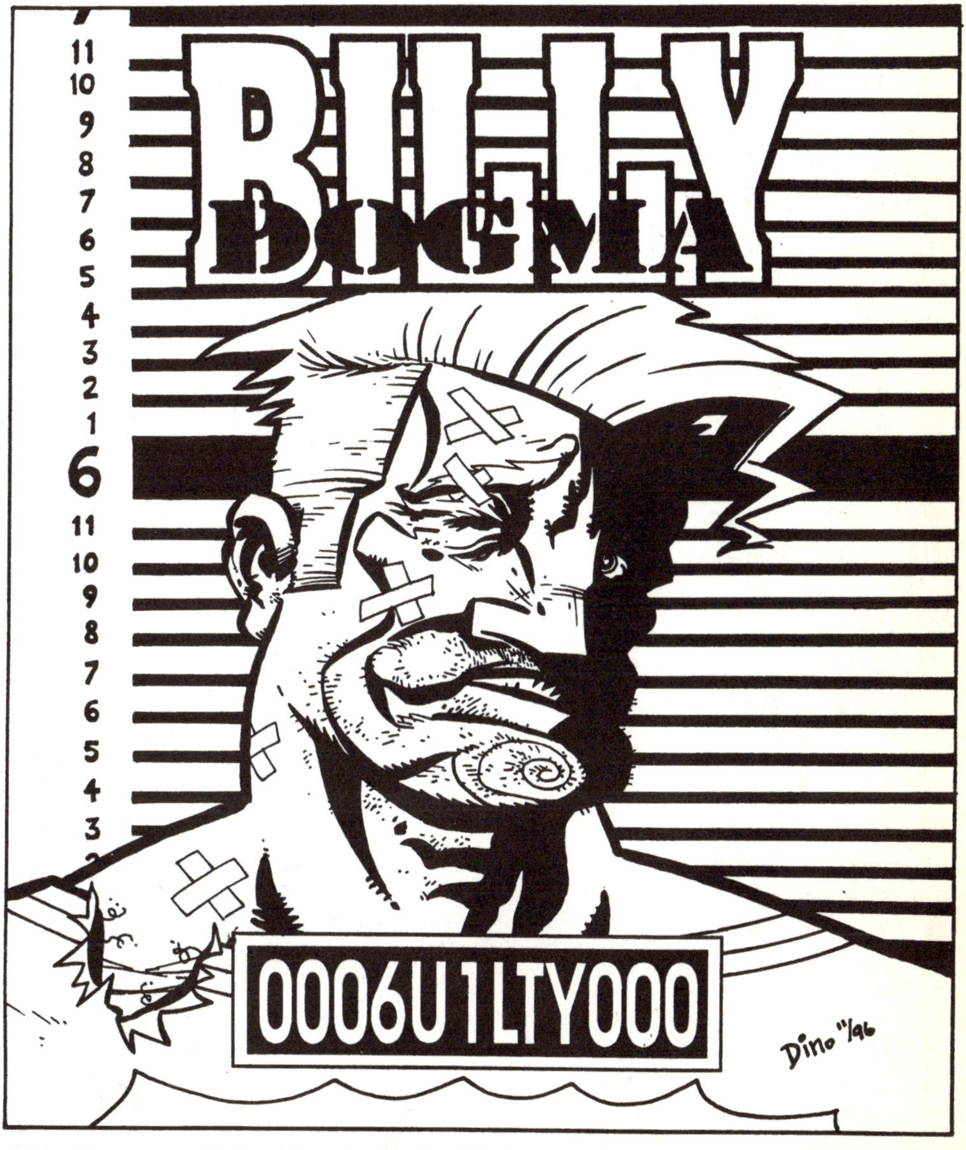
BILLY
DOGMA
11
10
9
8
7
6
5
4
3
2
1
6
11
10
9
8
7
6
5
4
3
0006U1LTY000
Dino '96

THE ABOVE SUSPECT IS CHARGED WITH 4 COUNTS OF CRIMINAL NEGLIGENCE:
1) TRAFFICKING UNSOLICITED BELIEF SYSTEM 2) PANHANDLING FOR PURPOSE
3) COMPROMISING SELF-DIGNITY 4) DAY DREAMING OF A BETTER TOMORROW

IF YOU HAVE ANY INFORMATION PLEASE CONTACT YOUR LOCAL AUTHORITIES

photograph by Seth Dinnerman

ABOUT THE AUTHOR

Dean Haspiel's experiences growing up on the mean streets of the New York City ghettos has served as the backdrop for informed, existential expression in his sociological comics. In the early 80's, Dean worked as an assistant for Howard Chaykin on *American Flagg!*, for Bill Sienkiewicz on *New Mutants* and *Elektra:Assassin*, and for Walter Simonson on *Thor*. In 1987, Dean inaugurated his solo comics career when he co-created and illustrated The Verdict with writer Martin Powell, and went on to draw two DC Comics Bonus Books for *Detective Comics* and *Justice League International*. His work has appeared in *Keyhole*, *Top Shelf*, *Non*, *Minimum Wage*, *SPX*, and *The New York Hangover*. Dean recently illustrated Sony Pictures Classics' *SLC Punk!* for Westhampton House. Coming soon: The *Y2-401-Special-K Problem: a Billy Dogma experience*.